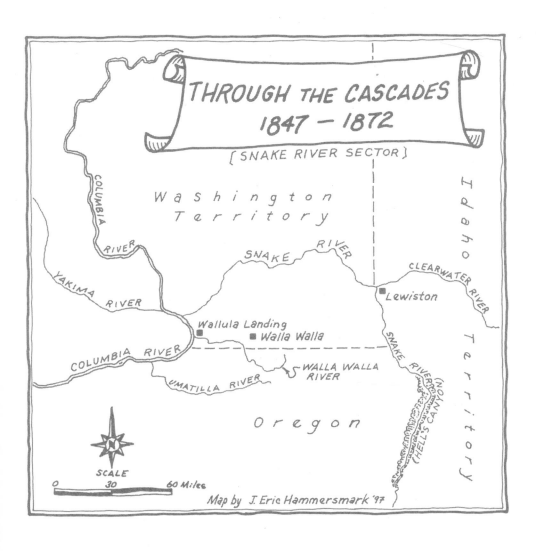

THROUGH THE CASCADES
1847 – 1872

[SNAKE RIVER SECTOR]

Washington Territory

Idaho Territory

COLUMBIA RIVER

YAKIMA RIVER

SNAKE RIVER

CLEARWATER RIVER

Lewiston

Wallula Landing

Walla Walla

COLUMBIA RIVER

UMATILLA RIVER

WALLA WALLA RIVER

SNAKE RIVER (HELL'S CANYON)

Oregon

N

SCALE

0   30   60 Miles

Map by J. Eric Hammersmark '97

Roll On, Columbia

ROLL ON, COLUMBIA

A Historical Novel

BOOK TWO
Through the Cascades

BILL GULICK

UNIVERSITY PRESS OF COLORADO

Copyright © 1997 by Bill Gulick
International Standard Book Number 0-87081-457-5

Published by the
UNIVERSITY PRESS OF COLORADO
P.O. Box 849
Niwot, Colorado 80544

All rights reserved.
Printed in the United States of America.

The University Press of Colorado is a cooperative publishing enterprise supported,
in part, by Adams State College, Colorado State University, Fort Lewis College,
Mesa State College, Metropolitan State College of Denver, University of Colorado,
University of Northern Colorado, University of Southern Colorado, and Western
State College of Colorado.

The paper used in this publication meets the minimum requirements of the American
National Standard for Information Sciences—Permanence of Paper for Printed
Library Materials. ANSI z39.48-1984

Library of Congress Cataloging-in-Publication Data

Gulick, Bill, 1916–
    Through the Cascades / by Bill Gulick.
        p.   cm. — (Roll on, Columbia : bk. 2)
    ISBN 0-87081-457-5 (casebound : alk. paper)
    I. Title.   II. Series: Gulick, Bill, 1916– Roll on Columbia : bk. 2.
PS3557.U43T48   1997
813'.54—DC21   97-15917
                                                                        CIP

10 9 8 7 6 5 4 3 2 1

Roll On, Columbia

Folk song by Woody Guthrie

Green Douglas firs, where the waters cut through,
Down her wild mountains and canyons she flew;
Canadian Northwest to the ocean so blue;
It's roll on, Columbia, roll on!
   Roll on, Columbia, roll on!
   Roll on, Columbia, roll on!
   Your power is turning
   Our darkness to dawn,
   So roll on, Columbia, roll on!

Tom Jefferson's vision would not let him rest;
An empire he saw in the Pacific Northwest;
Sent Lewis and Clark and they did the rest;
So roll on, Columbia, roll on!
   Roll on, Columbia, roll on!
   Roll on, Columbia, roll on!
   Your power is turning
   Our darkness to dawn,
   So roll on, Columbia, roll on!

At Bonneville now there are ships in the locks;
Waters have risen and cleared all the rocks;
Shiploads of plenty will steam past the docks;
It's roll on, Columbia, roll on!
   Roll on, Columbia, roll on!
   Roll on, Columbia, roll on!
   Your power is turning
   Our darkness to dawn,
   So roll on, Columbia, roll on!

And on up the river is the Grand Coulee Dam;
The mightiest thing ever built by a man,
To run the great factories and water the land;
It's roll on, Columbia, roll on!
Roll on, Columbia, roll on!
Roll on, Columbia, roll on!
Your power is turning
Our darkness to dawn,
So roll on, Columbia, roll on!

Used by permission
"Roll On, Columbia"
Words by Woody Guthrie
Music based on "Goodnight, Irene" by Huddie Ledbetter and John A. Lomax
TRO © 1936, 1957, 1963 Ludlow Music, Inc., New York, New York

Author's Note

In 1941, the Bonneville Power Administration paid folksinger Woody Guthrie $266.66 to spend a month writing twenty-six songs in praise of the development of government water and power projects. The ballad "Roll On, Columbia" was one of the songs he composed.

Used as background music to the twenty-minute documentary movie on the building of Grand Coulee Dam, it has been heard by millions of visitors to the site since that time, so has proved to be a real bargain as a musical score.

Though I never met Woody Guthrie, I long have been an admirer of his songs. As I researched and wrote this book, I came to realize that we had a number of things in common. We both were raised in Oklahoma during the Dust Bowl and Depression years of the 1930s. I spent two years working for a private utility that was building electric lines to serve rural Oklahoma areas in need of power, flood control, navigation benefits, and irrigation water, just as he later worked for BPA, which was doing the same thing in the Pacific Northwest.

Called a "radical" in his day, all Woody Guthrie asked of the politicians was a job for a decent rate of pay. Coming to know construction workers as I did, I found them to be the salt of the earth and the strength of a nation in peace and war, just as he proclaimed them to be in his ballads.

Some fifty years ago I settled in the heart of the Columbia River watershed near its juncture with its largest tributary, the Snake. Since then, all my writings have dealt with some aspect of the past, present, and future of the two rivers. During these years, I have followed, reported on, and taken part in controversy as to what uses should be made of the waters of the legendary "River of the West."

In planning what probably will be my last book on the Columbia River, I decided that the best way to tell the story of what man has done to the river was from the viewpoint of six generations of white and Indian families whose fictional lives were closely entwined with the use and development of the Columbia from the establishment of Astoria in 1811 down to the present day. All other characters in the book are real.

Some twenty-five years ago in the introduction to my nonfiction book *Snake River Country*, I wrote: "Somewhere along the way I learned that a great river influences the lives of the people in its watershed just as surely as the acts of those people influence the life of the river. Without water, people die. Without people's concern, a river dies. Thus, this book ..."

That statement still holds true today. So to all the river people I have known—both real and fictional—over the years, as well as to the memory of Woody Guthrie, this book is dedicated.

—Bill Gulick

Synopsis of Book One

Aboard the sailing ship *Tonquin*, which is attempting to cross the stormy Columbia River bar in order to establish Fort Astoria in 1811, sixteen-year-old Seaman Ben Warren hates Captain Jonathan Thorn for the ruthless way he drives his ship and crew. One of the eight men lost in crossing the bar is Ben's father, Thomas Warren. Blaming Captain Thorn, young Ben swears to kill him, if he ever gets the chance.

The opportunity never comes, for the *Tonquin* and its mad captain are lost while trading with the Nootka Indians in northern water, leaving the fledgling post of Fort Astoria without support at a time when England and the United States are on the verge of war. In 1818, the Treaty of Ghent proclaims the Joint Occupancy policy in the Oregon Country, so Ben Warren decides to remain as the only resident at Astoria. He is not interested in fur trading, but he does love the river and the sea. He determines to spend the rest of his life in the Pacific Northwest.

Forming a friendship with Conco, son of the great Chief Concomly, Ben starts a pilot business of guiding sailing ships across the dangerous bars and up the Columbia River as far as the Lower Cascades. On a trip to Hawaii, Ben meets and marries Lolanee, the beautiful granddaughter of King Kamehameha. Conco chooses as his mate a young Chinook girl, who is shocked when he makes her break tradition by not forcing the head of their first son into a press that will give it the slanted appearance which has long been a mark of royalty in the Chinook tribe.

Thus begins a dynasty of white and Indian families whose lives will be closely tied to the Columbia River for five generations.

When steam comes to the Columbia in 1836 with the British ship *Beaver*, Tommy, Ben's son, becomes a river captain while Sitkum, Conco's son, assists him as engineer. While the Joint Occupancy Treaty is in effect from 1818–1846, traffic and trade develop on the lower Columbia. Rivalry grows between the British Hudson's Bay Company and American emigrants, who are beginning to settle in Oregon's Willamette Valley. In late spring of 1843, a vote is taken as to whether the Provisional Government will be British or American. The Americans win 55–53. Later that year, the Great Emigration of 1843 brings one thousand Americans to the Willamette Valley, thus assuring this part of the Oregon Country will be American.

Included in the 1843 wagon train is a young Swedish girl, Freda Svenson, who catches the fancy of Tommy Warren. Coming west as an indentured servant, she needs to be taught what freedom means, Tommy thinks, while she feels that he needs to be taught some lessons in manners. On a visit to the Astoria home of Tommy's father and mother, Ben and Lolanee, Tommy and Freda decide to get married, filing a land claim near Rooster Rock just downriver from the Cascades.

Before they get married in 1846, news reaches Oregon that the Joint Occupancy Treaty has been ended and that the boundary between Great Britain and the United States has been set at the 49th parallel, just north of what will become Washington State.

Steam-powered boats now dominate the lower Columbia. To the east of Rooster Rock lie six miles of rapids known as the Lower, Middle, and Upper Cascades. In the heart of the ten-thousand-foot-deep Gorge through which the Columbia pours, fifty miles of tranquil water exist, which can be navigated by stern-wheelers. Knowing that sector of river as they do, Tommy and Sitkum will play important roles in its development from 1847–1872. Later, their sons, Lars Warren and Alex Conley, will be involved in the events related in Book Two.

Roll On, Columbia

1.

$\mathscr{S}$HORTLY AFTER their marriage in the Oregon City Methodist Church on March 1, 1844, Thomas Reginald Kamehameha Warren and his bride, Freda Svenson Warren, filed on the square mile of land they had chosen under the Donation Claims Act recently passed by the Provisional Government. Located on the south side of the Columbia River downstream from the six-mile stretch of rapids called the Upper, Middle, and Lower Cascades, the knoll upon which Tommy and Freda planned to build their cabin fronted a long, low, sandy beach on the river side. Behind the knoll, a sheer lava bluff rose eight hundred feet into the lower slopes of the tree-covered, mist-shrouded, waterfall-laced Cascade Mountain range, which here blended with the plains of the Willamette Valley.

Directly to the west, a fifty-foot spire of caramel-colored rock ten feet in diameter jutted boldly skyward, so strikingly unusual in its shape that all passing white emigrants noticed and commented on it, as had the local Indians from time beyond recall. Intrigued by the size and shape of the rock, Freda asked Tommy if it had a name.

"Why, yes," he answered uneasily, "I believe it does. It's called Ee-wash in Chinook Jargon, Sitkum tells me. White people call it 'Rooster Rock.'"

"That's a strange name. It looks nothing like a rooster to me."

"Well, as a matter of fact, Rooster Rock is sort of a euphemism."

Freda gave him a puzzled look. "A what?"

"A polite word substituted for one not used in mixed company. When you're more familiar with the English language, I'll explain it to you."

"Why can't you explain it now?"

Considering the fact that in Chinook Jargon, "Ee-wash" meant "penis," which male white emigrants cleaned up to "Rooster Rock" in mixed company, though they still called it "Cock Rock" amongst themselves, Tommy changed the subject and let the explanation wait for another day.

In a show of magnanimity forced upon them by local public opinion, Gustav and Emma Mueller, Freda's former employers, gave her the twenty dollars she had earned during her year of servitude, returned her late father's gunsmithing tools, and even accepted an invitation to the wedding. Afterwards, Mr. Mueller told Tommy Warren that he might give him a steady job in the new brewery he was building near Willamette Falls, if and when Tommy decided to give up his berth as First Mate aboard the Hudson's Bay Company steamer, *Beaver*, and settle down ashore. Earlier, Freda would have urged Tommy to do just that, but now that they had claimed a square mile of land at the western end of the Columbia River Gorge, she insisted that they use her twenty-dollar dowry and the money he had saved out of his Hudson's Bay Company wages to start building their cabin and "prove up" on their claim.

" 'Prove up,' " she said proudly. "I like those words, Tommy. They promise that the Provisional Government will reward us for being good citizens."

Following the Great Migration of one thousand people led west by Dr. Marcus Whitman in 1843, fifteen hundred Americans made the trek to Oregon in 1844, while in 1845 the number increased to three thousand. Even before the boundary dispute with England was settled in 1846, it became clear to the directors of the Hudson's Bay Company that Great Britain was going to have to close out its operations south of the 49th parallel and relinquish its land and water claims in Puget Sound. Though Tommy and Sitkum retained their berths as First Mate and Assistant Engineer aboard the *Beaver* until the spring of '46, the very nature of the cargo the ship was carrying between Fort Vancouver on the north bank of the Columbia River and Fort Langley in British Columbia made it clear that the Company was preparing to move north.

Shortly after Tommy and Freda hired a carpenter to help build their cabin near Rooster Rock, Sitkum announced that he, too, was getting married and planned to make his home on the river.

"Who's the lucky lady?" Tommy asked. "Where on the river do you plan to live?"

"Her name is *Ka-e-mox-nith*, which means 'Spotted Fawn' in the Yakima tongue," Sitkum answered. "She belongs to the Klickitat band, which has fishing rights on the north side of the Columbia just below Celilo Falls. We'll live in her people's village there. She is a round-head, like me."

It was a matter of pride to Sitkum, Tommy knew, that as the grandson of the renowned Chinook Chief Concomly, he had been the first high-born male child in tribal history not to have had his head flattened following his birth. The deep, abiding friendship between Sitkum's father, Conco, and Tommy's father, Ben, had been responsible for what then was a radical violation of custom among the Chinook Indians and other lower Columbia River tribes.

As Sitkum had been told the story by his father, Conco had valued his friendship with Ben Warren so much that he wanted his first-born son to grow up to be as much like him as possible, even if that meant violating a long-honored tribal custom.

Since Sitkum's birth, which had occurred a few years after the establishment of Fort Astoria across the Columbia River from the village long ruled by Chief Concomly, other Chinook parents had abandoned the head-flattening practice, which long had been a mark of distinction for high-born children. But to the elders of the tribe, Conco's insistence that his first-born son's head not be flattened had been shocking; it was regarded as the beginning of a degeneration of morals in what once had been a great race of people. Furthermore, because Sitkum had joined Tommy in deserting native canoes and ships propelled only by oars and sails and gone to work on a noisy, stinking steamboat that consumed wood and "stones that burn," the elders condemned him as a rash young man who now was embracing outlandish, newfangled ways.

Resenting their attitude, Sitkum found little reason to remain in the main village just inside the north entrance to the Columbia. Instead, he relished his job as Assistant Engineer aboard the *Beaver,* cruising from Fort Vancouver down the Columbia one hundred miles to its mouth, out to sea along the Northwest Coast, then into Puget Sound and on up the coast of British Columbia as far north as Alaska. Growing interested in the portion of the Columbia River where it had cut its massive gorge through the Cascades east of Fort Vancouver, he had become acquainted with interior tribes such as the Klickitats, Yakimas, and other bands that met to fish and trade at Celilo Falls. No longer marked by a slanted head as a lower river Indian, as his father's generation had been, he was attracted to the round-headed Klickitat woman, Ka-e-mox-nith—Spotted Fawn—married her, and agreed to live in her country when his work aboard the *Beaver* was done.

Both Tommy and Sitkum knew that it was only a matter of time before the little Hudson's Bay Company steamer carried its last shipload of cargo north from Fort Vancouver to Fort Langley, which would end their employment by the British concern. There was a crying need for a steamboat on the fifty-mile stretch of river between The Dalles and the Upper Cascades, Tommy pointed out, and since he and Sitkum were the only experienced American steamboat men in Oregon, they were well qualified to run it. Certainly, the potential for passenger and freight traffic for such a boat was there, for at The Dalles the wagon trail to the Willamette Valley ended. With the forbidding heights of the Cascades looming ahead, bone-weary travelers who had already negotiated two thousand miles of deserts, mountains, plains, and river crossings faced a final bitter choice of sticking to the Columbia or going up and over the Cascade Mountains.

"Whichever route they take," Tommy told Sitkum, "most of them wish they'd gone the other way. Traveling conditions are terrible both ways."

"The road over the mountains is very bad, I hear," Sitkum said. "Yet the Provisional Government gave Samuel Barlow, the man who laid it out, the franchise for a toll road and allows him to charge five dollars a wagon."

"Well, the Barlow Road *is* passable if their oxen are in good shape and they don't get snowbound. If they take the river route, the local Indians charge them a fortune to carry their goods downriver, then are apt to steal them blind when they get through the Gorge. What most of the poorer emigrants do, I hear, is chop down trees, lash together log rafts, dismantle their wagons, then try to float them through the Gorge on their own."

"I have seen some who have done this. They suffer greatly."

"We need a steamboat below The Dalles, Sitkum. Plus a portage railroad around the Cascades. But so far nobody with the money to build them has come along."

Having heard Freda relate her experiences traveling with the Gustav Mueller family, Tommy appreciated how fortunate the 1843 wagon train had been in getting through the Gorge with a minimum of trouble. Of course, the Mueller party had been well organized. Most of its members had money, its oxen were strong and healthy, and the

Celilo Falls Indians had not yet realized how much at their mercy these white emigrants were, for this was the first sizable migration they had seen. Furthermore, when word reached Fort Vancouver that a large party of Americans had reached The Dalles and was preparing to come on downriver, Dr. John McLoughlin, who long had been friendly to Americans, put all the resources of the Hudson's Bay Company into making sure that the emigrants made it through.

Since then, the increasing number of Willamette Valley–bound Americans had so alarmed Company directors that they had ordered Dr. McLoughlin to give them no more aid. This meant that late-comers with exhausted livestock and little cash now were at the mercy of both the local Indians and a growing horde of white speculators posing as traders and guides—people who had no scruples against fleecing travelers out of their last healthy animal, family heirloom, or dollar.

"Oh, I do wish we could help them," Freda told Tommy, after watching yet another party of worn-out, destitute travelers pass by the knoll on which their cabin sat. "They look so unhappy. Is there not something we can do?"

"We can provide food and shelter for a few of them, Freda. Maybe loan them a boat now and then. But there's so many of them ..."

Freda looked thoughtful. "In Sweden, we have societies of people with money and material goods who help newcomers who have neither until they are able to take care of themselves. Perhaps an Emigrant Aid Society could be organized in the Willamette Valley."

"Who would run it?"

"I will be glad to get it started. First, I will make a list of people I think should help—beginning with Mr. and Mrs. Mueller ..."

Because of his duties aboard the *Beaver*, which required him to be gone a great deal, Tommy was not able to give Freda much help as she organized Willamette Valley settlers into a society of volunteers willing to supply food, shelter, clothes, medical services, and carpenter, blacksmith, and farming skills to new arrivals. What he did do was assemble a fleet of leaky scows, water-logged boats, and abandoned Indian canoes, then persuade his river-wise white and Indian friends to patch them up and make them available to stragglers. Though he did not expect the impoverished emigrants to pay a fee for the use of the craft, Freda insisted that they be charged rent.

"Even if they are poor, these are proud people. Have them sign notes for a few dollars in cash, when they get it, or a few days' work, when they have the time. That way, the Emigrant Aid Society will benefit and be able to help others."

Because of the location of their cabin at the lower end of the Gorge, it was the first place to be seen by the exhausted emigrants that resembled the kind of civilization they had left six months ago and half a continent away. To most of them, Freda's sparkling blue Swedish eyes, her unfailing good humor, and the sympathy with which she greeted and helped them made the disheartened newcomers regard her as something of a saint.

Though at first worried about leaving his young wife alone at the isolated river cabin, Tommy soon learned that Freda was perfectly capable of taking care of herself. Having been taught the gunsmith trade by her late father, she was a crack shot with a pistol, rifle, or shotgun; could stalk and kill waterfowl along the river and deer or elk in the woods; and could repair any damaged weapon for which she could find or make essential parts. Since she had insisted that an extra room be added to the cabin in which she could install her father's gun-smithing tools and weapon racks, it soon was filled not only with her own guns but with those given to her as payment by grateful travelers for her help.

By the time Tommy and Sitkum finally left the *Beaver* in the spring of 1846, the trickle of westering American emigrants coming into the Willamette Valley either through the Columbia River Gorge or over the Cascade Mountains by way of the Barlow Road had swelled to a torrent that could never be stemmed. By then, Freda and her Emigrant Aid Society had collected a number of incredible stories of hardship, endurance, and the indomitable spirit of the kind of people that were coming west over the Oregon Trail.

One of these was the saga of Elizabeth Smith, who, with her husband, Cornelius, and their seven children, finally made it through the ice, sleet, and snow of the Gorge on Thanksgiving Day, 1847.

2.

*B*EFORE HER MARRIAGE to Cornelius Smith in La Porte, Indiana, in 1830, Elizabeth Dixon had been a lover of words, reading every newspaper, magazine, and book that she got her hands on, keeping a diary from an early age, and making the vow that if she ever did anything interesting she would record the events as they occurred in a daily journal so that her family or whatever posterity survived her would know what her life had been like. Since nothing interesting happened to her during the first seventeen years of her marriage, other than giving birth to seven children, she did not bother to record these events. But when she and her husband embarked on their overland journey to Oregon April 12, 1847, she felt that the trip would be worth detailing. Acquiring a journal book that could be protected from the weather, she began a sporadic notation of the trials and tribulations of the long trek west.

Following the arrival of the wagon train at The Dalles on October 27, she wrote:

> Here are a great many immigrants in camp, some making rafts, others going down in boats which have been sent up by the speculators.

Two harsh, practical facts were clear to Cornelius and Elizabeth Smith: first, that the season was very late, with winter already at hand in the high mountain peaks south and west of The Dalles; second, that they had no money to spare with which to pay the exorbitant prices demanded by the speculators for transporting their wagon and worldly goods from the point of land two miles west of The Dalles on which they were camped through the fifty-mile-long Gorge, around the six-mile portage that bypassed the unnavigable rapids, and then on by river or road the final forty-five miles to the settlements in the Willamette Valley. By one means or another, they would have to make the last leg of the journey on their own.

Finding two other families—those of Adam Polk and Russell Welch—in a similar situation, the Smiths decided to join forces and build a raft together. "October 29 was rainy and cold," Elizabeth wrote, then added:

> The men are making rafts, women cooking and washing, children crying. Indians are bartering potatoes for shirts. They must have a good shirt for half a peck of potatoes.

She and Cornelius were aware that there was an alternate route west, which, if winter not been so near, they might have taken.

> Snow is close by. We should have gone over the mountains, but they are covered with snow; consequently we must go down by water.

This late in the season, both routes were forbidding. Clouds covered the heights; near-freezing fog hung low in the Gorge. Plains-born and raised, she dreaded traveling by raft with their seven children, who ranged in age from a boy of sixteen down to a babe in arms, but she tried her best not to let her fears show. With the clumsy raft finally completed, the three families waited several days while the wind blew gusty and strong directly against them from the west. Finally, on November 2, the weather moderated and they pushed off from shore.

> We took off our wagon wheels, laid them on the raft, placed the wagon beds on them, and started, three families of us, on twelve logs, eighteen inches through and forty feet long. The water runs three inches on our raft.

Because the oxen would be needed to pull the wagons on the trail beyond the Gorge but could not be taken aboard, Russell Welch and two of the younger Smith boys undertook to drive them downriver over a steep, rough, narrow trail that ran parallel to the south shore of the river, at times climbing to a two-thousand-foot elevation, where the slopes were treacherous with ice and snow. Cornelius Smith, his sixteen-year-old son, and Adam Polk handled the raft, maneuvering it with clumsy hand-hewn poles and oars. Weakened by constant exposure and a worsening case of consumption, Adam Polk fell seriously ill after a couple of days and was forced to seek shelter within his wagon, shivering, coughing, wracked by chills and fever.

Though they had anticipated that the trip through the Gorge would take no more than a week, violent, howling headwinds held their progress in the near-freezing weather down to ten miles by November 8, only one-fifth of the journey in a week's time. Pulling

into a sheltered cove, they waited for the white-capped waters to sub- *Roll On*
side. Finding it impossible to sleep on the raft, they *Columbia*

> clambered up a side hill among the rocks and built a fire to warm
> ourselves and children, while the wind blew and the waves rolled
> beneath.

Next day when the wind eased, they pulled out from shore, floated
a few miles, then when the water grew rough again, pulled into the
bank and tied up. Provisions were running low. With his wife unable
to keep him warm and dry, Adam Polk began to wheeze and cough,
fighting for every breath. Clearly, he was dying. Russell Welch, the
cattle, and two of the Smith boys still were battling the icy trail on the
heights above. Cornelius Smith decided that he must get off the raft
and go on foot along the shore, where he hoped to find an emigrant
party, a band of Indians, or Russell Welch from whom he could obtain
enough food to keep his people from starving to death. This left the
sixteen-year-old Smith boy alone to handle the clumsy raft. While her
husband was gone, Elizabeth wrote starkly:

> The waves are dashing over the raft, and icicles hanging from
> the wagon beds to the water. Tonight, at dusk, Adam Polk expired. No
> one with him but his wife and myself. We sat up all night with him
> while the waves were dashing below.

Two days later, Cornelius Smith returned, carrying fifty pounds of
tough, stringy beef hacked off the carcass of one of his own oxen he
had found and butchered. But at least it was food. Once more the raft
was pushed into the sluggish current and headed downriver; once
more strong headwinds forced it back to shore. Elizabeth wrote:

> Husband and boy were an hour and a half after dark getting the
> raft landed and all made fast, while the water ran knee-deep over the
> raft and the wind blew freezing cold. We women did not attempt to
> get out of our wagons tonight.

Meanwhile, the stiff, frozen corpse of Adam Polk, covered by the
wet, cold blankets in which he had died, lay unburied, while his wife
silently mourned.

On November 11, the party made three miles downriver, where
they

> found Welch and the boys waiting with the cattle, which could be
> driven no further on this side of the river. Here is a ferry for the pur-
> pose of ferrying immigrant cattle across the river.

9

What the ferryman's charges were, Elizabeth Smith did not record, but it may be safely assumed that they were all the traffic could bear in cash, livestock, or personal belongings. After two days spent ferrying the animals and wagon beds across the river, Adam Polk was buried in a shallow, poorly marked grave on the north shore. Then, Elizabeth wrote:

> We got the ferryman to shift our load to their boat and take us down to the falls where we found quite a town of people waiting for their cattle to pull them around the portage.

Actually, the "falls" mentioned by Elizabeth Smith were the Upper, Middle, and Lower Cascades, a six-mile stretch of white-water rapids so severe that no boat could pass through them and live. Here, the dismantled wagons must be put back together again, the oxen yoked, and the journey resumed by land. In the endless rains of early winter, the primitive road was a sea of mud. After waiting three days for the rain to cease and traveling conditions to improve, the desperate travelers were forced to start despite the terrible weather. Elizabeth wrote:

> It rains and snows. We start this morning around the portage with our wagons. We have five miles to go. I carry my babe and lead or carry another through the snow and mud and water almost to my knees. It is the worst road a team could possibly travel. I went ahead with my children and was afraid to look behind me for fear of seeing the wagons turn over in the mud and water with everything in them. My children gave out with cold and fatigue and could not travel, and the boys had to unhitch the oxen and bring them and carry the children into camp. I was so cold and numb that I could not tell by the feeling that I had any feet at all. We started in the morning at sunrise and did not get to camp until after dark and there was not one dry thread on one of us.

Because the oxen had been unhitched and used to carry the children on into camp, it now was necessary for someone to take the stock back to the spot where the wagons had been left, hitch the oxen to them, and bring the wagons forward. Because of the pitch-black night and the raging rainstorm, the effort could not be made until daylight. Huddling in a makeshift shelter, the bedraggled family shivered and waited for dawn. When it came at last, Cornelius Smith was so worn out from his labors and exposure of the past three weeks, that he found himself unable to rise off the ground. Elizabeth faced the bitter fact that even though they were on the threshold of their long-sought goal, her husband's strength was gone.

While she made him as comfortable as she could, the older boys took the oxen back along the trail to where the wagons had been abandoned, then brought them on. Thanks to boats supplied by the Emigrant Aid Society, the Smith family would make the remainder of the trip to the Willamette Valley by water, but during the nine days they had to wait for the boats to arrive and carry them to shelter, Cornelius Smith grew steadily worse. Knowing that her husband was dying, Elizabeth recorded her first complaint:

> It is an impossibility to cook and quite impossible to keep warm and dry. I froze or chilled my feet so that I cannot wear a shoe, so have to go around in the cold water barefooted. The whole care of everything falls on my shoulders. I am not adequate to the task.

On November 27, after twenty-five days in the Gorge, the family arrived in Portland and at last they had a roof over their heads. But the exposure had been too much for Cornelius Smith, who never arose from his bed. On February 1, 1848, Elizabeth wrote:

> Rain all day. This day my dear husband, my last remaining friend, died. Now I know what none but widows know: that is, how comfortless is a widow's life; especially when left in a strange land without money or friends, and the care of seven children.

But thanks to the good people of the Emigrant Aid Society, Freda Warren told her husband, people like Elizabeth Smith and others who had suffered so greatly during the long journey west did not remain friendless in a strange land for long. Six months later, Elizabeth wrote:

> I became poor as a snake, but I was in good health, and never so nimble since I was a child. I could run half a mile without stopping to breathe. Neither I nor my children have had a day's sickness since we came to Oregon.

Before the year was out, she had met and married a widower named Joseph Geer, himself the father of ten children, six of whom were already married and starting families of their own.

"Think of what a wonderful future they have, Tommy," Freda said in awe. "Why, do you know when those children come of age and file land claims, they will own seventeen square miles of beautiful Willamette Valley land? In Sweden, that would be a kingdom."

3.

Terrible though the river route through the Gorge was for many emigrants, the way over the Cascade Mountains by what became known as the Barlow Road was even worse so far as physical difficulties were concerned. At first, attempts were made to build a trail just above river level, but at many spots vast moraines slanted steeply down toward the water, so that if a single rock were pried loose and moved, the entire mountainside came sliding down upon the builders, making the spot more impassable than ever. In other places, sheer lava bluffs two thousand feet high bordered the river, leaving no room at all for a trail.

How much credit Captain Samuel K. Barlow, the "builder" of the road, should have been given for pioneering a route later traveled by thousands was as questionable as his military title gained in whatever obscure Indian war he may have fought in. But the fact was that he did lay out enough of a road to be given a franchise by the Provisional Government to charge toll. So the Barlow Road it became.

By 1845, Willamette Valley–bound travelers had become so sick of waiting weeks at The Dalles for boat passage downriver to be provided by white or Indian speculators whose demands became more outrageous each year that several parties decided to find another way, no matter how difficult it might prove to be. One of these was a train of fifteen wagons led by a strong, intelligent, stubborn man from Indiana named Joel Palmer. Joining forces with a train just ahead led by Samuel K. Barlow, then with another catching up from behind led by William Rector, the now-combined train of sixty wagons felt itself resourceful enough to force a passage across the mountains by one means or another. By mutual consent, Joel Palmer was chosen to be its leader.

At that time and place, history was often recorded for posterity by a participant whose powers of observation were better than the quality of his grammar. Such a man was William Rector, who, with his wife and seven children, heard shortly after he reached The Dalles that the two wagon trains directly ahead had turned south and were going to try to find a way across the mountains. Letting the chips of misspelling fall where they might, he began to write a vivid account of what would be an epic journey:

> When we arrived at the Dalles, this being the end of the journey for wagons at that time, the accumulation of emigrants was already large. The only way possible at that time of getting from the Dalles to the Wilamette valey was by way of the Columbia river. Soon after I arived at the Dalles other companys began to come in. They were in a deplorable condition, completety woren out with heardship and starvation. The suplys of provisions at the mission were well neigh exhausted.

Hearing that the Palmer party had gone ahead and was seeking to find some sort of pass across the mountains, William Rector and his people hastened to catch up. On October 6 in a mountain meadow east of the Cascades, he found sixty wagons camped, waiting to learn what the small advance party of trailblazers led by Joel Palmer had discovered in the way of a trail across the mountains.

Truth was, Palmer was deeply troubled by the fact that his optimistic prediction he could find a way across the mountains had induced so many people to gamble on his promise. He and the five men with him had ascended a narrow, winding creek bed for fifteen miles, scaled a steep ridge, and finally came out on an open plain from which they got a wide view of the terrain to be crossed.

Behind them to the north lay the depths of the Gorge. Ahead to the south loomed Mount Hood, a huge, forbidding peak whose crest rose to an elevation of 11,235 feet, its upper slopes already covered with snow. Faintly visible far to the west through the tall trees lay the plains of the green, lovely Willamette Valley, their ultimate goal.

It was clear enough to Joel Palmer that the wagons could be brought up to this spot, though the effort would be a laborious one. Sending the other members of his scouting party back to guide the wagon train to this high meadow, Palmer went on alone, moving into increasingly rough, stony, timbered country as he sought out a feasible

trail. Since his leather boots had worn out weeks ago, he was using Indian moccasins as footwear now. The rocky trail soon cut them to rib-
bons. Exploring westward along the edge of a deep ravine, he found
himself struggling through icy water and newly fallen snow, where the
untanned moccasins fell apart, leaving him barefoot.

After a few miles of struggling through the thick brush, he came to
an open spot from which he got a good view of the country ahead.
What he saw appalled him. Lying directly across the route that the
wagons must take was a canyon at least three miles wide and so deep
that the two-hundred-foot-tall trees growing on its far slope looked
tiny. Just below where he stood, the slope grew even steeper, becoming so sheer that only a few scattered mountain laurels clung precari-
ously to its side. Despite his slashed and bleeding feet, he followed the
canyon rim twenty miles in a southerly direction, seeking an easier
way across. Finding none, he was forced to return to the spot where
the sixty wagons were camped, traveling close to fifty miles between
breakfast and midnight. When he gave his fellow emigrants the bleak
news that the mountains ahead were impassable, William Rector refused to accept his word as final, later writing:

> After informing Palmer the condition of affairs at the Dalles when
> I left there, I advised that we go as far as we could with the wagons,
> and that two men should go through on foot to the settlements and
> get fresh horses and assistance to pack through. Some of the party
> were not willing to abandon the wagons. To remedy that objection I
> proposed that if they would open the road to the sumate pararie whare
> there was grass, and that if the wagons had to be left I would insure
> their safety until next June, at which time the road would be opned.

None of the emigrants wanted to go back and winter at The Dalles,
so, when put to a vote, the proposal was accepted. Though the wagons would have to be left short of the summit, with the prospect of
help coming up from the Willamette Valley there was a good chance
that the women, children, and cattle could make it through to the settlements. Though Rector himself had not seen the country ahead, he
was confident that he and Samuel Barlow, who had been with Palmer
in the scouting party and would accompany Rector on this trip, could
reach Oregon City in a couple of days, then guide a rescue party back
to the stranded travelers. Rector wrote:

We started the next morning at daylight with only two days ration, which was supposed to be ample. Barlow and Palmer had been heigh up on Mount Hood so as to overlook all the mountains and see the valey but they were not competent to judg of distance from such an elivation, and though two days was time enough to get into the valey, we found to our sorrow that it required six days to reach Oregon City.

At that time I was nearly forty years oald in the prime of life. Barlow was my cenior by fifteen years, very spry and a good walker, but had not the botom of indurance that I had. He became very frail but did not seem to sufer with hunger as I did. I had a light shotgun but with the aproach of winter everthing had left the mountains for lower ground. So sharp was our apetites that Barlow remarked after the first days travle that he could eat all his food for super. I realy felt the same way, then Barlow made a very sencible proposition that we eat just half every time and we would never get out of provisions, to which I readily ascented and lived strictly up to it.

The second day was heard traveling, a light misting rain all day. We had to descend a long way into the kenion to get to water. It was geting dark. In trying to start a fire the maches was wet. We tryed the gun but that was no better. Barlow was disponding and believed we would never get out of that kenion. It was very coald and raining and without fire our chances to survive was truly bad.

I got stride of a dry fallin tree with a dry lim and began to rub violently. Called Barlow to help. We set fase to fase on the log with a blanket over our heads and both took hold of the stick and rubed with all our power until the place was very warm, then laid maches on the place to dry. In this way we succeeded in drying the maches so we got fire. I worked all night geting wood and keeping fire. Barlow slep.

After a scant brekfast we started again but had to asend out of the kenion to the mountain side to travle. The rain had stoped but there was a heavy fog all day. After traveling several hours paralell with the kenion, Barlow thought we were below the kenion and there was the valey he had seen when he was on Mount Hood. We tryed to cross but found it worse. I then determined to go no further in that direction, knowing that the cattle trail was north of us and we would have no chance to fall in with som one driveing catle. I had a smal compas and proposed to Barlow that we travel as near north as the country would permit until we found the catle trail, to which he agreed, and we started out.

That course led directly up the mountain. It was steap and tiresom. At length we got above the fog and saw the mountain get heigh above us. At length we reached the top. Here I discovered Barlow's mental faculties was failing as well as his fisical powers. He persisted in saying he had been on that identical spot before and it was not one mile from the wagon camp, though it was more like twenty-five. I found it was not posible to reach his reasoining facultys and took absolute controle of him. He complained biterly because I did control him, but he kept on with me.

He got frail and would frequently fall and hurt himself. I carried the axe and the gun so as to relieve him of any incumberance. He walked behind me, sulen and silant. Once he spoke in a kindly way and said, "Mr. Rector, if I should brake a leg in sum of these falls, what would you do with me?"

"I wud eat you," was my reply.

He said no more. I looked around at him and saw him sheding tears, so I stopped and went back to him and said, "Why, Barlow, you old fool, I wont eat you and neither will you brake a leg. We will get to the trail early tomorrow."

But he insisted that it was very likely he would never be able to get out of these mountains and made the solemn request that if he should get disabled so that he could go no further that I would knock out his braines with the axe and not let him linger in pain. But he took good care not to fall any more.

Well, as I had predicted, we got to the trail the next day and had the good luck to fall in with a partie driveing catle. We got refreshed and went on to Oregon City.

After they reached the settlements in the Willamette Valley, the helpful people of the Emigrant Aid Society supplied the manpower to send assistance back to the high meadow where the sixty wagons were waiting. Before winter came, the women, children, and cattle were brought on across the mountains, while a few of the men stayed with the wagons to guard their contents until a road could be built and the wagons could come on the rest of the way.

Though Samuel Barlow returned the following spring and did some work on the so-called road, along with a number of other party members, their efforts consisted mainly of chopping through a fallen tree here, prying aside a protruding rock there, and doing a bit of pick-and-shovel work on a stream bank so that it could be forded. By no stretch of the imagination could the result be called a toll road such as travelers were used to back in the more civilized East.

Two particularly bad stretches were Zigzag River and Laurel Hill. Roaring down off the snowfields of Mount Hood in a late spring flood, Zigzag was a terrifying chute of white water, its narrow canyon full of mud, boulders, and downed trees, which must be crossed time and again. So far as Laurel Hill was concerned, this infamous mile-

long slope slanted downward over a terrifying sixty percent grade, Roll On Columbia
which meant a drop of two thousand feet vertically in that mile-long
distance. Yet somehow the river was crossed and the hill descended.

At first, wagons were lowered down Laurel Hill one by one, prevented from tumbling too fast by restraining ropes belayed around tree trunks and bushes on the heights above. Later, a daring driver improved on the technique by locking all the wagon's wheels, tying a tree ten inches in diameter and forty feet long on behind as a brake, then angling back and forth down the steep slope in a zigzag pattern. Attached to the rear of the wagon by its small end, so that its outspread branches dug into the ground, the tree used as a brake was unfastened at the base of the hill and left behind.

There, of course, it blocked the way of the next wagon to come down the hill, whose driver would complain bitterly about the inconsiderateness of the driver ahead. Unyoking his oxen, he would drag the offending tree out of the way, pass the spot, then leave the tree *he* had used as a drag in exactly the same place.

By the time Samuel Barlow applied for and received permission to charge toll on his "road," a great scar crossed the face of Laurel Hill, deepening year by year as traffic coming over the Oregon Trail increased to the extent that it was said each emigrant train on the two thousand miles of the Oregon Trail was never out of sight of the column ahead or the one behind.

One emigrant described his experience descending Laurel Hill by writing: "We went down it like shot off a shovel." Another observed:

> The road on this hill is something terrible. It is worn down into the soil from five to seven feet, leaving steep banks on both sides, and so narrow that it is almost impossible to walk alongside of the cattle for any distance without leaning against the oxen.
>
> Our wagon was all shapes coming down the hill. Sometimes one fore wheel would drop nearly three feet from a boulder in the road, while at the same time the opposite rear wheel dropped two feet or more into another hole.
>
> Bad as the hill was, we got down in safety.

That seemed to be the sentiment of most of the travelers who passed over the Barlow Road. Bad as the road was, it took them to the Promised Land. Collecting a fee of one dollar for each animal and five dollars for each wagon that passed through the tollgate, Captain Samuel K. Barlow was too busy most of the time to do much work improving the road. But members of the Emigrant Aid Society later spoke kindly of him, saying: "Many a settler arrived at the gates unable to pay. But Mr. Barlow would always accept a note. And he always permitted widows to pass without payment."

4.

*N*o longer employed as First Mate aboard the *Beaver,* Tommy Warren kept busy from the spring of 1846 into the fall of 1847 helping emigrants in need of boats on the last leg of their trip from the Lower Cascades to the Willamette Valley. For many of them, their goal was the rapidly growing settlement where the Willamette River joined the Columbia, which now went by the name of Portland.

Though Tommy could not vouch for the truth of the story, gossip had it that a recently arrived merchant from Boston, Massachusetts, and a visiting sea captain from Portland, Maine, had acquired a large piece of land near the junction of the two rivers, then laid out the site for a city and began to sell lots. Because the wet, low-lying area recently had been covered with trees, most of which had been cut down to build cabins and stores, the city-to-be had been called "Stump Town" at first. This would not do as the name of what its promoters hoped would become the leading metropolis of the Pacific Northwest, of course, so they flipped a coin to decide whether their new city would be called Boston or Portland, Oregon.

Portland won.

With the *Beaver* gone north to British waters, no steam-powered ships were left to cross the bar, enter the Columbia River under the guidance of his father and Conco, then tediously work their way against wind, current, and tide one hundred miles upriver to Portland or Fort Vancouver. Knowing that Tommy was without employment, Ben Warren often sent word that a river-piloting job was available at Astoria, which Tommy usually accepted despite the fact that he was not as comfortable working a sailing ship as he was when handling a steam-powered craft. For both types of ship, the channel, the sandbars, the winds, and the tides were the same, of course; but the penalties for grounding on a mudbank and the time and effort required to work the ship free were far different for sail compared to steam-propelled craft.

Having no experience in sail, Sitkum did not participate with Tommy in his lower river piloting jobs. Living on the north side of the Columbia River above Celilo Falls, Sitkum did work now and then as a boatman or raftsman helping emigrants negotiate the fifty miles of relatively quiet water that lay between the launching site two miles west of The Dalles to just above the Upper Cascades. Usually when he completed such a trip, he would drop on downriver to Tommy and Freda's cabin near Rooster Rock, seeking news of their doings and relating his own. Since his wife was a Yakima woman whose people were in close touch with the upriver tribes, he always seemed to know what was going on in the interior country.

"A bad sickness has come to the people at the Whitman Mission," he told Tommy and Freda when he visited them in mid-November. "It was brought by whites in wagons coming west over the Oregon Trail."

"We have heard about it from people passing through," Freda said. "When they took their sick children to Dr. Whitman for medicines and treatment, he told them it was a mild disease called German measles. With rest and proper care, their children soon got well."

"So Spotted Fawn tells me," Sitkum said, shaking his head. "But among the children of the Cayuse tribe living near the Mission, the disease is far more serious. Many of them who have caught it from the emigrant children have died."

Disturbed by the stories that were being brought downriver by both white and Indian travelers, Tommy asked Sitkum if the Cayuse Indians were letting Dr. Whitman treat their children when they came down with the disease.

"At first, they did," Sitkum answered. "But as more and more of them died, their parents refused to let Dr. Whitman enter their lodges. Instead, they sought help from their own medicine men—the *tewats*."

"A lot of good that does them," Tommy said in exasperation. "A tewat just shakes some rattles and bones over the sick child, tells the parents to parboil the poor kid in a sweat bath even though it's already burning up with fever, then dunks it in freezing water—which is usually fatal."

"This is true," Sitkum agreed. "But the Cayuse parents are out of their minds with grief. Many of them believe the stories Tom Hill and

Joe Lewis have told them about the way the white missionaries intend to poison their people so that they can steal their land."

According to Freda, the half-bloods Tom Hill and Joe Lewis had been living in the Cayuse village near the Whitman Mission when the wagon train she was in stopped there in 1843. Even then, the two malcontents had been spreading lies about the missionaries. Part Delaware Indian and well educated in religious schools in the East, Tom Hill had turned bitter over some real or fancied abuse and begun to preach the deadly doctrine: *"Kill the whites or they will destroy you!"*

Coming west from Maine, Joe Lewis, who was half French-Canadian and half Iroquois, knew what white men had done to his people in the East, so soon had become Tom Hill's disciple. Events transpiring at the Whitman Mission seemed to be proving the two half-bloods right. When Indian youngsters persisted in swiping melons out of the Mission garden patch, an exasperated white employee tried to teach them a lesson by inserting purgative powders into temptingly convenient melons. The boys stole and ate the melons and got sick as poisoned pups. In scolding a Cayuse brave for a minor offense, Whitman inadvertently laid a hand on his shoulder. That night, the Indian got a bite of meat stuck in his throat and choked to death.

If the Cayuses failed to see ominous significance in these occurrences, the older people among them certainly remembered the grandfather tales they had heard regarding the chilling event that had happened in the lower Columbia River area shortly after the establishment of Fort Astoria. Left in charge of the newly completed post after their supply ship *Tonquin* sailed north in late spring of 1811 to trade with the Indians of Nootka Sound, the dour, testy Duncan McDougall, who was a senior partner in the Astor enterprise, had felt so threatened by the growing hostility of the local Indians that he decided the time had come to take strong measures.

Calling a council of all the chiefs of the lower river tribes in the yard within the stockade walls one afternoon, he served them a treat of well-sugared hot tea, gave them presents of blue beads and red cloth, then said he had an announcement of great importance to make.

"The white men among you are few in number," he said. "But we are mighty in medicine." Taking a small black bottle out of his pocket, he held it up so that all the assembled Indians could see it. "In this bottle I hold the smallpox, safely corked up. I have only to draw the cork and let loose the pestilence, which will sweep every man, woman, and child from the face of the earth."

Horrified at the threat of a disease, which in time past had wiped out more than half the natives through whose villages it had raged, the Indians present were stricken with abject terror. Imploring Tyee McDougall not to uncork the bottle, all the local chiefs fervently swore that they were firm friends of the white men and would always remain so.

From that day on, Duncan McDougall would be known and feared by all the natives as the "Great Smallpox Chief."

Though the Whitman Mission was 350 miles east of Chinook country and three thousand miles west of the lands in which Tom Hill and Joe Lewis claimed their people had been abused, the Cayuse Indians heard the tales and became convinced that the white missionary doctor and his associates were deliberately poisoning their children.

So on November 29, 1847, the Cayuses took the course of action that Tom Hill, Joe Lewis, and grief for their own dead long had urged them to take. By the time their bloody work was done, Marcus and Narcissa Whitman and twelve other white people had been killed, fifty-one other whites were being held hostage, and terror stalked the land.

Though Sitkum first brought word of the massacre to Tommy and Freda at their cabin near Rooster Rock on December 1, the incredibly swift Indian grapevine by which the news traveled had supplied few details. It remained for a half-blood interpreter named Matthew Bushman, who was employed at Fort Walla Walla by Factor William McBean, to bring further news downriver on the dark, cold, rainy night of December 3, when he and four Indian canoe paddlers straggled up from the landing just before midnight, pleading for food and warmth.

"What's happened?" Tommy demanded, as Freda set mugs of hot tea liberally laced with rum on the table for the bedraggled visitors.

Shaking his head, Bushman mumbled, "I cannot tell you, M'sieu Warren."

"I hear a lot of Americans have been killed. Is that true?"

"Do not ask, M'sieu. It is not permitted for me to speak."

"Who won't permit you to speak, for God' sake?"

"*Le Bourgeois*, my boss, M'sieu William McBean. When he sends me downriver, he warns me I must tell no one what has happened.

Particularly, I am forbidden to stop at the Methodist Mission at The Dalles to tell young Perrin Whitman that his uncle has been killed. Being only seventeen years old, you see, it is feared he will foolishly seek vengeance."

"Then the story we've heard *is* true," Tommy interrupted. "There's been a massacre at the Whitman Mission. How many people are dead?"

Assuming that since Tommy already knew part of the story, he might as well hear it all, Matthew Bushman told the rest, as Freda encouraged his disclosure by setting out generous portions of food for the famished Hudson's Bay Company couriers. This was the essence of Bushman's story:

First word of the killings, which had taken place in early afternoon Monday, November 29, had been brought to Fort Walla Walla by a carpenter named Peter Hall, who had managed to escape and make his way to the trading post on the east bank of the Columbia River. Though not at all happy to see him, McBean provided him with food, had him rowed across the river to the far bank, and warned him of the dangers he likely would encounter in his attempt to flee to safety at The Dalles.

Truth was, Factor McBean was in a precarious situation. Because this now was American territory, neither Great Britain nor the Hudson's Bay Company had any authority over whites or Indians here. Any quarrel arising between the natives and the American missionaries was not Company business. Being a Catholic and a Britisher, McBean could profess neutrality and say that whatever happened was not his concern.

But as a white man and a Christian, he could not ignore his fellow human beings.

Anxious to get more information about what had happened, he sent Matthew Bushman to the Whitman Mission Tuesday morning to make an inquiry there, knowing that the interpreter's status as a half-blood and a Company employee should protect him from harm. Seeing with his own eyes the dead, mutilated, still unburied bodies of Marcus and Narcissa Whitman and the other victims of the massacre, Bushman was so frightened that he immediately turned around and hastened back to Fort Walla Walla, making the fifty-mile round-trip in a single day.

"I tell M'sieu McBean what I see," Bushman muttered to Tommy and Freda between mouthfuls of food. "At first, he does not know what to do. But he feels he must do something. Finally, he says he will write a letter to officials of the Hudson's Bay Company in Fort Vancouver, telling them what has happened. Then he gives the letter to me to carry downriver."

"Swearing you to secrecy, you say."

"*Oui*, M'sieu Warren. He knows that many American men, women, and children living at the Mission have been captured and are being held as hostages by the Cayuse. If the white settlers at The Dalles or in the Willamette Valley hear of this and raise an army of volunteer soldiers to go to the rescue, the captives will surely die. He tells me when I get to Fort Vancouver I must give the letter to the only man who will know what to do in such a dangerous situation."

"That man being Peter Skene Ogden. Right?"

"*Oui*, M'sieu. He is the man."

Knowing Peter Skene Ogden as he did, Tommy nodded his approval. Never mind that the "Prince of Good Fellows and Terror of All Indians"—as he used to be called—was a Britisher living in a country now American; that he was pudgy and old and his muscles and bones were filled with an old man's aches and pains. No person living in the Pacific Northwest was as respected by the Indians of the interior as he. If the situation could be resolved without a massive shedding of white and Indian blood, he would know what to do …

5.

*E*VER SINCE the Joint Occupancy Treaty had been terminated and the country south of the 49th parallel ceded to the United States, the Hudson's Bay Company factors of the area had devoted their energies to winding up business affairs. Conflicts between Indians and Americans in the region were not their concern. But in Fort Vancouver, the Company headquarters, Peter Skene Ogden reacted to the tragedy at the Whitman Mission with the coolheadedness that had long marked Company dealings with the Indians.

Twenty years had passed since Ogden had made his grueling treks across the upriver country. And the years had taken their toll. Domesticated at last by his lovely Salish Indian wife, Julia, who had gone with him on most of his travels, borne him ten children, and now was making a comfortable home for him within the walls of the most civilized post in the Pacific Northwest, he could have said this was not his problem, sent Oregon's Governor George Abernethy a sympathetic note, and gone back to his paperwork.

Being Peter Skene Ogden, he did no such thing.

Instead, he ordered three bateaus filled with trade goods drawn from Company stores. He sent a brief note to the governor requesting that he make no move that might jeopardize ransom negotiations. Then he stepped into the lead bateau and headed upriver.

His protective force, if such it could be called, consisted of sixteen French-Canadians—men notorious for their lack of enthusiasm when it came to fighting Indians—and his well-deserved reputation for never making a promise he did not keep.

Reaching the Warren cabin well after dark, Peter Ogden asked permission to pull the bateaus into a sheltered cove on the sandy beach, where he and the men paddling the flat-bottomed boats would make a fireless camp for what remained of the night.

"No point in letting the local people know we're heading upriver," he told Tommy. "From what Matthew Bushman tells me, the Cayuse are so jumpy they'll start killing the captives at the first sign of a white attack."

"It is cold and rainy outside," Freda protested. "Without a fire or shelter, you and your men will suffer greatly."

"Your kind thoughts are appreciated, ma'am," Ogden said with a deprecating shrug. "But it won't be the first time we've bedded down with no cover but wet capotes."

"The inside of our house is warm and dry, Mr. Ogden. No one will think it unusual that we should have a fire in it. Bring your men inside. I will give them hot tea, then cook them a good meal. Afterwards, they can sleep on the floor."

"They smell like wet goats, ma'am, and eat like starving wolves."

"That does not matter. Bring them in."

"Do what she says, Peter," Tommy said with a chuckle. "She's a mighty stubborn woman."

Bringing most of the crew up from the beach to be fed and warmed while a couple of men stood guard over the bateaus, then relieving that pair and changing the guard frequently during the night, Ogden made sixteen French-Canadians happy and Freda sixteen friends for life. Having known Tommy for years from his service aboard the *Beaver*, Ogden freely voiced his fears regarding his rescue mission.

"To the Indian mind, when a *tewat* fails to cure a sick child, its father has a right to kill the medicine man. I warned Doctor Whitman about that. But he wouldn't listen."

"He knew the risks he was taking," Tommy said. "As a doctor, he felt he could not neglect a sick child."

"The Cayuse claim he cured only the white children, while he let theirs die."

"That's not true, Peter. His doctoring was the same for all. But the white children were kept dry, warm, and full of liquids, while the Indian children were given sweat baths and then dunked in ice-cold water—which was sure death."

"Well, whatever kind of treatment they got, I'm told that half of the Cayuse tribe died during the epidemic—most of them children. It's no wonder their parents went crazy."

"What do you plan to do?"

"Calm the Cayuse down as much as I can. According to William McBean, the only woman killed so far has been Narcissa Whitman. Fifty-one people living at the Mission have been taken captive and are being held for ransom, he says. Since some of the hostages are white women, they're in danger of being carried off and raped by the hot-headed young Cayuse bucks who did the killings. I hope to stop that before too much damage has been done."

"Has the Hudson's Bay Company authorized you to pay a ransom?"

Ogden shook his head. "I didn't have time to ask permission from Montreal, Tommy. I just lifted a batch of trade goods out of the store-room—blankets, shirts, tobacco, knives, powder and lead, stuff like that—and loaded it into the canoes. According to my reckoning, the stuff is worth around a hundred and thirty dollars in American money. I signed a receipt for it, writing Sir George Simpson a note saying that if it's going to make trouble for him with the stockholders, he can charge it to my account."

"Surely the Provisional Government will reimburse you."

"Well, I'm not going to lose any sleep over it if they don't. Saving lives is all that matters."

Keeping an event of this magnitude a secret from the white residents of Oregon, as Peter Skene Ogden had suggested to Governor Abernethy be done, proved impossible. But because of the explosiveness of the situation and the delicacy of the weeks of bargaining between Ogden and the Cayuse, no overt action was taken by the whites living at The Dalles or in the Willamette Valley while the talks were going on.

The legislature of the Provisional Government had been in session when Governor Abernethy received Ogden's letter telling about the massacre. Next day, it authorized raising a regiment "not to exceed five hundred men" for the purpose of marching into Cayuse country after the captives had been freed to apprehend the murderers. Since the term of service was to be ten months, this was tantamount to a declaration of war against the Cayuse.

On December 14, a "peace commission" was appointed consisting of three men: Joel Palmer, Robert "Doc" Newell, and Major H.A.G.

Lee. It was directed to proceed to the Walla Walla Valley, Tommy learned, as soon as the captives had been rescued and hold a council with the chiefs and principal men of the various upriver bands to prevent, if possible, the coalition of the other inland tribes with the hostiles.

"Which is a polite way of saying we ain't to make peace with the Cayuse," Doc Newell told Tommy Warren, "just do our damndest to make sure none of the other tribes join them in making war on us."

Already the Cayuse had sent a courier to Chief Kamiakin of the Yakima tribe, Sitkum told Tommy, urging him to persuade the fourteen related bands which regarded him as a leader to support the Cayuse in a war of extermination against the whites. He had turned them down, saying bluntly: "Your young men did a bad thing, killing the white doctor and his wife. Only blood will pay for their crime. But it will be the blood of your people, not of mine."

During the cold, gray, rainy month of December, details of the massacre and its aftermath were brought downriver to Tommy and Freda by white and Indian travelers who stopped at their home for food and shelter. As Ogden had feared would happen, half a dozen hot-blooded young Cayuse braves had raped several young white women captives. In one horrible instance, Crockett Bewley, the brother of one young lady, was forced to watch from his sick bed as Edward *Tiloukaikt*, the son of a Cayuse chief, violated his sister, Lorinda. Afterwards, she was compelled to witness her brother's murder as the same young savage bludgeoned Crockett to death with a nail-studded war club while she looked on in horror. When told about the atrocity, Tommy gasped:

"God in Heaven! The whites will make the Cayuse pay for that!"

Even before the arrival of the Ogden party, some of the older Cayuse chiefs had appealed to the Catholic priests to intercede for them, proposing a four-point program for peace:

1. That the Americans should not come up to make war.
2. That the Americans should send up a "great man" to make a treaty of peace.
3. That when the great man arrived, all the captives would be freed.

4. That the Americans should forget the lately committed murders, just as the Cayuses would forget the deaths of so many of their children from disease brought by the white men. To avoid trouble in the future, the chiefs suggested, no more Americans should travel through their country, where the young Cayuse braves might do them harm.

Though he doubted that the Americans would consider the last proposal, Bishop Blanchet, who put the request of the chiefs in writing, prefaced the document with the statement that the Indians had been convinced that Dr. Whitman was poisoning them. Signing the paper for the Cayuse were *Tiloukaikt, Camaspelo,* Young Chief, and Five Crows. Even before the ink was dry on the laboriously crafted document, news arrived that the "great man" sent up to negotiate the release of the captives was not an American but a Britisher—Peter Skene Ogden—which pleased the Indians. Meeting with him at Fort Walla Walla a few days after his arrival, the apprehensive Cayuse chiefs listened as he opened negotiations in his typically blunt, plain-spoken way.

"We have been among you for thirty years without the shedding of blood," Ogden said. "We are traders of a different nation from the Americans. We supply you with ammunition, but not to kill the Americans, who are of the same color, speak the same language, and who worship the same God as ourselves. Their cruel fate causes our hearts to bleed. Why do we make you chiefs, if you cannot control your young men?"

Edward *Tiloukaikt*, son of the Cayuse head chief and known to be the brave who had raped Lorinda Bewley and then clubbed her brother Crockett to death, spoke sullenly.

"I am one of those young men. *Tai-tam-nat* Whitman was an evil *tewat* who was poisoning our people."

"When Indians all over Oregon are dying of measles and other diseases, that is a foolish thing to say," Ogden responded. "How could Dr. Whitman be responsible for the deaths of so many in such widely scattered places?"

"We were told he was responsible. Tom Hill and Joe Lewis said it."

"I did not come here to argue with rash young men," Ogden said coldly. "I came here as an official of the Hudson's Bay Company. I left

Fort Vancouver before the Americans had been notified of the killings."

"What will the Americans do?" Chief *Tiloukaikt* asked anxiously "Will they come upriver and make war on us?"

"I cannot say. If you wish it, on my return I will see what can be done for you. I will pay you a ransom. That is all."

The talks went on all day, stalling time after time on the Cayuse demand that Ogden guarantee that the Americans would not make war on them—which he would not do—and his demand that the captives be brought to Fort Walla Walla within six days before the ransom would be paid—which the Cayuse were reluctant to do without a no-war guarantee.

"Fifty blankets, fifty shirts, ten guns, ten fathoms of tobacco, ten handkerchiefs, and one hundred balls and powder."

These were the goods, Ogden told the Cayuse, that he would pay them upon their delivery of the captives. Over the strenuous objections of guilty participants in the massacre such as *Tamsucky, Tomahas,* and his son Edward, Chief *Tiloukaikt* at last agreed to the terms, returned to the Whitman Mission, and told the captives that they were free to go. Five wagons were needed to carry their baggage, food, and the women and children for the twenty-five-mile trip, which was completed on December 29. With the hostages surrendered, Ogden kept his promise and paid the ransom goods on Thursday, December 30. After the goods had been distributed, he allowed the Indians to celebrate with a dance inside the fort enclosure, though he made sure that the former women and children captives stayed in locked rooms with guards on the doors.

The fact that a large band of angry Cayuse braves was camped just outside the fort worried Ogden. Adding to his anxiety was the news recently brought upriver by the courier, Matthew Bushman, that ten American volunteers under the command of Major H.A.G. Lee had come upriver from the Willamette Valley to The Dalles a week ago. Ostensibly, their purpose was to protect lives and property. But once the captives were out of harm's way, their position could quickly be converted into an advance base for a punitive expedition against the Cayuse. If the dissident Indians camped nearby learned about the presence of the volunteer force, they very well might renege on the promises they had made, overwhelm the small force at the fort, kill the captives, and launch a war.

Fortunately for the whites, the six adults and three children residing at the Lapwai Mission in Nez Perce country 140 miles upriver had been escorted to Fort Walla Walla by forty well-armed, friendly Nez Perce braves, who were more than a match for any group of rash young men who might try to break the peace, so no hostile acts occurred. Though the downriver trip would begin on Sunday, January 2, 1848, none of the religious people objected to traveling on the Sabbath—as many of them had done in time past.

The party being taken downriver by Peter Skene Ogden and his sixteen French-Canadian boatmen was a large one, taxing the capacity of the three bateaus. Reaching the Warren cabin a few days later, where Freda had alerted the Emigrant Aid Society to have a supply of food, blankets, and extra clothes available and Tommy had arranged for more boats to relieve overcrowding, the survivors were given a warm welcome there and at Fort Vancouver, where they arrived January 8.

Already plans were afoot, Tommy knew, to mount a military expedition to apprehend the Cayuse murderers and punish the tribe for what it had done. Ironically, the first group of people to be terrorized by the Oregon Volunteers were the recently ransomed captives.

After spending the weekend at Fort Vancouver, the former captives were taken by boat across the Columbia River to Portland. Assembled on the dock there was a company of fifty men, under the command of Colonel Cornelius Gilliam, getting ready to leave for The Dalles. As the boats approached the dock, the Volunteers gave them a typically noisy frontier greeting by raising their rifles and firing a salute into the rain-filled sky. Among the passengers in the boat which Tommy was steering were thirteen-year-old Catherine and ten-year-old Elizabeth Sager, orphan children who had endured all the horrors and bloodshed of the massacre, including seeing Narcissa Whitman and their older brother, Henry Sager, killed.

Terrified by the gunfire—which they thought was aimed at them—the two girls screamed hysterically, threw themselves down in the bottom of the boat, and tried to hide under the wet canvas.

"For God's sake, hold your fire, you idiots!" Tommy shouted angrily at the brave soldiers standing on the dock. "These poor kids think you're shooting at *them!*"

6.

$\mathcal{I}$N ALL, NINETEEN PEOPLE with white blood in their veins were victims of the massacre or died of exposure and neglect shortly thereafter. Included in this total were Mary Ann Bridger and Helen Mar Meek, the half-blood girls whose mothers had been a Ute and a Shoshone, the fathers, former mountain men Jim Bridger and Joe Meek, who had left their ten- and eleven-year-old daughters at the Whitman Mission to be schooled.

So far as the Cayuse tribe was concerned, it had lost 198 members to disease—most of them children—out of a total population of 400 people.

But by the rules of white justice, Tommy knew, the score was not even yet. The murderers must be apprehended, the Provisional Government demanded, given a fair trial in a white man's court, convicted, and hanged—even if that meant waging two years of brutal, relentless war against the Cayuse tribe ...

Which it did ...

Aware of the fact that most of the Volunteers could not distinguish between a hostile or a friendly Indian, Tommy warned Sitkum to give the soldiers coming upriver a wide berth.

"Keep your hair cut short, wear your cap and coat from *Beaver* days, and speak English whenever you deal with white people," Tommy told Sitkum. "No sense in losing your scalp to a glory-hunting Volunteer."

"I will be careful," Sitkum said, nodding. "As Chief Kamiakin told the Cayuse who asked him to go to war against the whites, this is their crime, not ours."

Because news of the Whitman Massacre would cause a national reaction once word of it reached the East, the suggestion by the Provisional Government that a special messenger be sent to Washington City was quickly endorsed. Joe Meek volunteered to make the trip.

"Been travelin' back and forth across the country fer more years than I care to remember," the ex–mountain man declared. "Happens President Polk is married to a second cousin of mine, so him and me are shirttail relations. Won't be no trick at all fer me to git an invite to the White House, where I can tell him and the other bigwigs how much this part of the country wants to become a territory of the United States."

For the past ten years, many memorials had been sent to the nation's capital urging that the jurisdiction of the United States be extended to Oregon—with no results. Now a new "Memorial to Congress" was drawn up, stating the case in stronger terms:

> Having called upon the government of the United States so often in vain, we have almost despaired of receiving its protection, yet we trust that our present situation, when fully laid before you, will at once satisfy your honorable body of the great necessity of extending the strong arm of guardianship over this remote, but beautiful portion of the United States.

Planning to go overland with a party of nine wilderness-hardened ex–mountain men, Joe Meek told Tommy that he'd heard the snow-drifts over the crest of the Blue Mountains would be twenty feet deep through January and February, so it would probably be the middle of March before his group could travel. Meanwhile, Tommy was kept busy transporting troops of Oregon Volunteers upriver from Portland to The Dalles, near which settlement the first shot of the Cayuse War was fired early in January 1848. The engagement occurred, Tommy heard, when a small group of Volunteers overtook a mixed bag of Cayuse and local Indians that had stolen three hundred cattle left in the area by emigrants the previous fall. In the skirmish, the Volunteers failed to recover the cattle but did manage to kill three Indians, wound a few more, and capture sixty Indian horses.

"If gaining sixty scrub Indian ponies while losing three hundred head of cattle is what you call a victory," Tommy told Doc Newell caustically, "you Volunteers better hope for a few defeats."

"Hell, I ain't a Volunteer," Doc Newell protested. "I'm a peace commissioner—with a paper that says so. Trouble is, I can't make peace till the shootin' stops."

Moving on up the Columbia toward Cayuse country, the Volunteers exchanged long-range shots with the hostiles on several occasions, with no significant effect. In an abandoned Indian village in the

Deschutes area, the Volunteers set fire to a dozen empty lodges. In retaliation, the Cayuses burned down all the buildings at the Whitman Mission except the gristmill—which they needed to grind their grain—then rode over to the Umatilla River and set fire to the Saint Anne Mission.

From what Tommy could learn from Sitkum, the Cayuse leaders were divided. Favoring war to the bitter end were *Tamsucky, Tomahas,* Five Crows, and most of the younger men, while *Stickus,* Beardy, and *Camaspelo* wanted a negotiated peace. Some of the Cayuse were boasting that "Americans are easy to kill," citing as an example the massacre victims they had clubbed to death. Believing that the Americans were poor fighters, young warriors from several inland tribes joined the hostile Cayuse faction, seeking glory and scalps, bringing the number of fighting men to four hundred by late February, when the Volunteers at last forced the Indians into a decisive battle in the Umatilla area.

One unpleasant surprise to the hostiles was the fact that a number of ex–Hudson's Bay Company employees, French-Canadians, and half-bloods had joined the Volunteers and were fighting on the side of the Americans. Included in Colonel Gilliam's regiment, which now numbered five hundred men, were Perrin Whitman, the late doctor's nephew; W.D. Canfield, one of the released captives; and half-blood Tom McKay, who had escorted the Whitman-Spalding party from rendezvous to Fort Walla Walla in 1836. Serving with Tom McKay, who was a Captain of the Volunteers, was his brother, Charles, ranked as a lieutenant.

According to talk among the Volunteers, a Cayuse *tewat* named Gray Eagle had bragged that his medicine was so strong no bullet could hurt him. "If he is shot, he says, he'll 'puke up the bullet.'"

In a sharp, bloody battle the next day, Gray Eagle got an opportunity to test his magic. Spotting Tom McKay fifty yards away during the heat of the skirmish, Gray Eagle gave a whoop of derision, lifted his rifle, and cried, "There's Tom McKay! I will kill him!"

But McKay fired first. A crack shot, he watched as Gray Eagle, struck squarely between the eyes by the bullet, toppled off his horse. Standing beside his brother, Charles McKay said laconically, "Reckon he'll puke it up?"

"Not likely. I shot him above his pukin' spot."

"Well, I got my sights on Five Crows. Let's see if I can get him."

Charles McKay fired. Struck in the right arm by the shot, Five Crows retired from the battle.

Counting their casualties when the battle was over, the Cayuses and their allies were shocked to discover eight dead and five badly wounded. With this stark lesson that the Americans could and would fight, all the allies deserted the Cayuse and headed for home. Divided and demoralized, the Cayuse abandoned organized resistance, broke up into small groups, and retreated into the wilderness of the Blue Mountains.

With the weather moderating and the snow melting in the high country, Joe Meek and his party of ex–mountain men crossed the Blues in early March, struck the well-established Oregon Trail in the Snake River country, and made good time on their journey to Washington City. There, as Meek had predicted, he was welcomed by his shirttail relative, President Polk, lionized by the press as Oregon's "Ambassador in Buckskin," and listened to with respect by Congress.

Reaching the fire-blackened ruins of the Whitman Mission in the Walla Walla Valley, the Oregon Volunteers established a military post called Fort Waters, from which, for the next few months, details ranging from squad to company size rode out in search of hostiles to capture or kill.

"Mostly, all they catch are friendly Indians," Doc Newell complained to Tommy, "who, after being mistreated and having their cattle and horses stolen, ain't in no mood to help me locate the leaders and negotiate a peace. But I have put out the word that the only way the Cayuse can end the war is for the chiefs to name the half dozen young bucks that done the killings, turn them over to me, and let me take 'em down to Oregon City for trial."

"Where they're sure to be found guilty by a white man's court?"

"Ain't much doubt about that, Tommy. But that's the only peace offer I can make."

As a result of his trip to Washington City, Joe Meek was appointed United States Marshal for Oregon Territory, whose enabling act Congress quickly passed. Returning to Oregon, he brought the good news that a regiment of Mounted Riflemen was on its way to assist the new territory in bringing peace to the area. Thus assured of federal support,

Governor Joseph Lane sent a strongly worded message to the leaders of the Cayuse tribe: *Give up the murderers or we will carry on a war of extermination.*

Shortly thereafter, five Cayuses surrendered and were brought downriver to Oregon City, where United States Marshal Meek took custody of them.

They were: *Tiloukaikt, Tomahas, Kia-ma-sump-kin, Clokamas,* and *Ish-ish-kais-kais.* All five, said their chiefs, "have blood on their hands."

An indictment for murder was issued against each of the five prisoners May 21, 1850, with the trial beginning the next day. Twenty-two prospective jurors were challenged and excused in an effort on the part of the defense to exclude all older Oregon citizens who might be Indian haters. Three hundred spectators jammed the courtroom each day to observe the proceedings.

Testifying for the five accused Cayuse were *Stickus*, Young Chief, and *Camaspelo*. Called as prosecution witnesses were young Eliza Spalding, Catherine and Elizabeth Sager, Lorinda Bewley, and a number of other white residents of the Whitman Mission.

After two days of hearings, the case went to the jury. The charge given the jurors by Judge Pratt was brief. In the opinion of Tommy Warren, who did not attend the trial but did follow the proceedings as reported in the *Oregon Spectator* with great interest, it was devastating to the defendants.

"You should bear in mind," Judge Pratt said, "that the Cayuse nation, which voluntarily surrendered the five prisoners, knows best who were the perpetrators of the massacre."

After deliberating for only one hour and fifteen minutes on Friday afternoon, May 24, the jury returned a guilty verdict against each of the five. Judge Pratt then sentenced the five Cayuses to be hanged on Monday, June 3, 1850. United States Marshal Joseph Meek, whose half-blood daughter had died of disease and neglect following the massacre, would act as executioner.

Though Tommy and Freda Warren felt as much sympathy for the grief-crazed Cayuse parents who had lost so many of their children as they did for the white victims of the massacre, they were grateful that this tragic chapter in the development of Oregon had finally come to an end. Now that peace had come to the upriver country at last, emigration over the Oregon Trail—which had ceased these past two years—could resume. With Oregon Territory established and travel between Portland and the interior expanded, interest in the upriver country was growing. Obviously, the Columbia River through the Cascades was destined to be the principal artery of travel to eastern Oregon.

Most important of all, so far as Tommy was concerned, boats powered by steam and owned by Americans had at last come to the great River of the West …

The first of these was the Army transport *Massachusetts*, which had been built in Boston in 1845 and put in service to carry troops where they were needed. Following Joe Meek's arrival in the nation's capital in late spring, 1848, the pressing need seemed to be in Oregon, so the transport had been loaded with soldiers, guns, and supplies and dispatched with all possible speed around the Horn and up the West Coast to the mouth of the Columbia, where it arrived in May 1849. Exactly how the ship's cannons and troops could be used against a small Indian tribe living 350 miles inland, military strategists did not attempt to say. Like other ships of her kind on long voyages, the *Massachusetts* was propelled by wind most of the time, but could fire up her boilers and be driven by steam for brief periods.

After piloting her in across the bar under steam power, Ben Warren sent word upriver to Tommy that a ship needing a river guide lay at anchor nearby. When Tommy came downriver a couple of days later, Ben took his son out to the ship in his Chinook Indian–manned pilot boat. Eyeing the *Massachusetts* as they approached the ship, Tommy frowned in puzzlement.

"She's a steamer, you say?"

"Aye, that she is."

"Where are her paddle wheels?"

"She doesn't have any, Tommy. She's screw propelled."

Observing the big troop transport more closely, Tommy noted the concave area below the stern under which he assumed the metal propeller that drove the ship was located.

"I've heard of such ships, Dad. But this is the first one I've seen. How well does the screw propeller work?"

"As well or better than paddle wheels on the open sea, Captain Bertrand tells me. But he isn't sure how it will work in the river, where there's more silt and sand to be stirred up."

During the daylong trip up the Columbia to the anchorage off Fort Vancouver, which was made at reduced speed, the screw-propelled ship behaved well enough, so far as Tommy could tell. After greeting the ship's arrival with a salute from the fort's brass cannon, just as Dr. John McLoughlin had done for the *Beaver* back in 1836, Peter Skene Ogden, who was now in charge, entertained Captain Bertrand and the ship's officers with a dinner. Next day, the troops disembarked and began forming an encampment that would transform the former Hudson's Bay Company trading post into an American military base which would retain the Fort Vancouver name.

Though the Cayuse War was over and there was no need to impress the Indians with the naval might of the United States, Captain Bertrand did accept Tommy's suggestion that he steam the *Massachusetts* on up the Columbia as far as Rooster Rock, where he circled close to shore and gave a toot of the whistle to Freda, who stood on the knoll waving as the ship passed by.

Dropping back downriver, the transport anchored near Portland for ten days, loading a deck cargo of newly milled lumber which Captain Bertrand planned to carry south to the new Army bases being built near San Francisco. Because of the vast number of prospectors pouring into the Sacramento area since the discovery of gold at John Sutter's mill in January 1848, most of the traffic west these days was headed for California rather than Oregon.

"Frankly, I'm worried about losing a lot of my crew to the goldfields," Captain Bertrand told Tommy. "On our way out from New York, we called at Hawaii rather than San Francisco, so had no problems with desertion. Now, I'm afraid we will."

"Probably you'll lose some sailors if you let them off the ship," Tommy said, nodding. "When news of the strike reached the Willamette Valley last spring, half of the settlers living there headed south, leaving their farms to the weeds and the Indians. Matter of fact, my kid brother, Emil, hired onto the first ship heading south from Astoria, then jumped it the minute it dropped anchor off San Francisco. He's in the gold fields now."

"Has he struck it rich?"

"Not that I know of. He writes Mom every now and then, telling her not to worry about him. Panning for gold is hard work, he says, but there are easier ways to get rich in the camps, if a person is smart enough to try them. Which he is."

"How old is he?"

"Twenty-one. He's as bright as a brass button, and twice as bold. He's never cared for the river or the sea. He says two sailors—Dad and me—are enough in one family. He intends to make his fortune ashore."

Tommy told Captain Bertrand that before the discovery of gold in California, plans had been made by the Pacific Mail Steamship Company to establish fast steamer mail service between New York and Portland. But the gold rush soon changed that. When the first Pacific Mail steamer, the *California*, sailed from New York in late spring, 1848, she was scheduled to stop at Monterey, then come north to the Columbia River and Portland. But when she touched at Buenos Aires on her way south, fifty South Americans who had heard of the strike swarmed aboard as paying passengers. At Panama on the west coast, seven hundred frantic men with money in their hands screamed to be taken aboard.

Knowing that his ship could legally carry only 250 passengers, the captain decided that since these were not American waters, American maritime law did not apply. In view of the fact that the fifty people that had come aboard at Buenos Aires were South Americans, who probably were used to being crowded anyway, they were shoved below decks into the steerage, while 350 of the waiting Americans who were waving money at him were taken aboard as deck passengers.

Reaching Monterey safely despite her overload, the *California* discharged the steerage and deck passengers, then, forgetting that her destination was supposed to be Portland, returned to Panama and picked up the three hundred and fifty cash customers left stranded there. Notwithstanding its agreement to serve Portland, the ship continued to make the highly profitable Monterey-Panama run for the next two years.

In May 1850, a new Pacific Mail steamer, the *Carolina*, did manage to sail west from New York around the Horn and then up the Pacific Coast to the Columbia and Portland. Only half the size of the *California*, she was a wooden twin-screw vessel, which also carried a rack of sail. Establishing what was advertised to be monthly service between San Francisco, Astoria, and Portland, she maintained that schedule until the weather turned bad and the seas grew stormy, under which conditions the "month" often turned out to have six or seven weeks in it.

Having learned by now that the prospectors in California were willing to exchange their gold dust for lumber, beef, potatoes, salmon, and butter, Willamette Valley farmers and Portland businessmen decided that it would be to their advantage to acquire a steamship of their own. When a majority interest in the side-wheeler, *Gold Hunter,* which had been built by an independent company for the Sacramento River trade, came on the market, a hastily thrown-together combine of Portland businessmen raised enough money to buy a controlling interest in the ship. Proud of the fact that they now owned what was bound to be a highly profitable steamship, the Portland merchants filled her hold with cargo and sent her on her way south rejoicing.

Unfortunately, when the *Gold Hunter* reached San Francisco, the minority shareholders residing there bought back enough shares from the ship's officers to give them a controlling interest in the ship, then put her into service between San Francisco and Panama. Quite literally, the Oregon owners—of which Tommy was one—had been "sold south."

Visiting his mother and father at Hilltop House in Astoria a couple of months later, Tommy was not surprised to hear his father snort derisively and say, "Serves you Portlanders right for trusting Californians, who are all born scoundrels and thieves. We Astorians intend to keep our money at home by building our own steamboat."

"I noticed a hull being framed on the bank just below the town dock. Is that your boat?"

"You bet it is. An experienced riverman named Jim Frost, who's run steamboats on the Mississippi for years, recently settled here. He helped us design it. We've got the parts for the engine ordered from San Francisco and are going to put it all together when they arrive."

"Does this mean you're giving up on sail?"

"Lord, no! Until wood grows on the open sea or coal deposits are discovered in the Pacific Northwest, we'll need sail on the ocean for years to come. But as you've said yourself, it's steam power that's needed on the river. We don't plan to take our boat out to sea. She'll just run between Astoria and Portland."

"What are you going to name her?"

"The *Columbia.* What else?"

Another interesting piece of news revealed by Tommy's mother at the dinner table that evening was that his father no longer was the only bar pilot licensed in Astoria under the new law passed by the Oregon Territorial Legislature. A recent arrival from San Francisco, George Flavell now had become a resident of Astoria and gone into the piloting business. Well qualified in the trade, he was in the process of forming a Bar Pilots Association which would set standards and fees for men guiding ships over the bar. Ben Warren had become the first pilot to enroll in the Association.

"You surprise me, Dad," Tommy said as he and his father sipped after-dinner brandies while Lolanee cleared the table. "I never imagined you'd work for any man."

"He's getting no younger, dear," Lolanee said gently. "And neither am I, in case you haven't noticed."

"Oh, you both have a few gray hairs, I can see that. But neither of you have lost your smarts. In fact, you both seem a lot brighter to me than you were ten years ago."

"Or you are," Ben said with a wry smile. "No, son, I don't think your mother and I have lost much so far as brain power is concerned. But our muscles and bones aren't what they used to be. Captain Flavell is a good man and a lot younger than I am. I'm perfectly willing to let him take over the lion's share of the bar pilot trade."

Before returning upriver to his home near Rooster Rock, Tommy had a quiet talk with his mother about a couple of things that were bothering her. The first was his father's insistence on taking his turn as a bar pilot whenever it came, no matter how stormy the weather. The second was the continued absence of Emil in the goldfields of California.

"Your father isn't as nimble as he once was, Tommy. After all, he's fifty-six years old. You know what it's like standing in a pilot boat and timing your jump to catch the rungs of a ship's ladder on a stormy sea. Your father is too old for that sort of thing."

"I know, Mom. But he won't accept being coddled."

"I don't ask that. But I wish you'd speak to Captain Flavell and ask him not to call on your father when the seas are rough. If he misses catching the ladder, he's gone."

"I'll do what I can."

"About Emil. He's always respected you, Tommy. Can't you persuade him to give up trying to make his fortune in California and come back to Oregon? From what he says in his letters, I'm afraid he's taking too many risks."

"I haven't heard from him for a while. What is he doing now?"

"He's involved in buying and selling claims, acting as an agent and taking a commission on every transaction. Since the gold rush started two years ago, over a hundred thousand people have come to California, he says. Most of them have no idea of how or where to begin digging. For what he admits is an outrageous fee, he shows them."

"What's wrong with that?"

"In a state that's been settled long enough to have established laws and courts to maintain order, there would be nothing wrong with it. But California is a lawless place, Emil says, where every man carries a gun. From what I read in the California papers—and what he jokes about in his letters—vigilante committees and vigilante justice are at work in all the camps, as well as in San Francisco. You know how reckless Emil can be. With all the money he's making, I'm afraid he's just asking for trouble."

"He's a sharp kid, Mom, with a knack for taking care of himself. But I'll do what I can. Maybe if I write and tell him about all the business opportunities that are developing in the Willamette Valley and along the Columbia River, I might be able to persuade him to come back home and apply his talents here. For instance, if he could convince some investors to build the steamboats we need so badly in the Gorge, he'd do us all a favor …"

Meanwhile, the builders of the home-designed-and-owned steamboat *Columbia* slid their nearly completed craft into the water below the Astoria dock in early June 1850. Even the most loyal local stockholder, Ben Warren, admitted that the craft was not much for looks.

"She's an ugly-duckling cross between a ferryboat and a scow," he told Lolanee. "But she floats. Now if her engine will run and turn her paddle wheels, we'll call her a success."

Built double-ended with a blunt stem and stern, the boat was a side-wheeler, ninety feet long, with a sixteen-foot beam and a hold depth of four feet. Unlike her distant relatives on the Mississippi, she was without an ornament of any kind, having not a single piece of gingerbread scrollwork on her. As boats went, she looked boxlike and clumsy. But when her wood-fired boilers were heated up and steam was fed into her cylinders, her paddle wheels turned and she moved through the water at a slow but steady rate.

Which was all that counted.

Lacking sleeping accommodations and a galley, she was not much for comfort, her passengers having to pack their own food and blankets aboard and sleep unsheltered under the open sky. Even so, the day of her maiden voyage from Astoria to Portland, July 3, 1850, was a memorable one in the annals of American steamboating in the Pacific Northwest. Every Astorian who could find an excuse to make the trip was aboard as the *Columbia* left the dock, leaving only Ben and Lolanee Warren, who did not wish to dim Captain Frost's glory by sharing the pilothouse with him, and George Flavell, who was expecting an incoming sailing ship, to cheer the steamboat on its way. But when the *Columbia* returned triumphantly a week later, the passengers who had made the trip gave the stay-at-homes an enthusiastic report on the trials and triumphs of the voyage.

"I'll say this for Captain Frost," an Astoria storekeeper named Jack Wilson told Ben, "he's a mighty cautious man. Like most of us aboard, he'd never gone further upriver than Tongue Point, so once we passed it none of us knew where the main channel was."

"I offered him my services as a river guide free of charge," Ben said. "But he told me anybody that had navigated the Mississippi as long as he had ought to be able to find his way up the Columbia."

"Well, his way worked—after a fashion. What he did was he hailed a couple of Indian boys we seen fishing from a small boat in a slough a couple of miles beyond the point. He asked if they knew the channel, they said they did, so he paid them a dollar to come aboard as river guides."

"Did they steer him right?"

"At first there was a communication gap, with them talkin' Jargon and him a Deep South drawl. But by using a lot of sign language, they finally managed to understand one another. We took it real slow, makin' only fifty miles the first day. Not wantin' to risk steamin' in the dark, Cap'n Frost pulled in to the bank and tied the bow to a tree for the night. Which turned out to be a mistake."

"Because of the tide, I suppose."

"Right. When we snubbed off, the tide was out. But around midnight it came back in—"

"Lifting the boat six feet and nearly pulling her under."

Jack Wilson frowned at Ben. "How'd you know that?"

"It happens twice a day, Jack. Everyday."

"Well, none of us knew that—including Captain Frost. We were all sound asleep when he suddenly woke up to find the boat's bow being pulled under water. If he hadn't jumped up and slacked off the line real quick, we'd have sunk for sure."

"He must have been a bit embarrassed."

"Yeah, Ben, he was. He said he'd never seen tides like that on the Mississippi."

"But you did make it to Portland the next day?"

"You bet we did! Matter of fact, by the middle of the afternoon we were steaming along so well Cap'n Frost took the *Columbia* into the Willamette River and we chugged all the way up to the falls below Oregon City, tootin' our whistle all the way. It was a sight to see, I tell you, with people linin' the banks on either side cheerin' till they was hoarse. Since it was the Fourth of July and they were shootin' off fireworks anyway, they gave us a real blast."

Following the success of her initial trip, the home-grown-and-built steamboat established regular service between Astoria and Oregon City on a twice-monthly basis, charging twenty-five dollars per passenger each way and the same amount for a ton of freight. Connecting with the Pacific Mail Steamship Company vessels to and from California, as well as towing sailing ships, barges, and keelboats at a brisk four miles an hour, the *Columbia* had a monopoly on the lower river trade for six months.

But even as she and the investors who had built her enjoyed the revenue from their enterprise, a professional shipbuilder was going to work at Milwaukie, Oregon, just downriver from Oregon City, with plans to build a steamboat the likes of which had never been seen in the Pacific Northwest.

His name was Lot Whitcomb …

7.

*E*MIGRATING FROM WISCONSIN to Oregon in 1848, Lot Whitcomb named the town he platted on the banks of the Willamette River seven miles upstream from Portland "Milwaukie." Since he had become its postmaster, as well as the owner and publisher of the local newspaper, his somewhat lame explanation—that the town's name had been derived from three Clackamas Indian words whose meaning had never been explained to him, rather than from his own misspelling of the Wisconsin city's name, Milwaukee—had to be accepted at face value.

After all, if the postmaster and newspaper publisher of a town didn't know how to spell its name, who did? So Milwaukie the metropolis to be, remained.

Most newcomers to Oregon shared the misconception that Portland was on the Columbia River. It was not. As a matter of fact, the first claim in what initially was called "Stumptown" had been staked out on the west bank of the Willamette River twelve miles upstream from its juncture with the Columbia. This was just downriver from what Lewis and Clark had called "Image Canoe Island" on their way west to the Pacific in November 1805, then renamed "Wapato (Wild Potato) Island" on their way east in early April 1806.

Both times, the explorers had missed finding the mouth of the Willamette itself, though Captain Clark suspected a river was there, for he wrote on the way west:

> Passed the lower point of the Island, which is nine miles in length....The Indians make Signs that a village is Situated back of these islands on the Lard. Side, and I believe that a chanel is still on the Lrd. Side as a canoe passed in between the Small Islands, and made Signs that way, probably to traffick with some nativs liveing on another chanel.

45

On the way east as the party again passed by the nine-mile-long island, the explorers shrewdly deduced that the wide valley between the Coast Range and the Cascades must be drained by a sizable river. They were correct; Sauvie Island masked the mouth of a river called Multnomah by the Indians, Willamette by the whites. After traveling half a day past it on their way east, the two captains met a pair of Indians who lived near the great falls of the river and described it to them. Lewis wrote:

> We readily prevailed on them to give us a sketch of this river which they drew on a mat with a coal. It appeared that this river, which they called the Mult-no-mah, discharged itself behind the Island which we called the Image Canoe Island. Captain Clark determined to return and examine this river; accordingly, he took a party of seven men and one of the perogues and set out 1/2 after 11; he hired one of the Cashhooks, for a birning glass, to pilot him to the entrance of the Multnomah and took him on board with him.

Because there was deep water from its mouth twelve miles to Portland, upstream to Milwaukie at River Mile 19, then on to Oregon City at River Mile 27, steamboats could navigate the Willamette all the way to Astoria without difficulty most of the year. The lone hazard was just below the mouth of the Clackamas River, two miles downstream from Oregon City, where the rapids were shallow at periods of low water.

In this land of a nine-month-long rainy season, bottomless mudholes, and poor roads, navigable rivers were by far the best way to travel. So Lot Whitcomb, who owned everything in sight, had good reason to believe that the town he had platted was going to be the most important port on the Willamette River. By building and launching the biggest and best steamboat ever to ply the inland waters of the Pacific Northwest, he was well on his way toward becoming a very important and a very wealthy man.

Not surprisingly, he decided to call the new steamboat the *Lot Whitcomb*.

When contacted in late October and offered the berth of First Mate aboard the still-being-built boat, Tommy Warren was inclined to say no, for what he really wanted was a captain's berth on a steamer of his own built to ply the Columbia between the Cascades and The Dalles. But right now no one seemed in the mood or had the money to build such a boat. And he did need a job, for Freda had just given birth to their first child.

A husky, blonde-haired boy whom they had christened Lars Thomas after her father, who had always wanted a son, and Tommy himself, the new baby was going to keep Freda busy for a while, forcing Tommy to take whatever river work he could get, pride and personal wishes notwithstanding. Until recently, Tommy had considered himself to be the most experienced steamboat man on the Columbia because of his years in the *Beaver*. Now that was no longer the case, for Lot Whitcomb had imported two well-qualified professionals from the Mississippi: Captain J. C. Ainsworth, a veteran pilot from the upper river, and Jacob Kamm, a licensed engineer from New Orleans. River gossip had it that he not only was paying them very well but had sweetened their employment contracts by giving them shares in his newly formed Oregon Steamship Company.

Since a First Mate's berth appeared to be the best he could do at the moment, Tommy felt compelled to go to Milwaukie, have a look at the boat whose hull was taking shape on the ways there, and talk to the boat's builder about his plans. Once there, he was favorably impressed, for it was plain to see that an enterprising owner, a crew of real shipwrights, a professional engineer, and a river captain who knew his business had been brought together under the best possible conditions.

"From her keel to her pilot house, the *Lot Whitcomb* is going to be a first-class steamboat," the brash, darkly handsome, black-mustached, energetic young entrepreneur who owned the boat proclaimed to Tommy as he showed him around. "Her keel is a stick of prime Oregon fir without a knot in it. She measures 160 feet in length, has a 24-foot beam, is 5 feet 8 inches deep in the hold, and is rated at six hundred tons."

"She's to be a side-wheeler, I take it, like the *Beaver*?"

"Right. Only much bigger, of course. Her side-wheels will be eighteen feet in diameter, set in housings well back from center. Fully loaded, we estimate she'll draw about three feet of water."

"You're starting to install the engine, I see. Where did you get it?"

"Jacob Kamm had it built to his exact specifications in New York and New Orleans, then shipped to us by way of San Francisco. He's a qualified marine engineer, with a degree from the best school in Missouri. I'll take you down and introduce you to him."

Picking their way carefully through the still-open framework of the boat, they approached a short, chunky, yellow-haired young man whose black-billed cap was pushed to the back of his head and whose hands were slick with grease. Speaking with a heavy Teutonic accent, he was scolding a pair of husky laborers as they attempted to lift a heavy metal part into place.

"*Nein, nein, dumkopfs!* First, ve geliften her oop, den ve gesliden her in! Not first gesliden, den geliften! Now, try und geliften again!"

With the workmen's efforts successful this time and the metal part in place, Jacob Kamm took off his cap and mopped his sweating brow, then turned and smiled apologetically at the two visitors as the laborers bolted the fitting into place.

"Dey are goot bhoys, Misder Whitcomb, only somedimes dey don't understand plain English too well."

"Jacob, this is Tommy Warren, who served as First Mate on the *Beaver* for ten years," Lot Whitcomb said. "I've offered him the same position on our boat."

"*Ya*, I haf heard of dot Hudson's Bay Company ship, de *Beaver*," Kamm exclaimed as he shook Tommy's hand. "She vas a goot steamer in her day. But ours vill be better."

"From what Mr. Whitcomb tells me, I'm sure it will be. When do you plan to launch her?"

"As soon as the lower part of the hull is sealed, we'll slide her into the water," Lot Whitcomb said, preempting the engineer's reply and making it clear to Tommy that *he* was in charge of the project. "If all goes well, we'll make it by the middle of December. I hope you'll come aboard."

After going back to their cabin near Rooster Rock and consulting with Freda, Tommy agreed to sign on as First Mate of the *Lot Whitcomb* at the respectable salary of fifty dollars a month and five shares of stock in the Oregon Navigation Company. During the six-week period between his taking the berth and the launching of the boat on Christmas Day 1850, Tommy came to know and respect Jacob Kamm, who, despite his youth, already had a great deal of experience as a marine engineer.

Born in Switzerland in 1823, Jacob Kamm had been eight years old when his father resigned his commission in the French Army and took his family to America in search of a better life. In New Orleans four years later, Jacob became an orphan at the age of twelve when his father, mother, and all the other children in the family died during an epidemic of yellow fever. Left to fend for himself, he worked as a copy boy for a daily newspaper for a couple of years, then, seeing no future in that, took passage up the Mississippi on a riverboat headed for St. Louis.

En route, a slick-talking stranger robbed him of all his money except ten cents, so he was forced to take employment as a cabin boy aboard the small steamer *Ark*. It was there that his interest in marine engineering began. Working first as a fireman, then as a mechanic aboard several river packets, he found that both jobs affected his chronic asthmatic condition adversely, making breathing difficult, so he studied textbooks, attended classes, and saved all the money he could in order to get a diploma from the Engineers Association of Missouri, following which he became part owner of the steamer *Belle of Hatchie*.

Increasingly frequent asthmatic attacks forced him to sell out and seek a change in climate. Leaving the miasmic lowlands of the Mississippi and emigrating to California in 1849, his health did improve. While working as an engineer on a steamboat running on the Sacramento River, he met Lot Whitcomb, who told him of his plans to develop navigation in Oregon, persuading him to come to Milwaukie as a partner in the company and to design and install the engine for the boat Whitcomb planned to build there.

"He's a real genius when it comes to marine engines," Lot Whitcomb told Tommy. "Give him a bellows, an anvil, and the help of good blacksmith, he can design and make every tool he needs to put an engine together."

Blueprinted in twenty-two sections, then manufactured and shipped to the West Coast by way of New Orleans and Panama, the boilers, pipes, valves, and fittings went together exactly as Jacob Kamm intended them to do. When fired up, the engine performed as flawlessly as a Swiss watch. In fact, when Captain J. C. Ainsworth arrived, he proclaimed the boat to be as good as any craft he had ever skippered on the Mississippi.

Big, bluff, and hearty, Captain John Ainsworth was a man Tommy liked on sight, for there was no pretense or self-importance in him. All he asked was that you know your job and do it without fuss or complaint. Because he was not familiar with this particular river system, whereas Tommy had navigated it for fifteen years, he was content to let Tommy read the river for him while he ran the boat.

With a top speed of twelve miles an hour, the *Lot Whitcomb* was by far the fastest boat on the river. It was a handsome craft, combining the traditions of Hudson River steamers with a few touches of Mississippi River boats. Twin smokestacks set well forward rose above a pair of boilers whose steam pressure turned the enclosed side-wheels with a great deal of power. She had a long cabin deck, a small Texas, and a modest-sized pilot house placed amidships just behind the chimneys. All her upper works were painted white and were without ornament, though each wheelhouse did bear her name in big black block letters.

Designed with what her owners called "simple elegance," she had ample mixed-passenger cabin space, a dining hall, and a small sheltered ladies' cabin where the fair sex would not have to endure such male crudities as tobacco chewing, spitting, cigar smoking, drinking, and strong language. On the boiler or freight deck, a substantial amount of cargo could be carried.

Following flowery speeches by Mayor Kilborn, Governor Gaines, and a stirring serenade by the Fort Vancouver brass band—all of which were duly noted by the local newspaper, *Western Star*, which Lot Whitcomb owned—the boat *Lot Whitcomb*—with Lot Whitcomb himself onboard—got under way two days after her launching. Her first order of business was to compete with the clumsy, lumbering, slow, Astoria-built *Columbia*, which now had a monopoly on the traffic of the lower river.

Charging twenty-five dollars for the trip between Milwaukie and Astoria, just as *Columbia* did, the *Lot Whitcomb* took most of the trade away from the older boat on her first round-trip. In retaliation, the *Columbia* reduced its fare from Astoria to Oregon City to fifteen dollars. Relying on the elegance, speed, and comfort of their new boat to beat the competition in all ways but price, the *Lot Whitcomb* cut its fare only to twenty dollars, announcing in January 1851, that it would leave Milwaukie on Mondays and Thursdays at noon, touching at Portland, Fort Vancouver, Milton, St. Helens, Cowlitz, and Cathlamet on the way to Astoria, with the return trip subject to favorable tides, scheduled for a more-or-less noon departure from Astoria on Wednesdays and Sundays, "Board not included in above rates."

Though the *Lot Whitcomb* got the larger share of the traffic for a couple of months, she did suffer the embarrassment of getting hung up on a reef at the mouth of the Clackamas River when the water across a riffle there proved to be too shallow for the boat's keel to clear. The way this misadventure happened was that as the steamboat was heading toward the rapid against a blinding, low-angled mid-afternoon sun, Captain Ainsworth called down from the pilot house to Tommy, who was standing on the starboard side of the deck just below.

"That riffle ahead looks a little shallow to me. Think we can cross it without bumping our bottom?"

"I don't know, sir," Tommy replied with complete honesty. "I've never been this far up the river before."

"Well, let's try it and see what happens," Ainsworth said gruffly. "That's the only way to learn."

It was typical of Captain Ainsworth that when the boat grounded and stuck on the reef, he assumed all the blame himself. After all, the Captain admitted, Tommy had told him the truth when he said he didn't know.

Because the boat had grounded while moving under full power, no amount of jockeying with first one wheel and then another, turning first in one direction and then in the other, would work her clear. But Captain Ainsworth was too old a hand at running aground on bars and snags in the upper Mississippi to be concerned with that.

"If we can't lower the sandbar, we'll just have to raise the river," he grunted. "First thing tomorrow, we'll get a crew of workmen to bring up some timbers from Lot's mill and build some cofferdams and weirs to raise the water level enough to float us off. The channel over this reef has to be deepened anyway, else all the river boats will have to stop two miles downstream from Oregon City."

Since a sawmill was among the many other enterprises Lot Whitcomb owned and operated in Milwaukie, getting enough timbers and skilled workmen to build the cofferdams and weirs was no problem. But damming the Clackamas and Willamette Rivers enough to raise their levels so that the grounded boat could be floated clear turned out to be much more of a project than anticipated, requiring two weeks to complete.

After bringing the boat back to Milwaukie, where she was docked and careened to make sure no serious damage had been done to her keelson, the *Lot Whitcomb*, went back into service on the Oregon City–Astoria run.

With plenty of water in the rivers during late spring and early summer and the engine performing perfectly under Jacob Kamm's precise control, the steamboat set new speed records, making the 120-mile run from Astoria to Oregon City in just ten hours against the current, with the final stretch from Milwaukie to Oregon City done in only fifty minutes. Using a trick learned on the Mississippi, Captain Ainsworth told Jacob Kamm to have the stoker toss half a dozen pitch-filled pine knots into the furnace just before the boat pulled into the landing, making billows of thick black smoke roll out of the chimneys and putting on a show for potential passengers.

"Das is goot for business but bad for my asthma," Jacob Kamm complained. "I do not like to vork in de boiler room, vhere my attacks get vorse. Yet dese dumkopfs ve hire as assistant engineers are goot for noddings but to throw wood into the furnace. No matter how many times I tell dem, dey do not learn how to take care of de engine."

"We had a good man aboard the *Beaver*," Tommy said cautiously. "Her engines got mighty cranky at times, but he always managed to keep them running."

"Dis man, he is a Britisher?"

"No, he's a Chinook Indian. His name is Sitkum."

Kamm scowled. "How did a Chinook Indian learn to be an engineer?"

"My father, Ben, and his father, Conco, worked together as bar pilots back in sailing ship days. Sitkum and I have been friends all our lives. When the *Beaver* first came out from England, we went to work on her, me as a third mate, him as a stoker. The Chief Engineer took a liking to him and taught him everything he knew. He's as good a steam engine man as you'll find in this part of the country. But if you don't like Indians—"

"It's dumkopfs of any color I don't like!" Kamm snorted. "Your friend could be a Fiji Island cannibal who eats babies for breakfast, for all I care, so long as he knows how to take care of an engine. Bring him to me, Tommy, und let me see vhat he can do."

Responding to Tommy's message that there might be an engineer's job for him aboard the *Lot Whitcomb*, Sitkum came downriver from his village near Celilo Falls, met Captain Ainsworth and Jacob Kamm, and impressed them favorably with his intelligence and quiet dignity. Making the next round-trip from Oregon City to Astoria below decks under Kamm's critical eye, he amply demonstrated that he indeed knew marine engines. Pleased with his work, Kamm went ashore and stayed there, leaving Sitkum in charge as the boat's Chief Engineer.

Just as the *Beaver* had done back in 1836, the *Lot Whitcomb* undertook a towing job in March 1851. Owned by the Pacific Mail Steamship Company, the iron-hulled propeller ship, *Willamette*, had been built on the East Coast, rigged as a schooner, and then brought around the Horn and north to Astoria under sail. Putting a hawser on the vessel, the *Lot Whitcomb* towed the *Willamette* upriver to Portland, where, during the next few months, her engines were installed, her propeller connected, and she was put into service on the lower river run. Scheduled to meet the bi-monthly Pacific Mail ship plying between San Francisco and Astoria, she was in direct competition with the *Lot Whitcomb*, of course, which did not seem to bother Captain Ainsworth a bit. In fact, it inspired him to challenge the rival boat to the first-ever steamer race on the Columbia River.

On a warm summer day in early July, the *Willamette* cast loose her lines from the Portland dock a few minutes after 1:00 P.M., heading downriver for Astoria just as the *Lot Whitcomb* tied up and put out its landing stage to discharge Portland ticketed passengers from Oregon City and Milwaukie. Seeing the other boat pull away, Captain Ainsworth stuck his head out of the pilot house window and shouted down at Tommy:

"Mister Warren!"

"Aye, sir?"

"It's a great day for a race, wouldn't you agree?"

"I certainly would, sir!"

"Then pull back your landing stage and cast off your lines! We'll take on the *Willamette* in spite of her head start. I mean to pass her before she clears Sauvie Island Slough!"

Scrambling aboard with or without downriver tickets as the landing stage was swung in, a dozen or so startled passengers managed to find footing on the deck as the lines were cast off. While they cheered lustily, the big side-wheels, which had barely stopped turning, came to life again, pulling the boat out into the river in a long arc, then pointing her bow downstream in the direction the screw-propelled *Willamette* had taken.

Unaware that she was being challenged to race, the *Willamette* was moving down the river, which here was constrained between ranges of steep hills, at three-quarters speed, so the *Lot Whitcomb* soon began to close the quarter-mile gap between the two boats. Seeing the *Whitcomb* gaining on her and hearing a pair of whistle-toots as Captain Ainsworth gave fair warning he was coming after her, the master of the *Willamette* accepted the challenge, gave two whistle blasts of his own, then poured on full power.

Because her screw was under water and did not disturb its surface, the propeller boat ran quietly, while the buckets of the side-wheeler

53

made a thunderous noise as they threshed the water. Standing on the starboard side of the deck just below the pilot house, Tommy felt the vibration of the planks underfoot and knew that the boat was moving faster than it ever had traveled before. Looking up, he saw Captain Ainsworth standing with feet widespread behind the wheel, reading the changing currents and eddies of the river as they unreeled before him, taking a spoke to the left here, one to the right there, as he made subtle adjustments to the boat's course. On a couple of occasions, Tommy saw Ainsworth lean down toward the speaking tube communicating with the engine room as he said something to Sitkum. Because of the noise of the engine and the thunder of the paddle wheels, Tommy could not hear the Captain's orders to the Chief Engineer, but he would have wagered his hearth and home that he had not said "slow down."

With the two boats running neck and neck abreast of each other as they raced half the length of Sauvie Island Slough, passengers lined the rails of both steamers, cheering and shouting at the top of their lungs. At the lower end of the nine-mile-long island, the channel narrowed until it was barely wide enough for two boats abreast, with the shallower water restricted by an invisible mud bank under the surface to port. Since both captains were familiar with the hazards here, neither had an advantage, so far as local knowledge was concerned. But as the captain of the *Willamette* knew very well, if a blade of his screw-propelled boat dug into the bottom and got twisted or bent, repairing it would be a major problem. On the other hand, a damaged bucket on a side-wheeler could be fixed with a lot less effort and expense. So as the two racing boats moved into the narrowing neck of the slough, Tommy was not surprised to see the *Willamette* move to starboard, seeking the deeper water of the right-hand channel, while the *Lot Whitcomb* stayed to port. Risking grounding on the mudbank to cut across the short side of the arc, the *Lot Whitcomb* forged into the lead by two boat lengths as the vessels cleared the lower end of Sauvie Island and moved into the deeper waters of the Columbia itself.

Acknowledging the cheers of the crowd by leaning out of the pilot house and lifting his cap, Captain Ainsworth shook a jubilant fist at Tommy, then bent down to the engine room speaking tube and grunted, "Good work, Sitkum! You can release your tie-down on the safety valve now."

In the years that followed, a number of steam-powered boats with engines designed and manufactured by Jacob Kamm were built in Milwaukie and Oregon City, operating as passenger and freight carriers on the Columbia and the Willamette Rivers below and above the falls. The tiny, iron-hulled propellers *Eagle* and *Black Hawk*, were only forty feet long, carrying no more than a dozen passengers and a ton of freight, plying the Willamette between Portland and Oregon City.

An even smaller craft, the *Hoosier*, was built out of a ship's longboat, which had been slightly altered to accommodate an engine originally designed to be a piledriver. When the engineer-captain-owner of this boat found business slack on the lower Willamette run, he put the vessel on rollers, portaged it around the falls, and put it into service to Dayton on the Yamhill and Salem on the Willamette.

He made history of a sort one day when he snapped the shaft of the *Hoosier* while trying to scramble over a rapid four miles downstream from Salem. Not at all concerned, he unshipped the shaft—which had broken in two pieces—shouldered one piece himself, gave the other to a deckhand, then walked into Salem and found a blacksmith shop. There, he had the pieces welded back together, then he and the deck hand carried the shaft back to the vessel and put it in place, following which the boat resumed its trip.

In a time and place when the writing and reading of poetry was considered to be an honorable pursuit, a genteel Oregon City lady named Elizabeth Markham immortalized the grounding of the *Lot Whitcomb* on Clackamas Rapid by witnessing the struggle, then rushing home and taking pen in hand. When her piece of "emotion reflected in tranquillity" was finished, she sent it to the *Oregon Spectator*, which dutifully published it, little knowing that seventy years later her son, Edwin Markham, would become a poet with worldwide renown. After seeing the Millet painting *The Man With a Hoe*, which showed a weary French peasant laborer in a field, the liberal-minded Markham wrote:

> *Bowed by the weight of centuries he leans*
> *Upon his hoe and gazes on the ground,*
> *The emptiness of ages in his face,*
> *And on his back the burdens of the world.*
> *Who made him dead to rapture and despair,*

A thing that grieves not and that never hopes,
Stolid and stunned, a brother to the ox?
Who loosened and let down this brutal jaw?
Whose was the hand that slanted back this brow?
Whose breath blew out the light within this brain?

The poem written by Elizabeth Markham was in a much happier vein, celebrating the triumph of the human spirit rather than its defeat. It read:

Lot Whitcomb is coming!
Her banners are flying—
She walks up the rapids with speed;
She ploughs through the water,
Her steps never falter—
Oh, that's independence indeed.
Old and young rush to meet her,
Male and female to greet her.
And waves lash the shore as they pass.

Oh! she's welcome, thrice welcome
To Oregon City;
Lot Whitcomb is with us at last.
Success to the Steamer,
Her Captain and crew.
She has our best wishes attained.
Oh! that she may never
While running this river
Fall back on the sand bar again.

8.

ITH THE CAYUSE INDIAN WAR over and the gold rush to California tapering off, emigration to Oregon from the eastern United States increased substantially in 1851. As promised, the Army had built posts at intervals all along the Oregon Trail, including a fort at The Dalles which was manned by a small detachment of troops. Despite the good climate, abundant sunshine, and proven fertility of the interior country east of the Cascades, most of the emigrants still regarded the Willamette Valley as the promised land, heading there either over the Barlow Road or along the river route through the Columbia River Gorge.

Though Tommy Warren still was convinced that the potential traffic warranted building and operating a steamer on the fifty-mile sector of navigable river between the Upper Cascades and The Dalles, he failed to sell the idea to Lot Whitcomb, J. C. Ainsworth, and Jacob Kamm, who were more interested in the lower river and the California trade. As that traffic dwindled and business began to develop above the Cascades, merchant D. F. Bradford and boatbuilder Van Bergen put together a hull and an engine for a small side-wheeler, the *James P. Flint*. When they asked Tommy and Sitkum to run it for them, both men welcomed the opportunity.

"The *Lot Whitcomb* isn't very busy these days," Tommy told Freda. "We get paid only when we work, which is less than half the time."

"Is all the gold gone in California?" Freda asked.

"No, but the boom days are done. Emil wrote Mom that he's thinking of moving to Portland as soon as he can convince Dolores she won't sprout web feet in the Willamette Valley."

"Dolores is the young lady he's going to marry?"

"That's right. Her family owned half of California before the Americans came, Emil wrote Mom. He can't get her to move north until he promises to give her half of Oregon."

"Which he cannot do, as you well know" Freda said firmly. "All a man and wife can own is a square mile of land—just like you and me."

"Well, according to Mom, Dad promised to make her Queen of Oregon before she'd agree to come to America with him. And the way things worked out, he did. At least the whole family has always treated her like a queen."

"Dolores sounds like a very intelligent young lady, Tommy. I hope they do get married and move to Oregon. We will make them welcome."

Tommy gave Freda a speculative look, then smiled and said, "It strikes me as strange that the men in the Warren family never have been able to find native-born American women to marry. Mom is Hawaiian, you're Swedish, and Dolores is Spanish. How come the Warren men always marry foreigners?"

"Because imports are always better than local stock when you're trying to improve the breed," Freda answered with a rare flash of humor. "Every farmer knows that."

Compared to the *Lot Whitcomb*, the side-wheeler *James P. Flint* was a modest-sized steamboat, measuring only sixty feet in length with a beam of twelve feet. But to the emigrants who put their wagons and cattle aboard for the fifty-mile downriver trip from The Dalles to the Upper Cascades, as well as to the soldiers whose horses and supplies were carried upriver to the newly established fort, she was a welcome change from walking and a sign that civilization at last was reaching this remote corner of the Pacific Northwest.

Unfortunately, with the coming of autumn and the chill rains, traffic on the middle river dwindled to the point of nonexistence, so Bradford and Bergen decided if business would not come to their boat, they must take their boat to the business. With the reluctant approval and assistance of Tommy and Sitkum, the boat was winched up onto the low north bank of the river, skids were placed under her, and she was dragged by the brute force of half a dozen yoke of oxen six miles downriver, then returned to the water below the Lower Cascades.

For the next year, the *James P. Flint* did a fair business transporting emigrants down and soldiers up the lower river. It became increasingly evident to Tommy and Sitkum from the way her valves wheezed and her bearings pounded that unless her engine was given an extensive overhaul, it was not going to last much longer. But her owners said no money was available for expensive overhauls at the moment, so her wheezing and pounding got progressively worse. On September 15, 1852, the inevitable happened. Blowing a valve just upstream from a spire of jagged rock on the north bank—appropriately named Cape Horn by Lewis and Clark—she lost power, drifted helplessly in the current, bashed a gaping hole in her bottom on a sharp lava reef, then sank where she struck, leaving only her upper works visible above the water.

Though her hull was a total loss and gradually rotted away, her engine was recovered, repaired so that it functioned after a fashion, then was reincarnated for a couple more lifetimes, first to power a sawmill on the lower river for a few years, then as a clanking steam engine on a homemade boat on the Yangtze River in China, where, Tommy suspected, it would probably outlive him …

With the coming of spring in 1853, several events of importance to the Pacific Northwest occurred. First, in March Congress passed legislation establishing Washington Territory, breaking what formerly was known as the Oregon Country into roughly equal portions, with the dividing line to be the Columbia River.

Appointed Governor of the new territory by President Franklin Pierce was an energetic, feisty, ambitious career Army man, Isaac Ingalls Stevens. Graduating from West Point at the top of his class in the Corps of Engineers a few years earlier, he had served with distinction in the Mexican War, then had resigned his commission when offered the position of Governor. On his way out to Puget Sound, where the capital of Washington Territory was to be established at Olympia, he would survey a proposed northern railroad route from Saint Paul to tidewater, he promised President Pierce. He also would talk to the Indian tribes encountered along the way, laying groundwork for his return a few months later to negotiate treaties with them "extinguishing title" to the lands they had lived on for time beyond recall.

In anticipation of his arrival, the white settlers living near the former Hudson's Bay Company post, Fort Nisqually, on lower Puget Sound, started building a wagon road east across the Cascades over which they hoped to encourage Oregon-bound emigrants to travel to Washington Territory instead.

Because of the lack of business on the lower Columbia, the *Lot Whitcomb* had been "sold south" to California and now was operating on the Sacramento River. Unable to compete with newer boats, the *Columbia* had given up the struggle, her hull being tied at a dock in Astoria while her engines were removed and placed in a smaller boat, the *Fashion*, which started running from Portland to the Lower Cascades. When a spring freshet tore the hull loose from the dock, sweeping it over the bar and out to sea, the boat that once had been the pride of Astoria "went south," too, after a fashion, for when last seen her storm-scattered timbers were floating in the direction of California.

In Oregon City that summer, the first-ever iron-hulled boat was built by a machinist and foundryman named Thomas V. Smith, who had recently come out from Baltimore. First called the *Belle of Oregon City*, then simply the *Belle*, the boat was ninety-six feet long and twenty-six feet wide. When finished, she was put into service on the lower Willamette run, where she established a standard for speed and dependability never before known in this part of the country.

Leaving the warehouse at the base of the falls at 7:30 each morning, the *Belle* stopped at Oregon City at 8:00 A.M., Milwaukie at 8:30, and arrived at Portland at 9:30. After giving businessmen travelers time for a full morning's work and a leisurely noon meal, the boat started back at 2:00 p.m., reaching home at 4:00 P.M. in plenty of time for the storekeeper to close up shop and get home for supper. Fare between the two terminals was two dollars. Compared to the time and effort required to travel the muddy or dusty roads of the area, this was the easy way to go.

As time passed, the *Belle* proved to be not only a dependable boat but also a durable one. Expanding her service to Fort Vancouver, the Cowlitz River, and the Columbia to the Lower Cascades, she proved her worth during the Indian wars of 1856–58, transported prospectors and settlers upriver as the interior developed in the 1860s, and continued to operate until 1869, when she finally went to the scrapper.

Even then, she lived on, as other boats did before and after her, when the dismantled sheet iron of her hull was shipped to China and her engines, still faithfully turning over, were used to power a sawmill.

Meanwhile, the master builder, Jacob Kamm, was hard at work designing and ordering parts for his latest concept in steamboats—a stern-wheeler. Financed by the Abernethy and Clark Company, in which Kamm and J. C. Ainsworth also had an interest, parts for the engines were manufactured in accordance with Jacob Kamm's detailed specifications in Baltimore, while the hull took shape in Milwaukie. To be called the *Jennie Clark* after the lovely wife of the principal stockholder, the craft would be the finest, most expensive, most efficient boat ever to ply the Columbia River.

Though Tommy and Sitkum were currently employed as captain and engineer aboard the *Belle*, it was assumed that they would transfer to the *Jennie Clark* after her launching, so they followed her construction with considerable interest. The cost of the engines by the time they were manufactured and shipped in parts from Baltimore, Tommy learned from Jacob Kamm, who kept meticulous track of every penny, was $1,663.16. Brought around the Horn on the clipper ship *Golden Racer*, the freight charges were $1,030.02. In an attempt to economize, Jacob Kamm had specified that the wheel by which the ship was steered be "neat and plain finish and not costly." Contrary to his instructions, it turned out to be of the most expensive mahogany the builders could find, inlaid with solid silver and polished until it gleamed.

"Vell, it does look nice und don't have no splinters," Kamm grumbled as he stroked the wheel with grudging admiration. "If de dumkopf helmsmen don't keep it polished, I'll peel off their hides."

Like Tommy, Ainsworth and Kamm agreed that a stern-wheeler was the best type of boat for the inland waters of the Pacific Northwest. Until now, all the others had been side-wheelers or propellers, but experience had shown them to have serious disadvantages. Propellers fouled in shallow waters, blades bent, and shafts snapped. So far as side-wheelers were concerned, they required docks with deep water on both sides and were hard to manage in swift currents and winding channels.

A stern-wheeler, on the other hand, was able to nose into or alongside a sandy beach, depending upon its slow-turning wheel and twin rudders to keep it in place. With her two engines connected so that one man could handle them both, the *Jennie Clark* maneuvered easily. Each cylinder had a four-foot stroke, their sixteen-foot connecting rod turning a stern-wheel that was fifteen feet in diameter. Because the slats of the wheel were simply lengths of one inch by four inch wood, they could easily be replaced if broken by even a poor carpenter, while repairing a damaged metal bucket on a side-wheeler was a major problem, requiring a mechanic's skill.

"Vith a stern-wheeler," Jacob Kamm told Tommy, "it vould even be possible to split de wheel into two sections set side by side. Vith three rudders—one on each end und one in the middle—und de engines turning de wheels in opposite directions, ve vould have a boat dot could spin around on a dime, like a puppy chasing its tail. Some day, I may build such a boat."

The length of the *Jennie Clark* was 115 feet, her beam 18 1/2 feet, and she was 4 feet deep in the hold. She had a single cabin, over which the boilers were centered; the two engines were set well aft, close to the stern-wheel, so that there was little lost motion. A single black smokestack rose from the boiler, with the pilot house set well forward and as high as possible for good vision lines. In these waters, it was most important that a boat's captain be up where he could "read the river" in all kinds of weather.

From the day she took to the water in February 1855, it was clear to Captain Ainsworth and her crew that the *Jennie Clark* was going to be queen of the river for years to come. She responded to her helm at the slightest touch, her stern-wheel bit into the water with powerful authority to give her all the speed she needed, and she handled the most delicate landings with ease. Though there was little doubt she could show her heels to anything else on the Portland-Astoria run, the only boat that might have challenged her to a race, the *Lot Whitcomb*, was now in California …

As Lewis and Clark had noted just below the Lower Cascades on their way west in 1805, the effects of the ocean tides were noticeable 145 miles inland from the mouth of the river. On November 4, Captain William Clark wrote in his journal:

Tide rose last night 18 inches perpendicular in Camp.

He also noticed an abundance of beautifully fashioned, seaworthy canoes, each of which could hold fifty paddlers.

I counted 52 canoes on the bank in front of this village, maney of them verry large and raised in bow.

Sitkum told Tommy and Freda when they asked him about it one evening that, in all probability, these had been the canoes of his people, the Chinook Indians, or of their neighbors across the Columbia, the Clatsops, for both tribes frequently came upriver to trade with inland bands such as the Celilos, Wishrams, Yakimas, and Nez Perces. Leaving their big seagoing canoes at the Lower Cascades, they would travel afoot around the six miles of rapids, then would be taken on upriver in smaller canoes manned by their relatives.

"They had relatives so far from their home village?" Freda asked in surprise.

"Yes," Sitkum answered with simple dignity. "Wherever my people go, we have brothers."

"What most white people don't know about Northwest Indians is that they're great travelers," Tommy explained. "Most tribes have strict taboos against marrying within the clan, so a lot of young men seek brides among neighboring tribes. Indian usage of the words 'brother', 'sister', 'mother', 'father', and so on is pretty loose. For instance, as soon as Sitkum married into the Yakima tribe, all his wife's male relatives became his 'brothers' while her female relatives became his 'sisters.'"

Freda smiled sympathetically. "Keeping track of your relatives must be very difficult for your people, Sitkum. How do you do it?"

"The grandmothers know," Sitkum said, shaking his head. "Always, they know."

While it was the duty of the grandmothers to keep track of family relationships, it was the task of the grandfathers to remember tribal history and pass it on to the younger generations. One local Indian legend that particularly intrigued Tommy and Freda was that of the immense natural bridge that the Indians claimed once spanned the Columbia River a few miles upstream from their Rooster Rock claim. Called "Bridge of the Gods," it was supposed to have reached from the base of the cliffs on the Oregon side of the river across the jumble of fallen rocks that formed the rapids called the Cascades to the base of equally sheer cliffs on the Washington shore. Geological evidence that such a natural bridge had indeed existed could be seen in several locations, but Tommy had found the local Indians reluctant to talk about where and when the bridge had spanned the river and how long it had been since it had collapsed.

"I've asked Sitkum what his wife's people have to say about it," Tommy told Freda. "All he will tell me is that Spotted Fawn says it's a *tah-mah-na-wis* thing."

"What does that mean?"

"Magic, ghostly, spiritual, supernatural—anything that's beyond the understanding of the Indians. It also has a religious connotation, I gather. That's why they don't like to talk about it."

"Do the Indians believe in God?"

"Not in our kind of God, Freda, but in some ways they are a religious people. They have a strict code of morals, believe in life after death, and are convinced that the world was created by an all-powerful being embodied in the form of the smartest animal they know, the coyote. They call this spirit-being Speelyi."

"Did this spirit they call Coyote build the bridge?"

"That's what they say."

"When?"

"In olden times—whenever that was. According to the grandfather tales, Speelyi hated water, so, in order to keep from getting his feet wet when crossing the river, he built a rock bridge across the Columbia reaching from shore to shore. To light his way in case he wanted to cross in the dark, he put a beautiful young Indian maiden named Loo-Wit in charge of a fire in the center of the bridge, promising that if she would tend it faithfully, he would let her live forever. She was a virgin, of course—"

"Tommy! You're making this up!"

"No, I'm not. I'm just telling it the way Sitkum says Spotted Fawn told it to him."

"All right. Then what happened?"

"Well, as Spotted Fawn tells the story, a big, brawny young chief living north of the Columbia saw Loo-Wit and began courting her. A short while later, a tall, handsome young chief living south of the river saw her and began romancing her, too. Coyote had warned her to have nothing to do with men. But she was flattered by their attention, so she encouraged them both."

"Coyote was jealous, I'll bet," Freda sniffed, "because he wanted to keep her for himself."

"Indian legend-tellers never criticize Speelyi, Spotted Fawn says.

Anyway, as Coyote watched, the quarrel got worse and worse. Finally, the two angry young chiefs began stealing burning brands out of Loo-Wit's sacred fire and throwing them at each other, then tearing rocks out of the sides of the cliffs on either side of the river and heaving them back and forth. Coyote got very mad and decided to take drastic action. Picking up the biggest rock he could find, he dropped it right in the center of the bridge, which broke into a thousand pieces, sending the sacred fire, the two quarreling chiefs, and Loo-Wit herself tumbling into the river."

"What about Coyote's promise to Loo-Wit that he would let her live forever so long as she tended the fire?"

"That did bother him a bit, Spotted Fawn says, because all he'd meant to do was teach all parties concerned a lesson. So to make it up to them, he turned the maiden and the two chiefs into mountains, which will live forever. As a matter of fact, all three mountains are still standing today, while the fire that Loo-Wit was tending still burns inside them."

Freda was silent for a time, then said thoughtfully, "If we are willing to believe the stories told in the Old Testament of our Bible, such as Noah and the Ark and Moses parting the Red Sea, I don't suppose we ought call the Indians' Speelyi stories ridiculous. What are the names of the mountains now?"

"Mount Hood, Mount Adams, and Mount St. Helens. They've all got fire inside them, I'll vouch for that, for I've seen all three erupt smoke, ash, and lava during the years I've been living in this part of the country. So far as the Indians are concerned, you can't pay one to guide you up to the top of the peaks, for to them that's forbidden territory."

So far as the geological evidence that a natural bridge once spanned the Columbia River in the heart of the Gorge was concerned, Tommy told Freda that on several occasions when the *James P. Flint* had been making the run between the Upper Cascades and The Dalles, Sitkum had come on deck and pointed out the remains of a phantom bridge resting on the bottom of the river deep under the water. Only when the surface was very still, the light just right, and the water crystal clear could the fallen bridge be seen. But when these conditions prevailed, entire sections of what looked to be a rock bridge could be viewed far below, on some of which fir and spruce trees thirty to fifty feet tall still appeared to be growing.

"Which would seem to prove that the natural bridge collapsed only a few generations ago," Tommy concluded. "Spotted Fawn says her grandfather once told her that when he was a boy he knew an old man who claimed to have paddled his canoe down the river and under the bridge before it fell. So apparently there is some truth to the legend."

The reality now was that the jumble of rocks and the six-mile stretch of unnavigable river did exist, thus must be bypassed in some way or other so that traffic and freight could proceed from the lower to the middle river. With a military post established at The Dalles and Washington Territory created, business began to pick up to the extent that two small riverboats were built and launched above the Upper Cascades and began making runs three times a week between there and The Dalles. Both boats were side-wheelers. The *Wasco*, which went into service in August, docked on the south side of the river, connecting with the *Fashion* from Portland. The *Mary*, launched a month earlier, connected with the *Belle* from Fort Vancouver.

On the Oregon side, goods bound upriver were transferred from the *Fashion* to the backs of pack mules, then carried around the portage and loaded onto the *Wasco*. On the Washington shore, the portage facilities were somewhat better, for the Bradford brothers had built a wooden tramway over which draft mules pulled small cars laden with freight. In order to protect the north side of the river from an Indian attack, the army had built blockhouses at the Middle and Upper Cascades, posting a squad of soldiers under a sergeant at the Middle Cascade blockhouse, while a lieutenant commanding thirty troops was stationed at the growing settlement clustered around Bradfords Store at the Upper Cascades.

When the Bradfords, who owned the *Mary*, offered Tommy and Sitkum the positions of Captain and Engineer, both men gave up their prospects of jobs on the *Jennie Clark*, even though taking berths on the smaller boat meant less pay.

"We'll be closer to home and on a section of the river that is bound to develop a lot of traffic," Tommy told Freda. "Small as she is, the *Mary* will be our boat to command."

"Will the *Wasco* hurt your business?"

"At the moment, there's more traffic than both boats can handle.

Matter of fact, bundles of freight bound upriver are being delayed at least a week at the portages on both sides for lack of space on the upriver boats."

"Where is all this freight going?"

"Mostly to the Walla Walla Valley, where Governor Stevens and General Palmer have set up a council with the inland tribes for late May. They're hoping to get the Indians to agree to go on reservations, ceding the rest of their lands to the whites."

"Why can't we all live together in peace as we're doing now?"

"Because conflicts like the Whitman Massacre, the Rogue River uprising down in southwest Oregon, and the troubles between the Clackamas Indians and the whites near Salem keep everybody stirred up. Both Governor Stevens and Joel Palmer, who's Superintendent of Indian Affairs for Oregon, agree that whites and Indians can't get along unless each race knows the boundaries of the lands they own."

"Your father and Conco get along well. So do you and Sitkum."

"That's different," Tommy said. "We've known each other all our lives. But the new settlers in this part of the country are suspicious of Indians, who they think have no respect for their land claims. So the federal government has authorized Governor Stevens and General Palmer to meet with the Indians and make treaties."

When Freda asked Tommy what war General Joel Palmer had commanded troops in, Tommy explained that it was the custom in the Pacific Northwest to promote any man who had led Citizen Volunteers during an Indian war to the honorary rank of General, while an enlisted man was entitled to be called Colonel. Although five thousand Indians representing half a dozen powerful inland tribes were expected at the council grounds, the military escort provided by Fort Vancouver and commanded by West Point graduate Lieutenant Lawrence Kip numbered only one hundred men.

From the quantity of supplies being shipped upriver on the *Wasco* and *Mary*, Tommy judged that the Indians would at least be well fed. But as massive amounts of food, tobacco, coffee, sugar, and trinkets meant for presents to the chiefs came aboard the *Mary* and were transported to The Dalles during the first two weeks of May 1855, Sitkum told Tommy that the people in his wife's village were alarmed at the rumors they had heard from their kinsmen west of the Cascades. There, Governor Stevens already had negotiated treaties setting up reservations for such tribes as the Nisqually on lower Puget Sound.

"At the Medicine Creek Treaty," Sitkum said, "Chief Leschi was told that all the land Speelyi gave his people must be cut up into little squares and divided between Indians and whites. Because the Indians who live in that part of the country are few compared to the number of white people who want to settle there, the Indians will be given only a few squares, while all the rest will be set aside for the whites."

"Did Chief Leschi sign the treaty?"

"He touched the end of the writing stick which the white man placed in his hand. But he did this only as a gesture of friendship, to show that his heart was good. When he was told that he could no longer go where his people have always gone, he said he did not agree to be put in a pen, so would not abide by the treaty terms."

"Will he go to war?"

"Not unless the whites try to take away his freedom. Then he will fight."

Beginning in late May, the treaty talks in the Walla Walla Valley lasted for nineteen days. Their end result was the creation of three reservations—Nez Perce, Umatilla, and Yakima—for the inland tribes, most of whom were horse Indians who traditionally roamed over an immense area of the upper Columbia River watershed. Ceded by the Indians to the federal government were thirty thousand square miles of land, for which the five tribes involved were rewarded in trade goods and annuities less than ten cents an acre.

Governor Stevens and Superintendent Palmer proclaimed the treaties a great victory for the cause of peace. But the Indians felt a great sadness, for they knew that they had lost their freedom. Under the terms of the treaties, no white man could travel across the reservations without permission from the Indians. It was further stated that the Indians would be permitted to fish in their "usual and accustomed places, in common with the whites" and hunt and travel across "unoccupied lands."

All the lands outside the reservations were to be thrown open to settlement by the whites once the treaties had been ratified by the United States Senate and signed by the president. Neither stipulation was understood by the Indians nor heeded by the whites. In fact, newspapers all over the Pacific Northwest publicized the treaties within two weeks of their signing, declaring the lands outside the reservations "open for settlement" even though three years would pass before the treaties would be ratified and signed.

Following the breakup of the council, Tommy and Sitkum were kept busy transporting troops, interpreters, and white civilians downriver to Fort Vancouver and Portland. It became increasingly evident to them both that the peace announced so grandiloquently by Stevens and Palmer was going to be an uneasy one. Even during the *"wa-wa"*—as the Indians called the talks—bloodshed had been averted by the slimmest of margins.

Shortly after the council began, Sitkum told Tommy, a group of dissidents in the Cayuse tribe had plotted to murder the commissioners, overwhelm the small military contingent, steal the supplies and the herd of beef cattle brought along to feed the Indians, then start a war of extermination against the whites. Though several chiefs among the Walla Walla and Umatilla bands, which were closely related to the Cayuse, approved the plot, they knew it could not succeed without the support of the Nez Perces and Yakimas, whose numbers were much greater. But neither Lawyer, head chief of the Nez Perces, nor Kamiakin, head chief of the Yakimas, would agree to the treachery.

"Since the coming of Lewis and Clark to their country fifty years ago, the Nez Perces have been good friends of the Americans," Sitkum said. "As for the Yakimas, Kamiakin always has followed the path of peace, even before the Commissioners made him a head chief."

"You mean he was not a head chief before they appointed him?"

"Not of what the whites call the Yakima Nation. Until Governor Stevens insisted that someone must speak for all the bands living in this part of the country, the Yakima tribe was just one of fourteen related bands. This I did not know until Spotted Fawn named them for me."

In what would have been a remarkable demonstration of memory for a white man but was commonplace among a people with no written language, Sitkum named the fourteen bands which long had recognized Kamiakin as a leader, if not as a head chief. They were: Yakima, Palouse, Pisquoise, Wenatshapan, Sjyiks, Ochechotes, Kamiltpah, Klickitat, Klinqyuit, Kowwassayes, Liaywas, Skinpah, Wishram, and Seapcat.

Apparently what Governor Steven and Superintendent Palmer did was appoint enough "chiefs" for each tribe so that all the Indians present at the council appeared to have been well represented. With up to fifty names appearing on the "X" (his mark) page at the end of each treaty, the Commissioners could tell Congress, the president, and the

American public that the treaties had indeed been negotiated in the democratic way.

The truth was, of course, that the white man's concept of democracy differed drastically from that of the Indians. To the white man, a majority vote meant that all citizens were obligated to obey whatever decision or law had been approved, no matter how slim the margin of approval had been. To Indians, a vote of approval regarding which particular individual should lead a hunting, fishing, or war party meant only that those people who had voted in favor of the leader were obliged to go along and to follow his orders. The dissenters were free to organize their own party or stay home.

"Spotted Fawn says that Kamiakin did not want to sign the treaty," Sitkum told Tommy. "But late one night Governor Stevens summoned him to his tent, where, in the presence of the Catholic priest, Father Pandosy, and the white interpreter, Andrew Pambrun, he made a threat that the Yakima people will remember all their lives."

"What was that?"

"Holding up the treaty paper, Governor Stevens waved it in Kamiakin's face and said: 'If you do not accept the terms offered and sign this paper, you will walk in blood knee-deep.' Later, Father Pandosy said that Kamiakin was so angry he bit his lips until they bled. But because he did not want to start a war, he signed the treaty."

Having once met Kamiakin during a visit to Sitkum's village on the north side of the Columbia near Celilo Falls, Tommy marveled that Governor Stevens could have made such a foolish threat. Standing well over six feet, with a strong, muscular build, a dark complexion, and piercing black eyes, Kamiakin was a man whose presence commanded respect. Upon arriving at the council grounds, he had demonstrated his independence by refusing to accept presents or provisions from the whites, saying: "I have never accepted anything from the whites, not even to the value of a grain of wheat, without paying for it. I do not wish to purchase your presents."

When asked to comment on the propositions put forward by the commissioners in long-winded speeches that had taken hours to complete, his answer was eloquent and brief: "The forest knows me; it knows my heart. I do not desire a great many goods. All that I wish for is an Agent, a good Agent, who will pity the good and bad of us and take care of us. I have nothing to talk long about. I am tired. I am anxious to get back to my garden. That is all I have to say."

According to Sitkum, Kamiakin's home was in the heart of the beautiful Yakima Valley, a day's ride north of Celilo Falls, where he had established the first irrigated farm in the area on Atahnum Creek near the Catholic Mission of St. Joseph. As a few other intelligent Indian leaders had done, he had accepted those facets of the white man's culture that he liked, such as cattle raising, gardening, irrigation, and the Catholic religion, while rejecting those which he did not approve, such as alcohol, poor housing, and moral degeneration. Forced to take a chieftanship he had not asked for and a reservation he did not want, he had made the best of a bad situation, signed the treaty, and come home.

The only thing he did have to show for the treaty council was that his wish for a good Indian Agent had been granted. The white man appointed as agent for the newly recognized Yakima Tribe was a person he liked and trusted—Andrew J. Bolon.

9.

$\mathcal{F}$ROM WHAT TOMMY WARREN knew about Andrew Bolon, whom he had met at Fort Vancouver several years ago, Governor Stevens had made an excellent choice in appointing him Agent for the Yakima Nation. A good friend of Kamiakin and the Yakimas, Bolon had been present as an interpreter at the Walla Walla council and was fluent in the Yakima tongue.

A tall, athletic man, with red hair and a full beard, he was renowned for being very fleet afoot. On one occasion in the spring of 1853, Tommy had been present as a spectator when Bolon challenged a mounted Klickitat Indian to a fifty-yard man-horse race, then beat the horse and rider by a margin of twelve feet.

Following the signing of the Walla Walla treaties, Governor Stevens ordered Bolon to purchase supplies west of the Cascades and transport them up the Columbia to the Spokane country in time for the talks scheduled to take place there. Traveling upriver on the *Mary* in mid-September with half a dozen men and the supplies, which he planned to transfer to pack horses at The Dalles for the journey on to the Spokane country, he told Tommy he was worried about rumors he'd heard of white prospectors trespassing on Indian lands.

"There's been talk on Puget Sound about a gold discovery in the Colville area north of Spokane Falls," he said. "A lot of damn fools have crossed the mountains and headed east across the Yakima Reservation without bothering to ask permission from the Indians."

"That could cause trouble, I imagine."

"It already has. Spokane Garry sent word that a party of whites had a run-in with a dozen young Yakima bucks a couple of weeks ago. He said he'd heard several white men were killed. After I've unloaded my supplies at The Dalles, I'm going to leave my party there, ride north, and investigate."

"Alone?"

"It's better that way, Tommy. Kamiakin and I are good friends. When he sees me ride in by myself, he'll know I come in peace."

Though it had been Bolon's intention to meet and talk personally with Kamiakin, he stopped short of the chief's village on Ahtahnum Creek when he reached the lodge of *Show-a-wai Ko-to-a-kin*, also known as Ice, a younger brother of Kamiakin. Bolon and Ice were good friends.

"The young men are angry and in an ugly mood," Ice warned him. "If you value your life, you will not ride any further north at this time."

"I'd like to talk to Kamiakin."

"My brother's heart is good toward you—this I know. But the blood of the young men is hot. As your friend, I urge you to go back to The Dalles. You can talk to Kamiakin later."

Knowing that Ice sensed the temper of the young men far better than he did, Andrew Bolon heeded his advice and turned back toward The Dalles.

Ironically, the timing and course of his retrograde journey caused him to overtake a moody, rebellious young Yakima brave named *Mo-sheel*, who was Ice's son. As a boy, *Mo-sheel* had attended the Methodist mission school conducted by Jason Lee in the Willamette Valley. Described as "spare, sinewy, quick in movement, and a wild young man," *Mo-sheel* had run away from the school in 1852 and had never gone back. Apparently the only lasting thing he had learned from the missionaries had been to hate all white men.

At the moment Bolon caught up with the small party of Yakimas, *Mo-sheel* had fresh reason to hate the whites. Via the Indian grapevine he recently had received word of the hanging of four Indians by federal troops along the Oregon Trail to the east. Just as frightened white people in this part of the country never bothered to inquire into the details or possible justification when whites were killed by Indians, neither did *Mo-sheel* bother to get straight the whys and wherefores of the execution of the Indians.

Actually, both provocation and retribution had taken place in the Fort Boise area, 350 miles away. During the summer of 1854 a band of local Indians attacked a party of emigrants and killed nineteen people in what was known as the Ward Party Massacre. Sent out to find and punish the perpetrators of this bloody deed, Major Granville O. Haller and his command of federal troops caught up with a group of Indians, gave four warriors a trial before a jury of three white officers, found them guilty, erected a gallows, and hanged them on the spot "as examples to other hostiles."

Unfortunately, instead of intimidating the Indians it made them so mad that for years thereafter they took vengeance against all travelers in their land. Word of the hangings spread rapidly to far-flung, unrelated tribes.

With *Mo-sheel's* party when Bolon overtook them were six men, several women, and a fourteen-year-old Yakima boy named *Suel-el-lil*. It was his eyewitness account of the event that later revealed what happened:

> Chief *Mo-sheel* was at the head of our party. He knew the white man, and he told the other Indians who he was.
> The white man said, "Hello, *Mo-sheel*."
> Then Chief *Mo-sheel* shook hands with the stranger, and, while the women kept on the trail, all the other men shook hands with him.
> Chief *Mo-sheel* spoke to his people. "This is the man who hanged my uncles and cousins at Fort Boise." *Mo-sheel* knew him and was mad.

As they rode on, *Mo-sheel* told the Indians riding with him that he was going to kill the white man. Two of the Yakima braves agreed that the deed should be done, but *Nou-yah* objected, saying:

> "No! We will all get into trouble. Let him alone. All at headquarters at The Dalles know of this white man. Do not kill him, all will be trouble."
> "You are not chief," *Mo-sheel* said. "I am chief. I will kill this man as he killed my brothers. I thought to meet him sometime, and now that I have met him this day, I will kill him."

Because the day was rainy and cold, the Indians halted toward noon near a sheltered spring called *Wahk-shum* and built a big fire to warm themselves. Agent Bolon unbridled his horse so that it could graze, took a package of food off the saddle, hung his canteen and holstered six-shooter on the saddlehorn, took off his overcoat, then brought his lunch to the fire, sharing it with the Indians while he ate and warmed himself.

The white man stood, holding his hands up to the fire, _Suel-el-lil_ related. _Wah-pi-wah-pi-lah_ stood by him, on the left. Chief _Mo-sheel_ stood on his right.

"We better hurry," somebody said.

I did not know what was up. I was eating hard-tack, which the white man had given me.

Chief _Mo-sheel_ again spoke to _Wah-pi-wah-pi-lah_, "We better hurry!"

Then _Wah-pi-wah-pi-lah_, the strong man, dropped quickly and caught the white man by the legs and jerked him to the ground. So-qiekt and _Mo-sheel_ jumped on him, each catching an arm, _Mo-sheel_ on the right. The white man cried out in Chinook.

"Do not kill me! I did not come to fight you!"

Stah-kin grabbed his beard, pulled back his head, and called, "Hurry!"

So-qiekt threw him a knife, and _Stah-kin_ cut the white man's throat. He struggled a short time and then lay still—the blood running from the big knife wound. He was dead.

I ran around, squealing.

After debating what to do with Agent Bolon's horse, saddle, gun, and clothes, the Indians decided to kill and conceal the horse and Bolon's body as best they could, keeping the rest of his possessions. Leading the horse to the brink of a canyon a quarter mile from camp, they shot it and dumped the body down the slope. They then buried the corpse of the agent in the cavity below a fallen pine tree.

Wah-tah-kon, father of the young Yakima boy who had witnessed the killing, had been absent on a hunt when the murder took place. When he rejoined the party and learned what had been done, he upbraided the warriors and told them they had done a bad thing.

"There will be trouble," he said.

Trouble there certainly was. Shocked and angered by the killing, the Army sent Major Haller, fresh from his glorious victory over four hapless Indians in the Boise Valley, north from The Dalles with a force of eighty federal troops, a mountain howitzer, and the firm resolve to teach the Indians a lesson.

From the reports Tommy and Sitkum received, it was not a brilliant campaign. Marching into a country they did not know, following streams and trails that left them exposed while the Indians made use of heavy timber, bushes, and rocks for cover, running short of water, food, and forage for their animals after two days in the field—Major Haller and his command spiked and buried their little cannon, made stretchers for their wounded, interred their dead, and began their retreat before the campaign had really gotten under way.

In all, Major Haller lost five men killed and seventeen wounded in the aborted Yakima campaign, plus a large amount of government property destroyed, lost, or abandoned.

A major Indian war had begun.

Because his wife was a Yakima and loyal to her people, these were unhappy times for Sitkum, Tommy knew. Spotted Fawn told Sitkum that while Chief Kamiakin deplored the senseless murder of his friend Andrew Bolon, and might even have been willing to turn the guilty Indians over to the white man's court of justice, he would not stand idly by and submit to an invasion of his country by the white soldiers.   It was Kamiakin's intelligence and strategy that had lured Major Haller's troops ever deeper into the canyons and forests of the homeland the Yakima warriors knew so well, until, when the defenders did choose to turn and fight, the bewildered, lost, exhausted soldiers were at their mercy. But it was not Kamiakin's plan to commit his people to a general warfare against the whites, Spotted Fawn said, despite the hysterical claims of the region's white settlers that nighttime fires on Cascade Mountain peaks as far south as California and as far north as Canada were signals from tribe to tribe that a massive uprising plotted by the wily Yakima chief was about to begin.

"She says all Kamiakin wants to do," Sitkum told Tommy, "is to protect the boundaries of the reservation agreed to at the Walla Walla council. If the white men wish to travel from Puget Sound to the Colville country, he will let them pass through Yakima lands, as long as they stay on the trail he will mark for them."

"The whites aren't listening, I'm afraid. With Governor Stevens cut off from home in the Blackfoot country and Lieutenant Governor Mason arguing with General Wool as to whether or not martial law should be declared, nobody in authority has time to talk peace with Kamiakin. In fact, one rumor I've heard is that Chief Leschi and the

Nisquallys are just waiting for word from Kamiakin to start a war of extermination against the whites on both sides of the mountains."

"Among Indians, when two chiefs do not agree," Sitkum said gravely, "each goes his own way, taking his followers with him. But when white leaders argue, they keep on talking endlessly, while their people suffer. What is the sense of that?"

Agreeing that the squabbles between the military and civilian leaders in the Pacific Northwest made no sense at all, Tommy told Sitkum all they could do was wait and see what happened, meanwhile tending to business, which, for the *Mary* and *Wasco*, now was substantial because of the increased traffic on the middle river.

Scattered attacks by dissident Indians in the lower Puget Sound area at the same time of the killings of the white trespassers on the Yakima Reservation spread panic among the settlers and gave credence to the rumor that a general Indian war plotted by Leschi and Kamiakin had begun. Planning to hit the hostiles from the west as well as the south, Major Raines led a column of federal troops east across the Cascades at the same time Major Haller marched north from The Dalles. Upon learning of Haller's defeat, the Raines contingent turned tail and hurried back to the safety of Fort Steilacoom without even firing a shot at an Indian. So the white settlers had good reason to doubt the ability of federal troops to protect them.

When hostilities began in Washington Territory, Governor Stevens and his treaty-negotiating party were on the upper Missouri River near Fort Benton, where he had just concluded a treaty with the Blackfeet, "extinguishing" their rights to a large expanse of land. By express rider, Secretary Charles Mason, Acting Governor in Stevens' absence, sent a message saying the whole Territory was aflame with an Indian war. Though he had appealed to General John E. Wool, commandant of federal troops in San Francisco for the Pacific Northwest District, for help and a contingent of federal troops to go to the upper Missouri River country and escort Governor Stevens and his party home, he feared General Wool might not respond favorably. Therefore, he suggested, it might be best if Governor Stevens and his party went down the Missouri and Mississippi by boat to New Orleans, whence they could eventually take a ship to Panama, cross the Isthmus by land, then board another ship for Puget Sound.

While this might have been the sensible thing to do, Governor Stevens refused to even consider it. To his way of thinking, it would be a cowardly act of retreat when the situation demanded a man of courage must charge. Rallying a hundred friendly Nez Perces to his support as an escort, he headed back to Olympia by way of the Spokane country and the Columbia River, determined to fight his way through the thousands of Yakima warriors supposedly blocking his path or die nobly in the attempt.

Because the alleged "hostiles" did not really care what he did and certainly did not want to go to war against the Nez Perces, they did not attack the feisty little Governor either during his overland journey or his half-day trip aboard the *Mary* between The Dalles and the Upper Cascades.

Though Tommy was intrigued by the opportunity to see Governor Stevens in the close quarters of the boat, he did not judge this to be a good time for idle conversation. Indeed, with a strong headwind blowing up the Gorge and the boat laboring against vicious whitecaps as it towed a fractious flatboat loaded with spooked horses, he was too busy himself to indulge in pointless conversation. On the wind-and-rain-swept deck below, he could see Stevens pacing back and forth, continually talking to his aides; it was clear from his jerky movements and impatient gestures that he was seething with anger.

"When I get back to Olympia, hell will pop!" Tommy heard him say. "Before I'll submit to that doddering old imbecile, I'll declare martial law and throw him out of Washington Territory with my own hands!"

From what Tommy had read in the regional newspapers, General Wool's response to the request that he send an escort to bring the Stevens' party back from the Blackfoot country had been the testy comment: "I have neither the resources of a Territory nor the United States Treasury at my command."

Since Governor Stevens had gotten himself into his present predicament, said General Wool, he could damn well get himself out of it on his own initiative—even if that meant coming home by way of New Orleans and Panama. Rumor had it that the General had chuckled and added: "Let him try to explain that travel voucher to whoever is paying his expenses in Washington Territory."

If the response seemed to indicate that General Wool did not like Governor Stevens, this was certainly true. Animosity between the two men dated back to a dinner party in San Francisco in December 1854, almost two years after Major Stevens had resigned from the Army and become Governor of Washington Territory. No doubt drinks were imbibed that evening, during which a discussion of the Mexican War played a prominent part.

When the talk turned to the Battle of Buena Vista, Stevens said later, General Wool "loudly claimed for himself all the credit for that battle, disparaging in an offensive manner General Taylor and the part he took in it."

Stevens had been only a lowly lieutenant at the time and had served in a different area of the Mexican War. But now he was out of the military, Governor of Washington Territory, and felt it his right to speak as an equal. According to his own account, his sense of justice was so outraged by the boastful and unfair tirade, that he spoke up and said: "General Wool, we all know the brilliant part you bore in that battle, but we all know and history will record that General Taylor fought and won the Battle of Buena Vista."

Satisfying though the statement may have been to Stevens' sense of justice and outrage, it was not a diplomatic thing to say under the circumstances, for a wounded general—like a wounded elephant—never forgets his attacker. When word reached Wool that an Indian war had broken out in Governor Stevens' bailiwick, he made a quick trip north to analyze the situation. During his visit, he censured everybody, not omitting Raines and Haller, but was particularly hard on territorial officers and volunteers.

When he heard that Secretary Mason was raising a company of volunteers to go to the aid of Governor Stevens, he ordered it disbanded and said Stevens would have to fend for himself. Furthermore, he declared that the war had been deliberately provoked by white businessmen eager to sell goods to the military. Claiming that the Indians were victims rather than aggressors, he closed the entire region east of the Cascades to settlement by the whites, ordering those who were there to move to the west side of the mountains. He then declared that he would use whatever political power he had in Washington, D.C., to persuade the Senate not to ratify the treaties Governor Stevens had made. Finally, he issued a statement that amazed and infuriated every white citizen in the Pacific Northwest:

> The Cascade Range forms, if not an impassable barrier, an excellent line of defense, a most valuable wall of separation between two races always at war when in contact. To permit settlers to pass The Dalles and occupy the natural reserve is to give up this advantage, throw down this wall, and advance the frontier hundreds of miles to the east, and add to the protective labors of the Army.

In retaliation, as soon as he reached the Territorial capital in Olympia, Governor Stevens declared all acts and orders by General Wool null and void, proclaimed martial law despite General Wool's statements to the contrary, issued a call for the raising of a Territorial Militia, and authorized the printing of a million dollars in scrip as a down payment for a major Indian war whose purpose would be to put the rebellious tribes in their place now and forever.

In a word, Tommy admitted to Sitkum, chaos reined supreme ...

Though normally the winters west of the Cascades were cold and rainy, with little snow and below-freezing weather, the bottom dropped out of the thermometer in early January 1856. Arctic air moved in from the north, the temperature fell to zero, and the Columbia River froze over so solidly from bank to bank between the Lower Cascades and Astoria that for three weeks no boats moved. No hostile Indians were moving either, nor did the deadlock between Governor Stevens and General Wool thaw in the slightest degree.

When the weather finally moderated and the ice broke up early in February, the *Fashion* and the *Belle* resumed bringing supplies upriver for the soldiers stationed at The Dalles, with the *Wasco* and the *Mary* picking them up above the portage and transporting them the rest of the way. Though no new Indian outbreaks had occurred, General Wool ordered that the thirty-man garrison at Bradford's Landing be transferred upriver to The Dalles, where Major Granville Haller had been replaced by Colonel George S. Wright, who was reputed to be a much more aggressive officer.

After spending three weeks with his wife in the Yakima village when the *Mary* was idle, Sitkum was unusually quiet following his return. As always, he kept the boat's boiler fired up and its engine producing at maximum capacity, but he had so little to say that Tommy knew something was troubling him. When his mood did not change after a couple of days, Tommy asked him what was wrong.

Standing beside Tommy in the pilot house as the *Mary* chugged laboriously against the current, pulling a heavily loaded barge, Sitkum stared out at the winter-brown bluffs on the near shore for a time, his face bleak, then he said, "My wife wants me to quit the *Mary*."

"Does she think you're gone from home too much?"

"No."

"Is the pay too low?"

"No."

"Then what's she unhappy about?"

"She says there's going to be bad trouble. She wants me clear of it."

"Is Kamiakin planning to start a war? Is that what she's worried about?"

"She won't say—though my guess is something is in the wind. All she'll say is she wants me to quit my job on the boat, cross the river, and go down to live with her and her relatives on the Warm Springs Reservation until the trouble is over."

Because Sitkum was one of the few Indians he knew who had learned how to read and write, shown and developed his outstanding mechanical skill, and was willing to take advantage of the opportunities offered by the white man's world, Tommy had encouraged him to keep his hair cut short, wear white man's clothes, speak English as much as possible, and become a part of the white man's culture. This was particularly important in these unsettled times, Tommy felt, when senseless killings by hot-bloods of either race could lead to disaster.

"What are you going to do?"

"Stick with my job on the *Mary*. If Spotted Fawn wants to go back to the blanket, I'll let her go. But I'll stay with my job on the river."

Apparently the military had heard rumors of Indian activity, too, for Colonel Wright was preparing to march east up the Columbia, "show the flag," and demonstrate to the natives that the Army intended to police the inland country and prevent white settlers from traveling across it. Carrying reinforcements and supplies to The Dalles, the *Mary* steamed upriver in mild, sunny weather on Monday, March 24, tied up for the night there, then returned to her dock below Bradford's Store near the Upper Cascades late Tuesday afternoon, March 25.

When the boat was busy, the four-man crew of the *Mary* took their meals and slept aboard, even though the quarters were cramped. In addition to Tommy and Sitkum, a big, lumbering, forty year old Negro named Dick Turpin served as cook, stoker, and deckhand, while a skinny, willing, but not very bright sixteen year old boy named Johnny Chance worked as a steward, helper, and general-purpose roustabout.

As usual, the fires under the boilers were extinguished for the night. When daylight came Wednesday morning, the crew ate breakfast, then Tommy and Sitkum went ashore to arrange for the loading of cargo and cordwood, which would take most of the morning, while the cook and his helper cleared away and washed the breakfast dishes. By eight o'clock of what promised to be a warm spring day, the settlement called Bradford's Landing was coming to life, with smoke curling upward from the chimneys of cabins, workmen shouldering their tools to labor on a bridge being built to connect the bank with a small island in the river, and tramway mules beginning to move downriver toward the stacks of freight deposited by the *Belle* at the lower end of the portage yesterday afternoon.

Suddenly a volley of shots rang out from the bush-covered slope above the settlement, followed by an ear-piercing series of savage yells that left no doubt as to the identity of the attackers.

"Godamighty!" Tommy shouted as he hit the dirt. "Indians!"

10.

$\mathscr{P}$ARTIALLY PROTECTED by the trunk of a fallen tree while the shots buzzed over his head, Tommy got glimpses of what was happening in the settlement just down the slope. Half a dozen men working at the sawmill made a break for the shelter of the blockhouse, were intercepted by a swarm of half-naked Indians, fought with them hand to hand for a few moments, then broke free and made it to safety, except for one poor wretch who was shot down, stabbed repeatedly, then scalped.

Entering an isolated cabin through an unlatched door, another band of Indians pulled a male settler, his wife, and two children out into the yard, tomahawked them to death, scalped them, then dragged their bodies down to the riverbank and dumped them into the water with whoops of triumph. Seeing the two groups preoccupied for the time being, Tommy got to his feet and yelled at Sitkum, who also was lying prone.

"Head for the boat! It's our only chance!"

Running down the hill half stooped over, both men heard bullets whizzing past them but neither was hit, bounding across the extended gangplank of the *Mary* and making for their respective stations, Tommy up to the pilot house, Sitkum below decks to the engine room. Aboard the boat, the big Negro cook, Dick Turpin, and his young helper, Johnny Chance, had responded to the attack with commendable rapidity, the cook coming on deck with a rifle and the boy appearing with an old Dragoon pistol; their covering fire made the attacking Indians keep their distance. Snatching up the loaded revolver which he kept in the pilot house, Tommy added its sting to that of the other two weapons.

"Sitkum!" he shouted down to the engine room. "Can you give me some steam?"

"The boilers are stone cold!" Sitkum yelled back. "But I'm stealing some fire from the cookstove and will give you some pressure as soon as I can!"

"How's your wood supply?"

"Enough to get us started. But don't cut loose the lines until I give you enough steam pressure to turn the wheels!"

Hearing wrenching, tearing, chopping sounds below, Tommy knew that Sitkum was prying loose and chopping up chairs, tables, lockers, bulkheads, or anything else made of wood that could be tossed into the furnace and burned. Without adequate steam pressure, Tommy knew, it would be suicide to cast off the lines and pull out into the main channel of the river where the current would sweep the *Mary* into the rapids a quarter mile downstream from the landing unless the boat had sufficient power to move its paddle wheels. Watching the Indians prepare to attack, Tommy yelled down from the pilot house, "Cover the bow, Johnny! Dick, watch the stern!"

Moving forward through the hail of bullets raking the deck, Johnny Chance suddenly crumpled, then reached down to seize his left calf, which was stained red.

"Ouch! That hurt!"

"Are you hit, Johnny?"

"Not so bad I can't shoot! I'll make the boogers pay!"

Crawling forward and crouching behind the port rail, Johnny fired a quick shot at an Indian about to set foot on the gangplank, causing him to topple backward to the bank, where two of his comrades picked him up and dragged him to safety. When Tommy added a couple of rounds from his pistol and Dick Turpin discharged his rifle in the same direction, the attackers decided the gangplank was too hot for them at the moment, retreated, and turned their attention to the less dangerous buildings of the settlement.

Unfortunately, a parting shot from one of the Indians struck Dick Turpin in the left shoulder, causing him to turn in panic and leap into a barge tethered beside the boat. Staggering around there as he cried out in shock and pain, he lost his balance and fell overboard into the river. With him went their most effective weapon, the rifle; neither man nor gun was seen again.

Going down to the main deck where Johnny Chance sat with his left trouser leg pulled up, staring at a wound in the fleshy part of the calf, Tommy knelt and said, "Give me a look, Johnny."

"My leg ain't broken, Captain. The bullet seems to have gone straight through the meat and missed the bone."

"Can you walk?"

"Sure, if I take it slow. Where do you want me to go?"

"Down to the engine room to give Sitkum a hand. I'll bandage the leg good and tight so it won't bleed too much. As soon as we get enough steam pressure, we'll pull out into the river and head for The Dalles, where we'll tell the soldiers about the attack."

"I've got more loads for my pistol in the galley, sir. Give me a yell if them damn Injuns come again."

"That I'll do, Johnny. But the important thing right now is to get the *Mary* under way."

As the boy limped below decks, Tommy climbed back up to the pilot house, reloaded his pistol, then stood waiting impatiently while the fire under the boilers burned higher and the steam-pressure gauge in the pilot house began to climb. For the time being, the attacking Indians were devoting their attention to the blockhouse, the store, the sawmill, and the scattered buildings of the settlement, though he knew that the moment the paddle wheels started to turn the Indians would realize the danger of letting the boat leave the dock.

Fed by the supply of pitch-filled pine knots the cook always kept on hand for a quick fire, the tubes of the rapidly heating boilers were thumping now as the metal expanded and the condensers compressed water into steam within the cylinders. Flat on the peg at zero a few moments ago, the steam-pressure gauge in the pilot house had risen from five to ten to fifteen and was climbing fast. Normal operating pressure for the boilers of the *Mary* was sixty pounds per square inch, but Tommy had no intention of waiting until normal conditions prevailed. Twenty-five would do. Or even twenty, so long as it was climbing.

When the gauge read eighteen, he stuck his head out of the pilot house and shouted down at the engine room. "Johnny! Sitkum! Cut loose the lines! Then give me all the power you've got!"

Appearing from below decks with axes in hand, Sitkum ran to the stern rail and chopped the line there, while Johnny hobbled forward, unfastened the gangplank, and cut the bow line. After casting off the lines connecting the barge to the boat, Sitkum ran back down to the boiler room and began valving the engine. As the paddle wheels began to churn, Johnny shouted a warning to Tommy.

"Look out, Captain! They're coming again!"

85

BILL GULICK

Aware of the danger to their cause if the *Mary* succeeded in pulling out into the river and heading toward the military post at The Dalles, a dozen hostiles armed with rifles came running down the slope, pausing frequently to kneel and fire at the pilot house, from which they knew the boat was controlled. Because the thin wooden sides of the structure offered little protection from bullets, Tommy dropped flat on his back, squirmed into a position beneath the knobs of the wheel, and prepared to guide the boat with his feet. Seeing what he was doing, Johnny scurried over to the well leading below decks to the engine room, where he would be protected from the volley of bullets ripping into the pilot house, could communicate with Sitkum, and see where the boat was going. From this spot, he called out instructions to Tommy.

"She's headed too much downriver, sir! Bring her a few spokes to the left! Sitkum, ease off power to the port side-wheel."

"Gotcha, Johnny!" Sitkum called up. Clumsily turning the wheel with his feet, Tommy asked, "How's that?"

"Fine, sir! Steady as she goes!"

"Are we drifting toward the rapids?"

"We were till you turned her. Now she's barely holding her own."

"Keep me on a course straight across the river till we've got more power, then I'll turn her upstream."

"Aye, aye, sir! We're a hundred yards offshore now and doin' fine!"

Knowing that the current grew stronger toward the middle of the river and hearing no more shots from the bank, Tommy rose to one knee and risked a look at the boat's position. Her course directly across the river had subjected her port side to considerable downstream thrust, putting her in danger of being sucked into the rapids, but she had sufficient steam pressure now to permit him to turn her bow into the current and head upriver.

"How much fuel do you have left?" he shouted down to Sitkum.

"Ten minutes' worth, at the most!" Sitkum yelled back. "After that, we'll have nothing left to burn but the hull."

"There's a settler's cabin a couple of miles upriver. If the Indians haven't hit it, we'll pull in there and raid his wood pile."

"We'd better, sir, else I'll have to begin chopping up the boat."

Feeling much better now that he had a live boat moving under him, Tommy gave audible encouragement to the besieged defenders of Bradford's Landing by using a brief burst of steam for two short

86

blasts of the boat's whistle, which he hoped they would interpret to mean, "Help is on the way!"

With Sitkum and Johnny still chopping and prying loose any parts of the boat not needed to keep her afloat, Tommy eased the *Mary* in toward the north bank as she passed the point of land two miles up the river, his eyes carefully scanning the shore line for signs of life in and around the settler's cabin. He saw none. The cabin was owned, he knew, by a middle-aged bachelor named Harry Lyle who worked at the sawmill near the blockhouse during the day, while in his off hours he tended a garden, added to the cabin, cared for a few horses and cattle, and tried to develop the half section of land he had claimed under the Donation Act.

Probably he had been at the sawmill when the Indians attacked, for there was no sign of life around the cabin now. Nosing the bow of the *Mary* into the sandy bank where an eddy created quiet water, Tommy called for Sitkum to cut off power, then descended from the pilot house, leaped ashore, and looped a line around a piling of the settler's dock. Hitting the beach right behind him were Sitkum and Johnny.

With all three of them moving as fast as they were able to, the woodpile in the lee of Harry Lyle's cabin was stripped bare in a matter of minutes and carried aboard, after which the captain and crew tore apart the rails and posts of the corral and fence separating the livestock from the garden. Thrown helter-skelter aboard the *Mary* without being chopped into furnace lengths, the six-foot-long X-shaped supports and the ten-foot-long rails would be burned hillbilly style—that is, thrust into the open furnace door without being cut into shorter lengths, then pushed on into the flames as they burned.

When the wood loading was finished and the *Mary* pulled out into the river again, Tommy could see smoke rising from the direction of Bradford's Landing, which led him to suspect that the attacking Indians had put some of the buildings of the settlement to the torch. Faintly on the upriver breeze, the rattle of gunfire could be heard, punctuated now and then by a deep-throated boom which he knew to be that of the cannon mounted on the blockhouse wall. Through the nine-power binoculars he kept in the pilot house, he could see a column of black smoke rising from the spot where the *Wasco* was docked near the Oregon shore, while in midriver three small boats apparently filled with settlers who had managed to make their escape from Bradford's Landing were pulling across toward the south bank.

No doubt the *Wasco* would head upriver to The Dalles, too, as soon as she got up steam, though it would be late afternoon before either boat reached the military post. Since they could not risk running at night, at least half the morning would pass tomorrow before military help could reach the beleaguered settlement. Downriver, the Middle Cascades' blockhouse was closer, of course, as was Fort Vancouver in terms of miles. But if this were part of a general Indian attack planned and ordered by the Yakima leader, Chief Kamiakin, as Tommy suspected it was, the hostiles no doubt had raided both the Middle Blockhouse and the Lower Cascades' settlement at the same time they hit Bradford's Landing. When informed of the attack, troops from Fort Vancouver could be transported upriver to the Lower Cascades aboard the *Fashion* or the *Belle*, but from that point on they would have to march six miles overland on a rough, muddy road, which would take time.

With the *Mary* running now under full power against a moderate current, Sitkum came above decks and stood beside Tommy, staring out at the spring-green hills of the north shore with a brooding look in his eyes. Tommy asked,

"Was this what your wife tried to warn you about?"

"Yes, I imagine it was."

"Did Kamiakin plan it?"

"The Yakimas are not my people, Tommy, so I cannot tell you who their leaders are or how they think. Kamiakin does not like or trust the white man, Spotted Fawn says. But I do not believe he would plan this alone."

"She wanted you to run away from the trouble she knew was coming, didn't she? She wanted you to take her and the children across the river and live on the Warm Springs Reservation, where you would be safe."

Sitkum shook his head, a misery in his eyes. "That's what she said she wanted, Tommy, but I would not do it. 'Go back to the blanket, if you must,' I told her. 'Take the children with you. I will stay on the river, using the skills my white friends have taught me so that I can live like a free man instead of a blanket Indian.'"

"Did she go to the Warm Springs Reservation?"

"No. She and the children are still living in the village near Celilo Falls. Now that war has come, I hope they will be safe there. But they will not go back to the blanket ..."

The attack on the white settlements had been planned by Kamiakin and a council of chiefs, it was learned later, as part of a general uprising all over the Pacific Northwest. Ironically, it would never have taken place if the fourteen bands now united as the Yakima Nation had not been forced by Governor Stevens to accept the boundaries of a large reservation and sign the treaty negotiated a year ago in the Walla Walla Valley. Guaranteed a homeland on which no white man could trespass without permission from the Indians, the Yakimas felt they had every right to be treated fairly. If they were not, they would go to war. Supporting their belief in the sanctity of their reservation, had been General Wool's edict closing the country east of the Cascades to settlement by the whites and ordering all white occupants presently living there to leave it and move west of the mountains.

Coming without warning as it had, the attack on the north bank settlements at first took a heavy toll among the white defenders, but they soon began to fight back. When the Indians struck the Middle Cascades' blockhouse, Sergeant Kelly, in charge of a squad of soldiers there, quickly responded by climbing to the parapet wall, charging the cannon, and blasting away at unseen targets on the brushy hillside, though he had no idea of where the attackers were. Frightened more by the noise than hurt by the effect of the cannonading, the hostiles pulled back, giving the soldiers and civilians caught outside the blockhouse walls time to seek shelter and grab up arms.

Three miles downriver at the Lower Cascades, which had no blockhouse, the crew of men transferring supplies from a flatboat to the portage tramway cars, heard the booming of the cannon only minutes before a friendly Washougal Indian called Fishhook Charley came rushing down to the wharf with word of the attack above. Taking a rapid inventory of their means and weapons of defense, the whites discovered to their dismay that they did not have a single pistol or rifle among them. Scrambling into the few small catboats and canoes that were available, the older men, women, and children set out down the river, promising to send back help.

The dozen able-bodied younger workmen who were left behind hastily piled sacks of flour, beans, rice, and wooden crates of hardware on one of the flatcars, building up a substantial breastwork, behind

89

which they hunkered and awaited the attack. Breaking open several crates in hopes of finding weapons, they discovered half a dozen three-inch steel points used in excavating hand-drilled wells, an equal number of metal bailers for lifting out dirt, and the handles and risers for several water pumps.

"Well, we can rig what'll look like cannons," one ingenious workman declared. "We'll point 'em over the barricade; then, when the Injuns come, we'll yell and pound like we're loadin' our big guns, makin' 'em think we're fixin' to blast 'em to hell and gone."

When the Indians did come and the ruse was tried, it worked, much to everybody's surprise. Seeing the white men well barricaded on the flatcar, with what appeared to be large-bore cannons pointed in their direction and ready to fire, the hostiles stayed well out of range all the rest of the day, contenting themselves with wild arrow and rifle shots now and then, but making no concentrated attack. When darkness fell, the defenders moved quietly down to the wharf, boarded the flatboat tethered there, cast off its lines, and drifted down the river toward Fort Vancouver.

Meanwhile at Bradford's Landing, any faint hope that the besieged white people there might slip down to the river under cover of darkness, board flatboats, and try the risky expedient of running the rapids vanished when the Indians set fire to the warehouse near Bradford's Store, making the area bright as day. Unable to breech the walls of the solid blockhouse or the well-defended store, in whose buildings the soldier and civilian survivors had taken refuge, the Indians tried to burn them out. Time and again during the night, a hostile would sneak down out of the brush on the brow of the hill and heave a red-hot iron or a blazing pine knot onto the roof of a building, setting it on fire. At the store, its defenders found that the blazes could be extinguished by cutting holes in the roof from inside, climbing up, then splashing brine from the pickle barrels stored in the basement on the flames. In the blockhouse, water drawn from cisterns built into the corner bastions against just that contingency, worked equally well.

Word of the attack reached Fort Vancouver just before dark that day, brought by the same friendly Washougal Indian, Fishhook Charley, who, after warning the workmen at the Lower Cascades, had gotten into his canoe and paddled swiftly downriver. Since General John Wool, commandant of the Pacific Northwest District, was six hundred miles away in his San Francisco headquarters, and Colonel

George Wright, local commander, was a hundred miles upriver at Fort Dalles, the ranking officer in charge at Fort Vancouver was an energetic, ambitious young lieutenant named Philip Sheridan. Recently graduated from West Point and eager for action more exciting than reviewing close-order drills on the parade grounds, Lieutenant Sheridan welcomed this opportunity to show his superiors his training had not been wasted. In a crisp dispatch, he informed the civilian authorities across the river in Portland:

> Word received of Indian attack upriver. Plan to move in relief early tomorrow morning, 27th, with company of dragoons aboard the *Belle*. If Oregon Volunteers wish to join my command, they may do so, though they probably will not be needed, for the Army has the situation well in hand.

Unfortunately for posterity, the original copy of this first-ever, hastily scrawled, command-decision made by an officer later to become famous as a Civil War leader, has not been preserved. But it indicates the kind of officer Phil Sheridan was at the time and would be for the rest of his long, distinguished military career.

In Portland, the response to the dispatch from Lieutenant Sheridan was immediate, if somewhat confused. Quickly a company of volunteers was formed, but when Territorial officials were asked to supply firearms they refused on the grounds that: (1) they lacked authorization from the Governor and the Legislature, and (2) they lacked firearms. Scurrying around town, the would-be volunteers managed to collect twenty rifles, so twenty men were selected to head upriver, though a day was lost in the process. Finally boarding the *Fashion* on the morning of the 28th, the Oregon Volunteers arrived at the Cascades too late to do any fighting, though they did take part in the cleanup work, such as it was.

A day earlier on the morning of the 27th, Lieutenant Sheridan, his company of dragoons, and a handful of volunteers living near Fort Vancouver, headed upriver aboard the *Belle*. Halfway to the Lower Cascades, he met the flotilla of refugees who had fled during the previous day and night. When a dozen of the younger men volunteered to return and fight with the troops, he swore them in as enlisted men, and the *Belle* chugged on up the river.

Meanwhile both the *Mary* and the *Wasco* reached The Dalles in late evening the 26th, only to learn that Colonel George Wright and most of his command had marched east earlier in the day. A courier mounted on a fast horse galloped through the dark to overtake them, finding the soldiers camped just above Five Mile Creek on the south bank of the Columbia near Celilo Falls. Not wanting to march in the dark, Colonel Wright held his forces in readiness there through the night, gave the order to move out at the crack of dawn next morning, and a few hours later began loading soldiers, baggage, howitzers, and enough horses to mount a company of dragoons aboard the *Mary*, the *Wasco*, and two flatboats. By the time men and baggage were aboard, the two boats were so heavily loaded that their guards skimmed the waters.

Since ferrying troops and horses down fifty miles of wind-whipped river was a new experience for the captains of the boats and the military commander of the expedition, the transport proved to be a slow, unwieldy operation. Jittery about their first water voyage, the spooked horses and the nervous soldier handlers had trouble maintaining their balance as the flatboats tilted dangerously on the choppy river. Struck by choppy waves and changing currents, the *Wasco* at times found itself being overtaken by her tow, which then took off on a course of its own. Because the wood supply he had picked up for the *Mary* at The Dalles was green and wet, Sitkum found that it burned poorly, with a consequent loss of power.

By nightfall of the 27th, the two heavily laden boats had covered only half the distance to the Upper Cascades. Not wanting to risk running at night because of navigational hazards and Indian dangers, the boats tied up in sheltered coves on opposite banks, the Wasco on the Oregon shore, the *Mary* on the Washington side.

Meanwhile, the *Belle*, which was carrying Sheridan and his troops upriver from Fort Vancouver, was having better luck, reaching the Lower Cascades in early afternoon that same day. Going ashore, the dragoons found that the hostiles had destroyed, burned, or looted everything in sight. Making a cautious advance along the portage road, Lieutenant Sheridan's command soon ran into stiff resistance from Indians lying in ambush, so he prudently pulled it back to the landing, his retreat covered by a real cannon mounted on the upper deck of the *Belle*.

At Bradford's Landing that night, the siege developed into a stalemate, with the defenders able to repel all Indian attacks while the hostiles set fire to buildings and lit up the area so that no attempt to escape could be made. When daylight came, Lieutenant Sheridan crossed his men to the Oregon shore, made a short march upriver, then recrossed to the Middle Cascades, where he found a group of Yakimas feasting on stolen beef, engaged them in a brief skirmish, and put them on the run.

A few miles above Bradford's Landing, Colonel Wright split his forces, putting Lieutenant Colonel Edward Steptoe and a company of dragoons ashore so that they could block the Indians from retreating to the east, while the *Mary* and the *Wasco* unloaded Colonel Wright's troops at the landing and drove the hostiles in that direction.

"Keep your eyes and ears open, Colonel," Tommy heard Wright say crisply to his subordinate officer just before they parted. "With the element of surprise in our favor, we should be able to end this Indian war before it's well begun."

"You can count on me and the dragoons to carry our part of the mission, sir," Steptoe replied smartly. "We'll nip this uprising in the bud."

Going ashore at Bradford's Landing, where the troops in the block-house and the civilians in the store cheered the arrival of Colonel Wright's relief force with shouts of joy and a wild waving of caps and hats, Wright was delighted to find that a fast-moving contingent of troops under Lieutenant Sheridan had just reached the beleaguered settlement after a rapid march upriver. Having been given a taste of action in the skirmish with the hostiles between the Middle Cascades and this point, Lieutenant Sheridan and his men were eager for more.

"Sir, we've got the hostiles on the run," Sheridan exclaimed. "May I have your permission to continue the pursuit?"

Well aware of the importance of encouraging a young officer in his first military triumph, Colonel Wright smiled and nodded. "Permission granted, Lieutenant. Keep the rascals moving upriver toward Colonel Steptoe's command, harassing them just enough to focus their attention on you rather than on Steptoe. With any luck at all, they'll be trapped between the two forces."

Unfortunately for the success of this well-conceived piece of strategy, Colonel Edward Steptoe's insistence on following the military dragoon handbook he had studied so assiduously at West Point doomed it to failure. With Sheridan and his men pushing the hostiles hard from the west and keeping them so occupied by peppering their rear with rifle fire that they had no idea another contingent of troops was coming toward them from the east, it was highly unlikely that they would have seen Steptoe and his company of dragoons until caught in the closing trap. But when an advance Steptoe scout galloped back to the head of the dragoon column, saluted crisply, and said that he had sighted hostiles just a mile ahead, Colonel Steptoe whirled around in his saddle and shouted, "Bugler!"

"Yes, sir!"

"Blow 'The Charge!' "

Crisp and clear into the early morning air rose the stirring notes of the classic call to action. Heard first by Steptoe's dragoons, it was also heard by Chief Kamiakin's forces, which, until now, had not known Steptoe's soldiers were there. Warned of the danger they were in, the hostiles abandoned their rear-guard action, wheeled their surefooted Indian ponies north into the foothills away from the river, and vanished like smoke before a rising gale. When the two Army forces met a few minutes later, they found the trap they had laid so carefully empty …

With the siege lifted from the settlements on the north bank of the Columbia, the task of counting casualties began. The numbers were grim. Eleven civilians and three soldiers had been killed outright, while fourteen people had been so seriously wounded that two more died within a few days. Though Indians dissatisfied with the terms of the recently made treaties had also attacked white settlements on Puget Sound and in southwest Oregon, the rumored assault on Portland—which had so alarmed its citizens that every able-bodied man between the age of fifteen and fifty had joined the militia, seized whatever weapon he could find, and prepared to defend home and hearth to the last red drop of his blood—had made its residents feel rather sheepish when not a single hostile appeared.

But on the Columbia River from Portland to the Cascades, on upriver to The Dalles, and beyond Celilo Falls to the big bend country where the river turned north at the site of the old Hudson's Bay Company trading post, Fort Walla Walla, a new day had dawned. Despite General John Wool's order that the whites abandon and vacate the country east of the Cascades, settlers voting with their feet showed that they had come to stay.

In direct violation of General Wool's edict, Governor Isaac Stevens declared martial law in Washington Territory, while Governor Joseph Lane did the same thing in Oregon Territory. Calling for a second Treaty Council in the Walla Walla Valley between the leaders of the Yakima Nation, the Umatilla Confederation, and the whites in late summer of 1856, the commissioners and their military escorts kept the river boats busy transporting supplies and men inland from Fort Vancouver and Portland.

When the talks ended not with peace but in a renewed outbreak of hostilities, even General Wool admitted that a state of war now existed east of the Cascades. In an effort to maintain order and "show the flag," he approved the establishment of a military post to be called Fort Walla Walla twenty-nine miles east of the former Hudson's Bay Company post of the same name, to be staffed by a company of infantry and three companies of dragoons. In charge of the post would be Lieutenant Colonel Edward J. Steptoe, whom Wool warned through his superior at Fort Vancouver, Colonel George Wright: "You will be on your guard against the whites and prevent further trouble by keeping the whites out of the Indian country."

Exactly what means the military was authorized to use to accomplish this aim General Wool did not say. But it did inspire more than one white gold-seeker, farmer, settler, or businessman determined to move across or occupy lands declared open to them under the terms of the recently negotiated treaties to ask caustically: *Whose side is the Army on?*

11.

*B*AD AS THE CHOKE POINTS at the portages had been before the outbreak of the Yakima Indian War, they became much worse now that the Army posts of Fort Dalles and Fort Walla Walla must be supplied with an ever-increasing quantity of troops, arms, building materials, and food staples. Because every pound of freight shipped upriver had to be unloaded and reloaded at the Cascades, then at The Dalles, and finally at Wallula Landing twenty-nine miles west of Fort Walla Walla, transportation charges paid by the military and civilian suppliers often exceeded the value of the merchandise itself.

Freight from Portland to The Dalles traveled at twenty dollars a ton, while a human passenger, a horse, or a cow was charged six dollars a head. Above The Dalles, passengers and freight must endure a fourteen-mile wagon ride over a rough, rutted, sand-drifted road around the rapids to the landing above Celilo Falls before returning to the river. Awaiting the traveler and packages of freight there were clumsy wooden barges rigged with square sails by which the craft hopefully would be shoved along by wind power when the wind blew strongly enough from the west, or, when it did not, be propelled by crews of husky men thrusting long poles against the bottom in shallow water or pulling at oars when it deepened.

From The Dalles to Fort Walla Walla, human and animal passengers were charged twenty-five dollars a head, while freight moved at one hundred dollars a ton. Since there was no alternative mode of transport, business was good despite the exorbitant rates.

As Tommy had hoped his younger brother would do, Emil Warren and his lovely Spanish bride, Dolores, moved north in April that year, filing a claim on a square mile of land near the Willamette Valley town of Albany, Oregon, sixty miles south of Portland. Bringing his wife to their Rooster Rock cabin in late May to meet Tommy,

Freda, and their chubby, tow-headed, five-year-old son, Lars Thomas, Emil quickly demonstrated that at twenty-seven he had not outgrown his mischievous charm nor his faculty for living by his wits rather than by his labors. But under his easygoing good humor now lay a calculating shrewdness, which Tommy had no doubt developed in the teeming California gold economy, where competition had been keen.

As for Dolores, she was a jewel—beautiful, gracious, and so warmhearted that Freda, Lars, and Tommy took to her immediately.

"Do you plan to live in Albany?" Tommy asked his brother.

"Lord, no!" Emil said with a laugh. "It's far too small a pond for Dolores and me. I've hired a couple of workmen to build a cabin we'll sleep in often enough to validate our claim. I may even vote and hang up my shingle there, after I've gotten my law license. If I decide to run for the Legislature, I'll probably claim residence in Albany. But Portland suits Dolores and me much better. I imagine we'll build our permanent home there—if a few business deals I'm working on pan out."

"Hey, you're going too fast for me!" Tommy interrupted. "When did you become a lawyer and a politician?"

"Oh, I got into law and politics down in California a couple of years ago, when I had a lot of spare time on my hands and got acquainted with a few well-heeled businessmen. What worked in California will work just as well in Oregon, I'm sure, once I learn my way around. It's just a matter of being in the right place at the right time, with money and nerve enough to take advantage of whatever opportunities come up."

"You made money in California, I take it?"

"So did a lot of other men, Tommy," Emil said with a nod. "But most of them stayed in the game a few hands too long. I was smart enough to cash in my chips and get out while I was still ahead."

"Do you plan to invest in some sort of business here?"

"Eventually, yes, after I've looked over the field. Now—tell me about yourself. Dad says you're captain of your own boat?"

"That's right. The *Mary*, running between the Upper Cascades and The Dalles once a week."

"For a while after the gold rush started down in California," Emil said, "we had some wild and woolly steamboat days. Back in '49 and '50, any ship that would float—and a lot that wouldn't—headed for San Francisco."

"So I've heard. We lost a few ships from Portland and Astoria that were supposed to operate in this area, but went down to California and never came back."

"Whatever ships deserted the Columbia for the goldfields didn't amount to a hill of beans compared to the losses suffered by East Coast ports—particularly New York. Ever hear of the *Wilson G. Hunt* and the *New World?*"

"Only that they were built in the East and made the run around the Horn when the gold rush began. I understand they're both operating on the Sacramento River now."

"That's right. But the way they got there is quite a story ..."

Built in 1849 for the Coney Island trade, the *Wilson G. Hunt* was a side-wheeler whose sedate mission was carrying excursionists from lower Manhattan to the fashionable seaside resorts along the nearby coast, a journey that never took her out of sight of land except on very foggy days. In appearance, she was something of an oddity, for between her two covered side-wheels, rising high above the cabin deck, was a tall, steeple-like frame in which the piston rods that drove the wheels rose and fell in guides, moving a pair of pitmans that turned each wheel. Such steamer designs had been common on the Hudson River for years, but were becoming rare when the *Hunt* was built. Normally left exposed, the engines and connecting rods were covered, making it appear that the boat was carrying a tall wooden wedge amidships, thereby spoiling the lines of what otherwise would have been a graceful-looking steamer.

"The *Hunt* made the run to Coney Island and back every day for six months or so," Emil said. "Then her owners got gold fever and announced a new excursion—New York to San Francisco by way of Cape Horn. Before the year was out, she was carrying passengers on the Sacramento River." He chuckled. "Of course, that was tame stuff, compared to the trip of the *New World* a couple of months later ..."

Also a side-wheeler, driven by a walking-beam engine uncommon at
that time, the *New World* was a big, sturdy, fast ship, 220 feet long,

capable of outrunning any craft sent to overtake her—as several would attempt to do—built to carry up to three hundred passengers, with the bunker capacity to make long sea runs between coaling stops—which also would prove to be a valuable asset. Setting an unusual precedent by being ready to go to sea immediately following her launching, she was kept tied to the dock after being skidded down the ways not by mechanical problems but by legal red tape. Because her owner was in deep financial trouble with the bank which had loaned him the money to build the ship, liens were placed against the vessel before her launching; two sheriff's officers came aboard her to enforce them; and the brand-new, ready-to-sail ship found herself securely tied to the dock not by thick rope lines but by paper writs.

Captain Edward Wakeman, skipper of the ship, was a big, muscular, red-faced man, Emil said, known far and wide in maritime circles for his explosive temper. If the two sheriff's men had been better acquainted with him, they would have become very suspicious of the calm way he accepted the restraining order they served on his ship, ordering it to remain in port, and the genial manner in which he extended them the hospitality of his cabin.

"You're only doing your duty, gentlemen," he said politely. "I realize that. Might as well come in out of the weather and join me in a few drinks and a good supper while the lawyers argue."

Pleased to see that he was being a good fellow and acting as a reasonable man should act under circumstances he could not change, the two deputies gladly accepted the captain's offer.

As the steward served yet another round of drinks halfway through supper, Captain Wakeman responded to a knock on the cabin door by getting up, opening the door, and chatting for a moment with an officer from below decks. Turning to his guests, the captain said, "My chief engineer wonders if you'd mind if he turns the engines over slowly for a bit. They're new and ought to be run now and then, he says, to keep them properly lubricated."

Consulting over their drinks, the two deputies agreed that the request was a perfectly reasonable one. Nodding, one of the deputies said, "Got to treat new engines right, no question about that," while the other lifted his glass, chuckling, "Sure, a lil' lubrication'll be good for 'em, just like it is for you and me."

Shortly after the Chief Engineer withdrew, a gentle vibration could be felt underfoot, which pleased both Captain Wakeman and the two deputies, for it indicated that the new engines were being properly broken in. With a delicious supper under their belts, a delectable dessert put away, and a fine brandy being served with coffee and cigars, the two deputies were feeling too mellow to notice that the intermittent slap of the tide against the hull of the ship had changed to a slow, steady roll. But when they got to their feet, staggered to the cabin door and opened it a few minutes later, they did notice that the New York skyline now lay a mile or so astern, where before it had been just adjacent to the dock. As for the dock itself, it had receded, too, with a lot of open water lying between the ship and the shore.

"Hey!" one of the deputies exclaimed. "We ain't tied to the dock no more!"

"We sure ain't!" the other deputy cried in dismay. "We're headed out to sea!"

Joining them in the doorway, Captain Wakeman looked outside, nodded soberly, and said, "Gentlemen, I do believe you're right."

When the two officers angrily declared that he was violating the writs and breaking the law, Captain Wakeman lost his temper. At sea, he told them, *he* was the law. If they did not like what he was doing, he would be only too glad to drop them into a dinghy and let them row themselves to shore. When they asked him where he thought he was going, he said to the sunny shores of California. When they reminded him that he had no clearance papers for his ship and would subject to seizure by any foreign government vessel or privateer that overtook the *New World* in international waters, he said he was quite aware of that, but since his ship had a full bunker of coal and was capable of outrunning any steamer afloat, he was perfectly willing to take his chances.

"Meantime, gentlemen, I suggest you answer my question. Do you want to row the dinghy—or would you rather walk?"

The adventures of the colorful Captain Edward Wakeman and his ship during the next few months, Emil said, would fill a book. As a matter of fact, the captain later told a curious newspaper reporter named Samuel Clemens that he fully intended to write such a book, if he ever he found the time. On the voyage south, he had a narrow squeak getting in and out of a coaling station at Pernambuco,

Venezuela. At Rio de Janeiro, a British frigate forced him to take his ship into port for a few days before he managed to slip out to sea under the cover of darkness and a thick fog and resume his dash to Cape Horn.

Coming north on the Pacific side of Panama, he was greeted with a different sort of reception at Balboa, when 250 frantic men with money in their hands demanded that he take them aboard and transport them to San Francisco immediately, or else they would toss him overboard, assume command of the ship, and steam north without him. Not wishing to displease them, he obliged ...

Finding Emil interested in the rapidly developing country upriver, Tommy suggested that he come along on the next trip the *Mary* made between the Upper Cascades and The Dalles. The moment his father mentioned taking a river trip, Lars Thomas ran across the room to him, hugged his knees, and begged, "Can I go, too?"

"Why, sure, son," Tommy said with a smile. "I can always use another hand."

"Can you do without us for a few days?" Emil asked Dolores and Freda.

"We certainly can," the two women agreed.

Pleased at the prospect of having the men out of the house for a few days while she got better acquainted with her new sister-in-law, Freda packed them a substantial lunch for their trip. Early the next morning, they went down to the landing just below the cabin, where the fourteen-foot skiff in which they would travel was moored. Here, the Columbia was a mile wide, placid and smooth except when a stiff wind through the Gorge whipped up whitecaps on its surface, and so deep that ocean-going ships could steam 145 miles up the river to the Lower Cascades, where the ebb and flow of the tides were still evident.

Single masted, carrying a sloop-type sail, with a modified bowsprit on which a jibsail could be raised when the wind was right, the skiff was equipped with a center-board keel, two sets of oarlocks, and two pairs of oars, in case the wind failed. Under ordinary circumstances, the ten-mile run up and across the river to the Lower Cascades could be made in two or three hours. Eyeing the skiff suspiciously before stepping into it, Emil said, "I don't see any engine. What makes it go?"

"Just get in, landlubber," Tommy laughed. "Lars and I will do the sailing."

"I don't have to row?"

"All you need to do is sit still and not rock the boat. We'll do the rest."

"Hey, Uncle Emil is funny!" Lars giggled. "He doesn't know *anything* about boats!"

"Young man," Emil exclaimed with a mock-serious scowl, "when I was born, your grandmother said it was high time at least *one* male member of the Warren family shed his gills and came ashore to stay. She was sick of living with sailors, she said. So I decided to make my fortune on dry land."

Sailing upriver before a brisk westerly breeze to the small settlement at the Lower Cascades, they went ashore and ate lunch before getting aboard the portage cars. Noticing the boxes and bundles of freight stacked alongside the tramway for a quarter mile or so, Emil asked Tommy where it was bound.

"Some of it's merchandise for Bradford's Store at the Upper Cascades," Tommy said. "The rest is military supplies headed for The Dalles or Fort Walla Walla."

"I've been reading a lot lately about the Indian troubles upriver. How serious are they?"

"To the white settlers and prospectors, they're damn serious. To the military commander of the district, General John Wool, they're just squabbles trumped up by the local merchants and stock raisers who hope to sell to the military."

"Looks like a lot of goods are piling up here. How long before they move on?"

"Two days to two weeks, according to what kind of shape the tramway on this side of the river is in, and whether or not the portage road on the Oregon side is flooded out. Right now, it is."

"Sounds like a real bottleneck to me. Somebody ought to fix it."

Ever since Oregon Trail days, one person after another had tried to do just that, Tommy explained, as he, Emil, and Lars got aboard one of the flatcars and found seats on boxes and bales of goods headed upriver. For the time being, the flatcars were being pulled by teams of nimble-footed mules, which must pick their way between narrow-gauge wooden rails. The rails now were in the process of being topped with strap iron, Tommy said, so that they could support the weight of a small locomotive built in Pittsburgh and hopefully now aboard a ship heading north from San Francisco.

"A man named Chenoweth built the first tramway on the north side of the river back in '51," Tommy said, "starting out with a single flatcar and one very stubborn mule. He charged seventy-five cents a hundred pounds for freight, with all the business he could handle for a while. Some of the wagon train emigrants thought his rates were too high, so they carved out their own road on the Oregon side of the river. Over the years, the ruts have gotten deeper and deeper, so nobody much uses it anymore.

"After a year or two, Chenoweth sold out to the Bradfords. Then a man named Bergen built another tramway on the Oregon side of the river, setting off a rate war and splitting up the business so that nobody made money. Of course, when one of the tramways is out of service or flooded, the other doubles its rates, which makes the shippers very mad. Now the Bradfords have ordered a steam locomotive and plan to dignify their tramway by calling it the 'Cascade Railroad.' The people on the other side of the river have ordered a locomotive, too, and are going to call their route the 'Oregon Portage Railway.'"

"Sounds like they're cutting each other's throats."

"That's exactly what they're doing, Emil. Each side of the river has its own boats—the *Fashion* and the *Wasco* on the Oregon side; the *Belle* and the *Mary* on the Washington side. It's a shameful waste of resources."

Looking thoughtful, Emil asked, "Do you know John Ainsworth and Jacob Kamm?"

"I certainly do. Kamm designed and installed the engines for the *Lot Whitcomb*, the finest boat ever built in this part of the country. John Ainsworth was its captain. I served under him for a year as First Mate. They're both good rivermen."

"So I gather. They've been talking to me about a plan I suggested aimed at bringing some sense of order to the transportation business in this part of the country, as we did down in California. After I've seen a little more of your operation, I'll tell you what we've got in mind ..."

Outwardly during the upriver trip of the *Mary* to The Dalles, Emil appeared to be nothing more than a casual tourist along for the ride, taking advantage of his older brother's position as captain of the boat to see something of the country. But wherever they went, Tommy noticed, no detail of what was happening escaped Emil's sharp, observant eyes.

With a faculty for making friends and getting people to talk about themselves by showing a genuine interest in what they were doing, Emil struck up conversations with everyone he met—stevedores, carpenters, store clerks, soldiers, teamsters, rivermen—managing to make them feel that it was a privilege to give this genial stranger all the information they could about their trade. Though the pocket notebook in which he recorded what he was told was never in evidence during his conversations with these people, as soon as he got a little time alone he took out a pencil and the notebook and wrote down whatever he had learned.

At Bradfords' Store, at Fort Dalles, and even at the barge landing above Celilo Falls, to which he rode in company with a supply sergeant on an Army horse that he had persuaded the post's commandant to loan him, he gathered a working knowledge of the transportation problems of the river that surprised Tommy by its completeness. But it was not until they had returned to the Rooster Rock cabin three nights later that Emil gave his older brother an outline of the proposal he had made to Jacob Kamm and John Ainsworth.

"Competition is wasteful, Tommy. What we need in this part of the country is a transportation monopoly."

"With a single company owning the boats, you mean?"

"The boats, the docks, the portages, the tramways—everything that has to do with shipping passengers and freight up and down the Columbia River. Eventually, it can be expanded to include California, Hawaii, Puget Sound, and Alaska. Everything that floats in the Pacific Northwest will be controlled by a single company."

"You'll never sell that idea to businessmen out here."

"We won't try to sell it. But it will come to pass."

"How will you accomplish it?"

"With the carrot and stick approach. With money and economic power."

"Who do you mean by 'we'?"

"To begin with, Jacob Kamm, John Ainsworth, myself, and half a dozen other Portland businessmen I'd rather not name for the time being. We're thinking of putting together a combine to be called the 'Oregon Steam Navigation Company.' Sure, it will be a monopoly. But a benevolent one, we hope, that will benefit everyone involved. To begin with, we'll acquire a few boats—"

"It'll never work," Tommy said, shaking his head. "Not in a million years will the bullheaded, stubborn, independent-minded business-men in this part of the country become part of a transportation mo-nopoly—benevolent or otherwise."

"Don't bet on it," Emil said quietly. "Shortly after I go back to Portland and confer with my people, I suspect we'll be making offers for the *Fashion*, the *Belle*, the *Wasco*, and the *Mary*. The next step will be to buy the portages on both sides of the river. If we can't acquire them both for a reasonable price, we'll keep raising the bid on first one, then the other, until an owner finally agrees to sell out to us. Once we've secured the portage facility on one side of the river, we'll cut rates so low we'll force the portage on the other side to sell or go bankrupt. Then we'll raise the rates back up to where we want them to be."

"Do you have enough capital to do that?"

"We will have, Tommy." Emil's smile was cold. "Would you like to buy some stock in the Oregon Steam Navigation Company? It could make you a rich man."

12.

$\mathscr{D}$ESPITE THE EDICT issued by General Wool ordering all white settlers to leave the area east of the Cascades, prospectors continued to cross the mountains and move up the Columbia. Even though large portions of these lands had been granted to the inland tribes, the 1855 Treaties still had not been ratified two years later, so technically the whites were not trespassers. Gold was found in the Colville area of northeastern Washington Territory in 1857. Fort Dalles and Fort Walla Walla continued to require an ever-increasing quantity of food and supplies, so preventing gold-seekers and merchants from moving into the region proved impossible.

All through 1857 and well into '58, the *Mary*, the *Wasco*, and the portage tramways on both sides of the river were kept busy hauling passengers and freight. But as Tommy had expected, the giant transportation company Emil and his backers were trying to organize did not fall together as quickly as they had hoped. The first problem encountered by the organizers, Emil said, was the fact that from its mouth below Astoria to its big bend northward at Wallula Gap—a distance of 340 miles—the Columbia River flowed between Oregon and Washington, thus was subject to the laws of both Territories. Even though the two political and geographical entities were both part of the United States and had been in existence only a few years, the legislators of each had wasted no time in drawing up some marvelously complex, often contradictory laws.

"To begin with, we're organizing what we call the 'Union Transportation Line,' with Captain Ainsworth in charge. At the moment, the laws are simpler in Washington, so we plan to incorporate there."

"You've bought a few boats, I hear."

"So far, we've acquired the *Mary*, the *Belle*, and the *Fashion*. We haven't had any luck yet buying out the portage owners on either side of the river, so we're at their mercy so far as rates are concerned. We may end up following the principle: 'If you can't lick 'em, join 'em,' offering them a piece of the company. Or we may wait until we see what happens when Oregon becomes a state—which appears to be in the wind."

"Jacob Kamm is building a new boat, I understand."

"You bet he is—the *Carrie Ladd*. From what he tells me, it'll be the fastest boat on the river and will set the style for years to come."

Launched in the summer of '58, the *Carrie Ladd* went into service between Portland and the Lower Cascades. Invited to come aboard as First Mate under Captain Ainsworth on her maiden voyage, Tommy found her a dream of a boat, living up to every prediction Emil had made for her. A stern-wheeler, she was a modest-sized boat, measuring only 126 feet from stem to stern, but she was well powered, her engine cylinders being sixteen inches in diameter with a sixty-six-inch stroke. Going back to his Mississippi River days, Jacob Kamm had designed her to look like a real racing steamboat, with sleek, clean lines.

Painted sparkling white, she carried a single tall stack and a pilot house amidships; her main passenger cabin opened into a parlor that could be used as a dining room. Forward toward the bow she boasted a "Ladies' Saloon," into which members of the fair sex could retire away from the whiskey, tobacco, and contamination of loud-talking, unwashed, burly males.

"She can travel," Captain Ainsworth announced approvingly at the end of her first trip. "From her dock in Portland, we made six miles down the Willamette, then up the Columbia and across to Vancouver in just an hour and a half. She cruised to the Lower Cascades against a stiff current in five hours and a half. Coming downriver, she took just four and a half hours from the Lower Cascades to the Portland dock."

"That's making mighty good time," Tommy said. "Particularly when she wasn't running full out."

"Got to take it easy when we're breaking in new engines." Captain Ainsworth gave him a quizzical smile. "Would you like to try to do better as her captain on her next run?"

"You bet I would!"

"She's yours, then. We'll schedule her for three round-trips a week between Portland, Vancouver, and the Lower Cascades. From now on, we'll give you the rating and pay of a Senior Captain in the Union Transportation Company fleet."

"I appreciate that, sir. What about Sitkum?"

"For the time being, we'll leave him aboard the *Mary* on the Middle River. But we'll give him a Chief Engineer's rating and a raise, too."

"He'll be glad to hear that."

"You're convinced that stern-wheelers are what's needed on the Middle and Upper River, I know—and I agree with you. I want you to get the feel of the *Carrie Ladd* for a few trips so that you can tell us what sort of boats we'll need upriver when we start operations there. Once the Indian unrest is settled, we expect the inland country will develop fast."

In May, that year, an event that would trigger that rapid development occurred when Lieutenant Colonel Edward J. Steptoe, commandant of the garrison at Fort Walla Walla, decided the time had come "to show the flag" and demonstrate to the hostile Indians of the inland country that the army was on the job. This was the same go-by-the-book officer, Tommy recalled, who had ordered the bugle call during the Yakima Indian War that had given the red warriors an early warning that the trap set so carefully for them by Lieutenant Phil Sheridan and Colonel George Wright was about to snap shut.

Because of General Wool's closure edict, a peace of sorts lay over the inland country all through 1857, even though prospectors and settlers continued to trickle in. The intruders were fiercely resented by the Indians. Hearing that two miners in the Colville area had been killed, Colonel Steptoe decided that the time had come to show the Indians that the army was present not to make war but to keep the peace. With 159 men and a large pack train, the colonel set out May 8, 1858, intending to make a leisurely march north through the country of the Palouses, Spokanes, and Coeur d'Alenes.

Later, Tommy and many other civilians would hear and believe a statement made by local reporter, who wrote:

> When the expedition started, 100 mules were required to pack the camping outfit. As the last one was loaded, it was found that no room remained for the ammunition.

This was an exaggeration, Tommy learned later, though it became part of the folklore attached to what history would call the "Steptoe

Disaster." In actuality, the three companies of dragoons and the partial company of infantry carried forty rounds per man, along with two mountain howitzers. But their arms were very poor. One of the surviving junior officers, Lieutenant John Mullan, who returned to take part in a more successful campaign a few months later, told Tommy aboard the *Mary*: "Two of the dragoon companies were armed with musketoons—short muskets with a very limited range, useless beyond fifty yards. The other dragoon company had Mississippi Yager rifles, which carry well but can't be loaded on horseback. There were ten good carbines in the infantry company. Some of the men had revolvers, while others had only old-fashioned muzzle-loading pistols. The cavalry did not have sabers."

From the best information Tommy could gather from Sitkum's Indian sources, a large force of Yakimas under Chief Kamiakin had joined the other inland tribes in their resistance to what they regarded as an unjustified invasion of their territory. Probably it was Kamiakin who devised the overall strategy, Sitkum said, though, once a fight started, the usual Indian way was every man for himself. Certainly, the defeat of Major Haller's force when it had tried to invade the Yakima country in October 1855, the successful attack of the hostiles on the Cascades in March 1856, and the official withdrawal of white settlements east of the Cascades a few months later, had given Kamiakin and his followers confidence in their power.

Since the time of Lewis and Clark, the Nez Perce Indians, whose large reservation lay to the east, had befriended and supported the whites. They did so again now. Reaching the Snake River at the mouth of Alpowa Creek, the command was joined by Chief Timothy and three Nez Perce warriors, who had agreed to go along as guides and scouts.

By May 16 the troops were ninety miles north of the Snake, deep in the heart of the Coeur d'Alene country, surrounded by increasing numbers of Indians who were strenuously objecting to what they regarded as a trespass on their lands. If the soldiers went any farther, the Indians said, they would attack. Since they greatly outnumbered his force, Colonel Steptoe told them that he would turn back the next morning.

Monday, May 17, the command broke camp and started the return march south. At first the retreat was orderly. Then, made confident by the withdrawal of the troops without so much as a token resistance, the Indians started sniping at them from the shelter of scattered pine trees and ridgetops along either side of the line of march. Soon a running battle was under way.

Later, Colonel Steptoe would be accused of cowardice, for he rode at the head of the retreating column with "H" troop and the supply train, letting the dragoon detachment protecting the rear of the column, where the Indians were concentrating their attack, fend for itself.

As the morning passed and the Indians began to attack the column from all directions, the pace of the retreat quickened, Lieutenant Mullan said.

"Captain Taylor and Lieutenant Gaston, who were in charge of the rear-guard detachment, were in a desperate situation. Their men were exhausted, their ammunition was running low, and they could not reload their weapons while moving. Finally, Lieutenant Gaston sent a courier named Tickey Highland to the head of the column, asking Colonel Steptoe to halt the command and give his men an opportunity to reload their guns. His request was refused."

Out of ammunition, badly outnumbered, and deserted by the rest of the command, Captain Taylor, Lieutenant Gaston, and members of the rear guard were reduced to fighting the Indians hand to hand, using clubbed pistols and empty muskets against the knives, lances, bows and arrows, and guns of the Indians. It was in this battle that Private Victor C. DeMoy, a former French officer who had served in both the Crimean and Algerian wars, began a legend when he cried as he swung his clubbed musket at the Indians: *"My God, my God, for a saber!"*

Wounded so badly that he could not ride or bear to be carried by a comrade on a horse, DeMoy asked that he be placed in a sitting position on the ground with a loaded revolver in his hand. After killing or wounding several Indians, he used the last bullet on himself.

For many of the new recruits, Lieutenant Mullan said, this was their first test under fire. So demoralized did they become that on one occasion, when Lieutenant Gaston called for volunteers to follow him in a countercharge, only ten men answered the call.

"When he led off in the charge with these, he chanced to look over his shoulder and found that not one of them was following him. He turned back, saying nothing to condemn them."

Hearing that the two officers and most of the enlisted men in the rear-guard detachment had been killed, Colonel Steptoe finally halted the command on the slope of a hill, where the weary soldiers dug in

and made a stand. At a council of war, it was decided to bury the howitzers and leave the balance of the stores, in hopes that the prospect of
loot would distract the Indians and give the soldiers an opportunity to
slip through their lines.

Sure that they had the troops surrounded, the Indians broke off
the siege as darkness fell, going into camp and spending the night
dancing and celebrating. Checking on the supply of ammunition,
Colonel Steptoe learned that the soldiers averaged only four rounds
per man. There was nothing to do but run for it.

Leaving behind the dead and badly wounded, muffling spurs, bridle
chains, and anything that would clink, covering light-colored horses
with dark blankets, and moving through the darkness with the silence
of ghosts, the soldiers filtered one by one through the loosely manned
lines of the hostiles until they were out of earshot, then mounted and
rode for safety as fast as their horses would run.

When muster was taken and the losses counted, the scope of what
came to be known as the Steptoe Disaster could be fully realized. Seventeen officers and men had been killed, fifty had been wounded, and
large quantities of arms, supplies, equipment, and pack animals had
been deserted or lost. Coupled with the losses and failures of earlier
engagements, this new defeat made the fighting ability of regular
army troops look very bad indeed.

This was a state of affairs not to be tolerated by the War Department or the American public. Corrective measures must be taken at
once …

General John E. Wool had been removed as army commander of the
Department of the Pacific in May 1857, with General Newman S.
Clarke named as his successor. Since a state of peace existed east of the
Cascades, Clarke had seen no reason to change the policy of exclusion
of American settlers from the interior country.

The Steptoe Disaster drastically altered his attitude.

Moving his headquarters from San Francisco to Fort Vancouver,
Clarke ordered the Hudson's Bay Company agents at Fort Colville to
stop selling arms and ammunition to the Indians and to turn over all
horses and mules taken by the hostiles from the Steptoe command
and later sold to the company. If the Indians wanted peace, he said,

they must return all property stolen or captured. Furthermore, they must identify and surrender for punishment any of their people who had committed acts of violence against the whites.

Failing to comply completely with these terms would result in only one thing—a war of extermination.

All through the months of June and July, the increased traffic of men, arms, and material being shipped upriver to Fort Walla Walla made it clear to Tommy Warren and the officials of the Union Transportation Company that this time the United States Army meant business. Put in charge of what was obviously meant to be a punitive expedition against the Indians was Colonel George Wright, a fifty-seven-year-old career officer who had distinguished himself earlier in campaigns against the Seminole Indians in Florida and in battles during the Mexican War. Stocky of build, prematurely white haired, with the stern-faced-manner of a cold-blooded martinet, Colonel Wright arrived at Fort Walla Walla July 19. Immediately, he undertook the task of turning the officers and enlisted men in his command into a crack fighting force.

On this expedition, Colonel Wright would be in charge of a seven-hundred-man force, while Lieutenant Colonel Steptoe and one hundred dragoons would be left behind to garrison Fort Walla Walla. With his critical daily inspections, reviews, and twice-a-day drills, Colonel Wright quickly corrected the lax discipline permitted by his predecessor.

Leaving Fort Walla Walla August 7, the formidable force consisted of one company of dragoons, six companies of artillery, thirty Nez Perce warriors enlisted as scouts, two twelve-pound howitzers, and two six-pound guns. Instead of short-ranged musketoons, the soldiers were armed with "rifle-muskets" shooting a minie ball that could kill at six-hundred yards. This time, the dragoons wore sabers.

Accompanying the expedition were two young army officers, Lieutenants John Mullan and Lawrence Kip, with whom Tommy had become acquainted earlier during their trips upriver aboard the *Mary* before and after the Stevens Treaty negotiations and the ill-fated Steptoe campaign. It was from them that he later learned the details of the brief, brutal war waged by Colonel Wright against a thousand or more hostile Indians reluctantly led by the brilliant, brooding, Yakima leader, Chief Kamiakin.

"Spotted Fawn says Kamiakin did not want to be a war chief,"

Sitkum told Tommy. "From the beginning, he knew his people could
not win. Better than any other Indian, he understood that whites and
Indians fight a different kind of war."

"In what way?"

"An Indian fights only to protect his home, his people, and his
family. Now and then a few rash young men will band together to go
on raid against another tribe, stealing a few horses or taking a few
scalps. But they seldom fight long or do much damage. Never does an
Indian war party attack a village containing women and children."

"That's true."

"But when a few white people are killed by Indian warriors, the
anger of the entire American nation is turned against the whole Indian
tribe. Even though only a few evil white men have started the trouble
by trespassing on Indian lands, stealing Indian horses, or raping Indian women, the death of a single white man must be revenged by the
whole country, no matter how many thousands of soldiers are needed
to do the job."

"That also is true, I'm afraid."

"Kamiakin knows this. But when his people asked him to lead
them into a hopeless war, his sense of honor would not let him turn
them down."

According to what the two officers told Tommy later, Lieutenant
Mullan had been in charge of the thirty Nez Perce auxiliaries, while
Lieutenant Kip acted as adjutant of the artillery battalion. After marching in stifling late-August heat across plains and hills whose scattered
bunchgrass cover had been set afire by the Indians and seared into
black, choking dust, Lieutenant Mullan and the advance party of Nez
Perce scouts he was supposed to command made contact and exchanged fire with a straggling group of hostiles.

"Once the bullets started to fly, there was nothing I could do to
control the scouts," Lieutenant Mullan told Kip that evening. "Each
warrior fights on his own."

Since men and animals were exhausted after several days of hard
marching, Colonel Wright decided to make camp some twenty miles
south of the Spokane River in order to give them a badly needed rest.
Reading this as a sign of indecision on the part of the soldiers, the
hostiles grew more aggressive, swarming over the nearby hills, shouting taunts, inviting an attack. After placing the four-hundred mules
and the stores under a strong guard, Colonel Wright prepared for

*Roll On
Columbia*

battle. Lieutenant Kip later filed an official report:

> After advancing about a mile and a half, we reached the hill and prepared to dislodge the enemy from it. Major Grier, with the dragoons, marched to the left, while the party of Nez Perces under Lieutenant Mullan wound round the hill and ascended it at the right. The main column came next, with Colonel Wright and staff at its head, followed by Captain Keyes, commanding the artillery, the rifles, and the howitzer battery.
>
> As soon as the dragoons reached the top of the hill, they dismounted—one half holding the horses and the other acting as skirmishers. After exchanging a volley with the Indians, they drove them off the hill and held it until the foot soldiers arrived. On our way up, Colonel Wright received a message from Major Grier, stating that the Indians were collected in large numbers [about five hundred, he thought] at the foot of the hill, apparently prepared to fight. Colonel Wright immediately advanced the battalion rapidly forward, ordering Captain Ord's company to the left to be deployed as skirmishers.
>
> My place, as adjutant of the artillery battalion, was, of course, with Captain Keye. We rode to the top of the hill, where the whole scene lay out before us like a splendid panorama. Below us lay "four lakes"— a large one at the foot of the barren hill on which we were, and just beyond it three smaller ones, surrounded by rugged rocks, and almost entirely fringed with pines. On the plain below we saw the enemy. Every spot seemed alive with the wild warriors we had come so far to meet.... Mounted on their fleet, hardy horses, the crowd swayed back and forth, shouting their war cries, and keeping up a song of defiance. Most of them were armed with Hudson Bay muskets, while others had bows and arrows and long lances.

Thus the Battle of Four Lakes, as it would be called, began.

> Orders were at once issued for the artillery and infantry to be deployed as skirmishers and advance down the hill, driving the Indians before them from their coverts, until they reached the plain where the dragoons could act against them. At the same time, Lieutenant White, with the howitzer battery, supported by Company 'A,' under Lieutenant Tyler, and the rifles, was sent to the right to drive them out of the woods. The latter met with a vigorous resistance, but a few discharges of the howitzer, with their spirited attack, soon dislodged the enemy, and compelled them to take refuge on the hills.
>
> In the meanwhile the companies moved down the hill with all the precision of a parade.... As soon as they were within six hundred yards, they opened their fire and delivered it steadily as they advanced. Our soldiers aimed regularly, though it was no easy task to hit their shifting marks....

But minie balls and long range rifles were things with which now for the first time the Indians were to be made acquainted. As the line advanced, we first saw one Indian reel in his saddle and fall—then, two or three—then, half a dozen.... The instant, however, that the "braves" fell, they were seized by their companions and dragged to the rear, to be borne off. We saw one Indian leading off a horse with two of his dead companions tied on it.

But in a few minutes, as the line drew nearer, the fire became too heavy, and the whole army broke and fled toward the plain. This was the chance for which the dragoons had been impatiently waiting. As the line advanced they had followed behind it, leading their horses. Now the order was given to mount, and they rode through the company intervals to the front.... Taylor's and Gaston's companies were there, burning for revenge, and soon they were on them. We saw the flash of their sabers as they cut them down. Lieutenant Davidson shot one warrior from his saddle as they charged up, and Lieutenant Gregg clove the skull of another.... It was a race for life, as the flying warriors streamed out of the glens and ravines and over the open plain, and took refuge in the clumps of woods on the rising ground.

If the horses of the dragoons had been fresh, the troopers would have made a terrible slaughter of the hostiles, Kip felt, but after twenty-eight days on the march, the mounts were exhausted. Entirely blown, the horses halted, their riders dismounted, and the foot solders passed through their ranks, pursuing the Indians across the broken, rolling country for two miles—then they, too, ran out of strength and had to stop and rest.

Thus the battle ended for that day with the Indians routed and the soldiers victorious. Because the hostiles had carried away most of their dead and wounded, their losses during the battle could only be estimated. Lieutenant Kip set them at seventeen seen to be killed, while forty or fifty appeared to have been wounded.

"Strange to say, not one of our men was injured. One dragoon horse alone was wounded. This was owing to the long range rifles now first used by our troops, and the discipline which enabled them so admirably to use them."

For three days the command rested, with the Nez Perce scouts sent out to reconnoiter. Resuming the march in cooler weather, the command covered some five miles before the Indians again resumed their attack. This time, they tried a different strategy. Lieutenant Kip wrote:

We had nearly reached the woods when they advanced in great
force, and set fire to the dry grass of the prairie.... Under cover of the
smoke, they formed round us in one-third of a circle, and poured in
their fire upon us, apparently each one on his own account. The pack
train immediately closed up....

It was curious to witness the scene—the dust and smoke, and the
noise and shouting of the Mexican muleteers driving forward to the
center four hundred overloaded animals, while the troops were formed
about them with as much order and far greater rapidity than if no danger threatened. Then on the hills to our right, if we could have had
time to have witnessed them, were feats of horsemanship which we
have never seen equaled. The Indians would dash down a hill five
hundred feet high and with a slope of forty-five degrees, at the most
headlong speed, and apparently with all the rapidity they would have
used on level ground.

Again, the long-range rifle muskets, the howitzers, and alternate
charges of horse and foot soldiers did deadly work. All day long the
running fight continued, with the column advancing until it reached
the banks of the Spokane River, where it camped for the night.

Incredibly, considering the number of hostiles involved and the
length of the engagement, only one soldier was slightly wounded. Estimating that some five hundred Indians had been in the battle, Kip
made no attempt to guess at their casualties, but from the number of
warriors seen to fall, it was clear that they had been heavy.

After camping near Spokane Falls the evening of September 7,
Colonel Wright began to see clear signs that the will of the Indians to
resist further had been broken. Though more than a thousand eager
warriors had urged Chief Kamiakin to lead them into the first battle,
their number had dwindled to five hundred before the second engagement took place. Now only a hundred or so Coeur d'Alenes, into
whose country the white soldiers had marched, were left to defend the
Indian cause. During the fight that day, an artillery shell had severed a
tree limb, which struck Chief Kamiakin on the head as it fell, knock-
ing him senseless to the ground. Though he regained consciousness
after a while, a *tewat* regarded the incident as a bad omen, so most of
the Yakima warriors decided to quit fighting and go home, taking
their still-dazed war chief with them.

Spokane Garry, a local Christianized Indian who long had been
known as a man of peace, expressed a wish to have a "talk" with the

colonel. When it was granted, he said he had always been opposed to fighting, but the young men and many of the chiefs were against him, and he could not control them. Now all he wanted was peace.

> "I have met you in two battles," Colonel Wright said coldly. "You have been badly whipped. You have had several chiefs and many warriors killed or wounded. I have not lost a man or animal. I did not come into the country to ask you to make peace. I came here to fight. Now, when you are tired of war and ask for peace, I will tell you what you must do.
>
> "You must come to me with your arms, with your women and children, and everything you have and lay them at my feet. You must put your faith in me and trust to my mercy. If you do this, I shall then tell you the terms upon which I will give you peace. If you do not do this, war will be made on you this year and the next year until your nations shall be exterminated."

While Chief Garry spread Colonel Wright's stark ultimatum among the Spokane and Yakima leaders, the command marched east into the heart of the Coeur d'Alene country. Overtaking a group of Indians who were trying to drive a large herd of horses into the shelter of timbered hills, the white soldiers attacked them with withering fire, forcing the Indians to flee and abandon the entire herd. Learning that it contained nine hundred animals, Colonel Wright issued an order that appalled Lieutenant Kip, who wrote:

> At nine o'clock this morning, Colonel Wright convened a board of officers to determine what should be done with the captured horses. They decided that one hundred and thirty should be selected for our use, and the rest shot. It was a disagreeable necessity, but one which could not be avoided. Nothing can more effectual cripple the Indians than to deprive them of their animals.

In the Southwest where the Spaniards had first introduced the horse to the natives, the priests had found that as soon as an Indian learned to control a horse, his first ride was toward freedom. In order to keep their converts at the missions, they had made *reducidos*—"reduced ones"—of the natives, setting them afoot and forbidding them to ride horses on pain of death. In this part of the country, the Indians had been mounted for so long that they knew no other way of life. Kip wrote:

> We learned subsequently that nothing we had done so much prostrated the Indians as this destruction of their horses.

With the Indians' will to resist broken, all that remained to be done now was to meet with the humbled chiefs and proclaim the surrender terms. They were harsh. All horses or property taken from the whites must be returned. All the rash young men accused of killing prospectors must be surrendered and tried by a military court. Those found guilty would be hanged on the spot. Though word was sent to Kamiakin that he would not be harmed if he surrendered, he refused to trust the white man's promises. Another Yakima chief, Ow-hi, did come in, and the rude treatment he received fully justified Kamiakin's suspicion.

Convinced of the truth of the stories that Ow-hi's son, Qualchen, had murdered at least nine white men, Colonel Wright told the older Indian that if his son did not surrender within four days, he, Ow-hi, would be hanged.

Though the message was sent, it did not reach the young brave. For some reason Qualchen rode into camp a few days later, not knowing that his father was a prisoner and that he had been condemned to death without a trial. In a report dated September 24, Colonel Wright stated laconically:

Qualchen came to me at 9:00, and at 9:15 A.M. He was hung.

A few days later, Ow-hi, still a prisoner, was shot and killed "while trying to escape."

Thus, the peace Governor Stevens thought he had secured by treaty in 1855 finally was brought to the region by force. It had been an expensive process. For the two years of war, the Territories of Washington and Oregon eventually handed the federal government a six-million-dollar bill—"for scalping Indians and violating squaws," as Horace Greeley acidly put it.

In September 1858, General William S. Harney was appointed to command a new military department embracing the area. Following his arrival at Fort Vancouver, his first act was to revoke General John Wool's order excluding Americans from lands east of the Cascades, throwing the interior open to settlement. On March 8, 1859, the U.S. Senate confirmed the treaties made with the Nez Perces, Umatillas, Walla Wallas, Cayuses, and Yakimas, and appropriated funds for their implementation.

When Tommy Warren heard this, he asked Sitkum if his wife

knew what Chief Kamiakin's reaction had been to the good news. Sitkum shook his head.

"Nobody knows where Kamiakin is. Like a wolf without a home, he wanders from place to place, with nowhere to lay his head."

"He's still head chief of the Yakima Nation, the government says, entitled to a house on the reservation and a federal annuity."

"He will not take it, Spotted Fawn says. He does not trust the promises of the white man."

"Do the Yakimas still acknowledge him as their head chief?"

"Most of them do, Spotted Fawn says. But he refuses to live in a pen and take orders from the white Agent who has been put in charge of the reservation. He has gone to Canada, some say, where he can live as a free man."

"Well, at least we have peace in this part of the country now. Business should pick up on the river."

13.

*A*T THE AGE OF NINE, Lars Thomas Warren was beginning to lose his baby fat and fill out his large-boned frame with muscle. Yellow haired, blue-eyed, and tall, he was going to look very much like Freda's father, she said, though the Swedish angular ruggedness of his facial lines was somewhat rounded and softened by the Hawaiian blood he had inherited from Lanee, his beautiful grandmother. If any room were left for traits inherited from his father and grandfather on the New England side of the family, they were not readily visible in his appearance. But from all his forebears he had inherited his love of water.

As both Freda's and Tommy's parents had done with them, Lars Thomas was being educated at home, taught reading and a respect for the written word with strict Swedish and New England discipline. At the same time, he was taught mechanical gunsmithing skills by his mother and nautical river skills by his father. Whether Tommy was making a run as Captain of a steamboat between the Lower Cascades and Portland or on the upriver sector between Bradford's Landing and The Dalles, Lars was aboard as a cabin boy, a deckhand, or a fireman assistant below decks to Sitkum or whoever else was acting as Chief Engineer.

On February 14, 1859, Oregon entered the Union as a state. Even the most rabid expansionist in the area admitted that statehood at this time was not a recognition of the region's population and resources but was part of yet another compromise aimed at balancing the growing split between the slave and free states.

When organized as a Territory a few years earlier, Oregon had attempted to avoid the slavery issue by simply declaring it illegal within its borders. In a cynical attempt to exacerbate the question, a flood of pro-slavery newcomers from Missouri had rammed through a provision that no person of Negro blood would be permitted to live in Oregon Territory more than thirty days, with violators to be flogged and forced to leave. As a consequence, several intelligent, well-to-do, freed Negroes who had emigrated to the Pacific Northwest in search of a more tolerant place to live had gone north of the Columbia River and settled in Washington Territory, where in a few cases they had been recognized as citizens and been given the right to file land claims and vote.

Quick to take advantage of Oregon's liberal monopoly laws, Emil Warren had advised the incorporators of the Union Transportation Company to dissolve the corporation and reorganize as the Oregon Steam Navigation Company. Becoming familiarly known as the "O.S.N." Company, the combine of aggressive capitalists continued to expand its operations.

But the spirit of free enterprise that had inspired many independent-minded Easterners to pull up stakes and head west was difficult to overcome. Though the Bradfords and the owners of the north-bank portage tramway joined the O.S.N., two successive proprietors of the south-bank portage railroad and several boat operators on the lower river refused to sell out, even though threatened with ruinous competition. Above Celilo Falls on the upper river, where only wind-pole-and-oar-propelled barges now carried freight, complete chaos reigned.

For example, one of the barge owners was an early-day pioneer named William H. Gray, a would-be missionary to the Indians who had come west with the Whitman-Spalding party in 1836. A cantankerous, opinionated, talented jack-of-all-trades, who was an excellent mechanic and carpenter, he was so disagreeable that nobody could get along with him. Despite this, Tommy and Freda treated him courteously whenever he stopped by the Rooster Rock cabin on his way up and down the river, for Lars and William Polk Gray, the man's fourteen year old son, were fast friends.

Always a man of strong opinions, Gray said of his son, who was born in 1845:

> I named him after President Polk. When I named him, the President had taken a strong stand on 54–40 or fight. Polk reversed his attitude on that question and I have been sorry I called my boy after him ever since. Sometimes I have a notion to wring the youngster's neck, I am so disgusted with President Polk.

If young William Polk Gray were at all afraid that his neck would be wrung by his father, his behavior did not show it. Certainly, he obeyed his father without question when given an order dealing with handling a line, a boat, a barge, or any other river equipment, just as Lars Thomas obeyed his father, for both boys loved the river and were eager to learn from their fathers. But when the elder Gray told Tommy and Freda on a visit one day that he had launched a barge above Celilo Falls and wanted Lars to work aboard it with him and his son, they hesitated.

"He's awfully young to be hiring out as a deckhand," Tommy said tentatively.

"Oh, Dad, please let me go!" Lars pleaded. "I've never been on that part of the river before."

"You'll learn something, boy," Gray said fiercely. "I'll guarantee you that."

"Lars is as tall as I am, and almost as strong," William Polk Gray chimed in. "He's even better as a swimmer. It'll be hard work, no doubt about that. But we'll have a lot of fun, too."

"What do you think, Freda?"

"If the Company builds a stern-wheeler above Celilo Falls, as you say they are going to do," Freda said thoughtfully, "they will need pilots who know that section of the river. If Lars really wants to go, I think we should let him. I am sure Mr. Gray will treat him as well as he does his own son."

During the next two years, Lars Thomas Warren spent much of his time working for the senior William Gray on the Columbia River above Celilo Falls. After gold was discovered in Idaho in 1860, his experience expanded to include the 140-mile sector of the Snake River from its juncture with the Columbia to the mouth of the Clearwater. East of the Cascades, both rivers traversed the bleak, barren country of eastern Oregon and southeastern Washington Territory. Though Lars never complained to his mother and father about the way Mr. Gray treated him, it was exactly the same way he treated his own son—with ironhanded discipline.

This was arid-looking desert land upriver from The Dalles, where little rain fell during the long, hot summer; the only vegetation that grew on the rolling hills was seared brown bunchgrass and twisted gray sagebrush. Because of the vast number of migrating salmon that must negotiate the chutes and rapids of Celilo Falls before they could move on up to the mountain streams where they were born and repeat the age-old spawning process, bands of Indians claiming fishing rights on both sides of the river came to Celilo to catch and cure their yearly supply of salmon. How a visiting family knew its traditional rights to a certain rock at a certain time for a certain number of days each year baffled young Lars. But he accepted Sitkum's assertion that they did.

"Don't they ever quarrel or fight over fishing spots?" he asked Sitkum.

"Almost never," Sitkum answered, shaking his head. "Now and then, the grandmothers hiss and spit at one another like bad-tempered snakes. But when that happens, a word from a chief soon settles the quarrel, for they know there are fish enough for all."

Unlike the middle and lower river sectors, which were deep enough to accommodate the largest of boats, swift-running tributaries such as the Deschutes, John Day, and Umatilla Rivers, which flowed into the Columbia from the south, created rapids, shoals, and riffles that could become a hazard to any kind of craft. Exactly how a vessel should ascend these rapids depended to a great measure upon whether the river was in flood or at a low-water period, the force and direction of the current and wind, and whatever recent changes had been brought about by the erosion of sand and gravel from upstream.

"Pa says you've got to learn how to read a rapid," William Polk Gray told Lars after the heavily laden barge had zigzagged its way across the foot of Deschutes Rapid. "He's been teaching me the signs."

"Like what?"

"Look at the shape of the land just above where it joins the river, he says. Likely that same contour will continue under water. A steep bluff above water means a steep drop below. Low, slanting ground above water means a gentle slope and shallow water below."

"That makes sense."

"Unless you know what kind of water you're getting into, Pa says, you should never try to run a rapid at high noon on a sunny day."

"Why not?"

"Because there are no shadows on the water then and you can't judge its depth by its color. At high noon, the water reflects the color of the sky. Early morning and late evening, with the sun behind you, is the best time to read a rapid."

Spreading the square sail when the wind was favorable and tongue-lashing the seven-man crew of husky laborers into rowing or poling when it was not, Gray moved the clumsy barge slowly upriver. Now and then he put Lars and "Pokey"—as he called his son when particularly exasperated with him—into a small boat and ordered them to take a line above the rapid which the barge was attempting to ascend, where they would secure it to a rock or a sturdy tree. When this had been done, the two boys would toss the line into the river and let it float down to the barge crew, which would attach it to a capstan in the bow of the craft, then crank the heavy barge laboriously through the rapid. If the boat in which the two boys were hauling the line capsized and dumped them into the river—as it frequently did—Mr. Gray simply told them to catch, bail, and right the boat, get back into it, and try again.

In this manner, the enterprising Mr. Gray and his heavily laden barge progressed to the big bend of the Columbia at Wallula Landing after three weeks of hard labor. There, the cargo he had contracted to deliver to Fort Walla Walla twenty-nine miles inland was unloaded and transferred to Army wagons.

And there every last member of his much-abused crew, except for the two boys, quit him.

"Good riddance!" he snorted contemptuously. "Not one of the rascals was worth the two dollars a day they made me pay them!"

Whether or not *he* was worth the fifty cents a day *he* was being paid, Lars Thomas did not ask. But secretly he felt he had earned every penny of it.

Following the discovery of gold in the Clearwater country, William Gray decided a great deal of money could be made transporting miners' supplies to the settlements 140 miles up the Snake River. Portland merchants were so skeptical of the Snake's navigability that they would give him no freight on consignment. Mortgaging everything he owned, he bought a stock of goods for the mines and shipped it up the Columbia to the landing above Celilo Falls, where his barge was waiting. Again, he set sail for the interior country, with his son, Willie, and Lars as members of the crew. On this trip, Lars *really* earned his pay.

Learning at Wallula Landing that their employer intended to take the heavily laden barge on upriver, the whole crew deserted, declaring the Snake too dangerous to be navigated. Managing to bribe and browbeat another seven-man crew to work for him, Mr. Gray and his unwieldy barge left Wallula on September 20, 1861. Because the prevailing wind and late-summer current were against them, it took three days of brutal labor to reach the mouth of the Snake, just eleven miles upriver, for the barge had to be cordelled most of the way.

When they entered the Snake, the real difficulties began. For starters, this was the low-water stage of the year, so in many places the river was less than three feet deep, with many rocks, riffles, and gravel bars exposed. Every mile or two, white water deep enough to float the barge poured over and through channels narrowed by sharp, unyielding basaltic rocks, in which the force of the water was so great that a line and the capstan had to be utilized time and again. This meant that the two boys were frequently called on to get into the rowboat, work their way upriver to a spot above the rapid, go ashore and find a solid anchor for the line. On one occasion while thus engaged, Lars got the scare of his life.

Carrying the heavy rope line ashore at the foot of a gravel bar, he found an uprooted cottonwood tree that had been deposited there during high water and stranded as the river level fell. As he stepped toward the base of the downed tree and started to loop the line over its exposed roots, he called over his shoulder to his companion, who was dragging the prow of the boat up on the beach.

"How's this for an anchor, Willie?"

"Looks fine to me. Tie her off."

Directly underfoot, Lars suddenly heard a sibilant, angry whir. In the same split second, his eyes caught the flash of a thick, glistening, reptilian body lashing out at his right leg between the ankle and the knee. He heard Willie Polk yell, "*Rattlesnake, Lars! Look out!*"

How high he jumped and how far he managed to twist his body in midair in order to land out of range of the striking rattlesnake, he did not know. But he was quite willing to accept Willie's later estimate of ten feet each way. Sprawled prone on his back, he was dimly aware of the fact that Willie had jumped out of the boat, run toward the base of the uprooted tree with a three-foot-long shovel in his hand, and was now doing an enthusiastic job of snake killing. Which was no easy task, for this was a monster rattlesnake, fully five feet long, three inches thick, and very, very mad.

"*Jesus Christ!*" Lars breathed hoarsely.

White-faced and trembling, Willie turned and stared at Lars, completely overlooking the fact that his young friend had risked the stern disapproval of his father by taking the Lord's name in vain.

"Did the son-of-a-bitch get you?"

"No, he missed me. But he sure scared the hell out of me. I'm not used to snakes."

"Got to watch for 'em in this part of the country, Pa says. I should have warned you."

"Now you tell me!"

Gingerly poking around the length of the stranded tree trunk, the two boys stirred up a dozen more rattlers of various sizes, which they either killed with the shovel or poked into the water with long sticks.

Though Willie seldom disagreed with his father, the task of taking a line upriver through the roaring white water of the lower Snake became so exhausting and risky that at a particularly bad place called Five Mile Rapids he openly rebelled.

"Pa, you're asking the impossible. The current here is just too dangerous to be swum if the boat upsets. Besides, there's no place to secure a line. It just can't be done."

"My son," Mr. Gray replied sharply, " 'can't' isn't in my dictionary. Anything can be done if you want to do it badly enough."

"But, Pa—"

"Get into the boat, boy, and take the line through the rapid. If you are overturned, you and the boat will both come downstream. You may not come down together, but you will both come down. You will then go back and make another attempt and continue to do so until you have succeeded."

Success did not come easily. On three consecutive tries, the boat upset, with it and the two boys bouncing like corks downstream through the swift, cold water. During their third swamping, Willie banged his head on a rock as he tumbled through the rapid, being saved from sure drowning by Lars' quick work in grasping his hair and keeping his face above water so that he could breathe until both boys made their way ashore.

"Thanks, Lars!" Willie gasped when he finally could speak again. "I knew you were a better swimmer than me."

"That evens us up, Willie. You're a better snake killer."

After forty days of wet, grueling, dangerous work, the barge finally reached the new settlement of Lewiston, where Mr. Gray sold the goods it carried at a substantial profit. At the age of eleven, Lars Thomas could join his sixteen-year-old friend, William Polk Gray, in his boast: "By the time we got there, my comrade and I had proved that there was not a single rapid in that stretch of the Snake River that could not be swum."

Though the lives of the two youngsters sometimes would take separate paths during their long careers on the Columbia and its tributaries, Lars also could say—as William Polk Gray later did: "After that experience there has never been any combination of wood, iron, or water that has ever scared me."

14.

$\mathcal{E}$VEN BEFORE the California Gold Rush in 1849, Tommy Warren had heard rumors of strikes in the Columbia River country. Back in 1840, a Catholic missionary priest, Pierre Jan DeSmet, was said to have found gold near his mission in the Coeur d'Alene region, but kept it secret because he feared word of the strike would be the ruination of the Indians.

In 1845, while passing through the Snake River country, a wagon train led by an inept guide attempted to cross the eastern Oregon desert by a new route up the Malheur, came to disaster, and, after many hardships, eventually reached the Willamette Valley.

Somewhere between Fort Hall and the John Day country—a stretch of 350 miles—children playing in a stream found some pretty yellow rocks, tossed them into a blue bucket, and then forgot them. Years later, the rocks were seen by a man who had prospected in California, were identified as gold, and the children were asked where and when they had found them. In a stream, they said, one afternoon along the way. Which stream? Which afternoon? Where along the way?

They did not remember.

Thus the legend of the Lost Blue Bucket Mine, for which men still were searching, was born.

But the wildest tale of all, which had been published in the *Oregon Spectator*, turned out to be true. According to the account:

> An Indian from the Nez Perce country found his way into California during the gold excitement in that State, and, chancing one day into a gulch where some miners were at work, made himself friendly and useful, and told them in his broken English where he was from and the name of his tribe.
>
> Among those miners was one named E. D. Pierce, who was a visionary and susceptible man, liable to be strongly impressed with a ro-

mantic tale that possessed points of plausibility. Among his strong characteristics was tenacity, and he was disposed to follow an idea, that might only be a delusion, with a persistence seldom equaled.

To this man one day the Nez Perce Indian told a strange, weird tale of how he, with two companions, had been camping at night in a defile among his native mountains, when suddenly a light like a brilliant star burst forth from among the cliffs. They thought it was the Great Spirit's eye, and watched with superstitious awe until the dawn, when, taking courage with the wakening day, they sought the spot from where the night twinkling had looked down upon them, and found a glittering ball that looked like glass embodied in the solid rock. The Indians believed it was a great medicine, but could not get it from its resting place, and were forced to leave it there.

This was just the kind of tale to make a strong impression upon Captain Pierce, who believed the Indian had found a diamond more valuable than the famed Kohinoor, and he determined to become its possessor. With that purpose he left California and became a resident of Walla Walla. He scouted through the mountains east of Snake River, and finally induced a party of men to accompany him, they hoping to find gold, he still searching for the mythical diamond.

With the Indian Treaties ratified and the interior country opened to settlement, the directors of the Oregon Steam Navigation Company felt that a steamboat launched above Celilo Falls would be a moneymaker. Even as William H. Gray and other barge owners began hauling supplies to the military post of Fort Walla Walla and the sprinkling of grog shops, stores, and "parlors of entertainment" springing up nearby, the timbers, ironwork, engine parts, and boiler sections for a stern-wheeler designed to operate on the upriver sector of the Columbia were being shipped to the launching ways just below the mouth of the Deschutes River. In honor of the military leader whose firm actions had recently opened up the interior country, the boat would be called the *Colonel Wright*.

Naming the nearby town that had come into existence near Fort Walla Walla was not so simple. When first established, the settlement had been called "Steptoeville" in recognition of the commander whose avowed duty was to bring peace to the interior country. Following his defeat, the name had been dropped for obvious reasons. Someone then suggested that the metropolis adopt as its name the Cayuse Indian word meaning "Place of the Rye Grass," which the ill-fated Whitman Mission had used for the eleven years of its existence. Since no one could agree on the pronunciation of the word, let alone whether it should be spelled *Waiilatpu, Wyeletpo,* or *Wyelatpu,* that name was dropped, too.

Why not call the town Walla Walla?

Why not indeed.

So it was on the very spot where the brush arbor had stood when the Nez Perce Treaty had been signed that the town of Walla Walla was built. Because of the lands ceded by the Nez Perces, the former council grounds now lay 120 miles west of the heart of the Nez Perce Reservation—upon which, it had been promised the Indians, no white man could trespass without permission.

But it was from this distant settlement that the first white trespassers came—drawn by the magnet of gold ...

Though Tommy Warren supposed that the man called Captain E. D. Pierce had been among the hundreds of passengers he had carried up-river on one of his boats during the past few years, he did not associate a face with the name. Like many newcomers to the country, the title "Captain" probably had been assumed by Pierce after taking part as a volunteer in some obscure Indian war. Even the Swiss immigrant, John Sutter, who had made the initial strike near his mill on the American River just above its juncture with the Sacramento down in California in 1848, had used the title "Captain," presumably after service in the Swiss army.

What soon became common knowledge was that in a Walla Walla saloon one day, Captain E. D. Pierce repeated the Indian's story to three friends, then led them on a prospecting trip into the mountains north of the Clearwater, he seeking the fist-sized diamond while they looked for gold. Halted as trespassers by Indian Agent Andrew J. Cain and a squad of Indian police, they were warned that if they were caught trespassing again, they would be arrested and thrown in jail.

Here, accounts of what happened next differed. One said that the Pierce party pretended to withdraw and leave reservation land, then circled around and came into the area again by a devious route, where Agent Cain and the Indian police would not see them. A more romantic version related that Captain Pierce bribed a pretty young Indian woman named Jane, whose father was a Christianized Nez Perce chief called Timothy by the whites, to act as the party's guide and lead it north, east, and then south into the remote mountain meadow which was their goal.

However they got there, the men immediately began digging and testing the sand and gravel in the nearby creek. Finding spots of "color" in the first few pans, they built a rough sluice of cedar bark and soon recovered eighty dollars in gold. Being short of supplies, Captain Pierce returned to Walla Walla, spread word of the discovery to a few trusted friends, re-outfitted, and, with a party of fifteen men, returned to the area and dug in for the winter.

It was now November and this was high country where the snows came early and stayed late. Agent Cain and the Indian police knew the white trespassers were there and set out from Agency headquarters at Lapwai to remove them. But the weather turned stormy, snow closed the trails, and the only thing the authorities could do was go back to Lapwai—and hope that the miners would starve or freeze to death.

Unfortunately for the Indians, the trespassers survived. Building a cluster of five solid log cabins, which they named Pierce City, they continued to pan for gold despite deepening snow. By January, they were so sure they had struck a bonanza that they sent two men to the settlements on snowshoes for more supplies. In March, another member of the party followed, carrying eight hundred dollars in dust to Walla Walla to pay off debts to the merchants. Sent downriver to Portland, the gold and news of the strike set off a blaze of excitement. Within weeks, men by the thousands were moving toward the interior.

This was in the spring of 1861. A continent's breadth away, Fort Sumter was under siege; President Lincoln was about to issue a call for seventy-five thousand troops; and the country soon would be rent asunder by the Civil War. But in the Pacific Northwest, there was bigger news.

Gold ...

Selected as Captain of the *Colonel Wright* for her maiden voyage was a veteran Willamette River pilot named Leonard White, who was recognized to be a man capable of taking a steamboat anywhere water slightly denser than a light dew happened to flow. One of his many eccentricities was his firm belief that the King's English would be greatly simplified if words were spelled the way they were pronounced. In the frequent letters he wrote to editors of local newspapers, he put his theory into practice. For instance, he wrote the editor of the Eugene, Oregon, paper:

> I anticipat that navigashun wil be opened as far as Ugen Siti the kuming winter, if the good inhabitants wil alou us to Bush-hwak above Korvalis [Corvallis] … the smal timber that gros along the eg wil be ov yus for Bush-hwaking.

When Emil Warren read the letter in the office of the editor of the Eugene paper, he scowled and asked, "What in the devil does he mean? I thought 'Bushwhacking' was a Missouri hill country term for shooting somebody in the back from ambush."

"It does mean that," the editor said with a laugh. "But according to *Webster's Dictionary*, it has other meanings, too. Pulling a boat against the current by grasping bushes along the bank, is one. In the early 1800s, the speaking style of a politician who sawed the air with his hands as he orated, was another. Len White is a well-read man."

Following the building of the *Colonel Wright* by Lawrence W. Coe and Robert R. Thompson, both of whom were stockholders in the Oregon Steam Navigation Company, at the mouth of the Deschutes River in 1859, Captain Len White piloted it on regular runs as far up the Columbia as Wallula Landing. The boat had a mast carrying a huge square sail, which was used when the wind was favorable. Fuel was a problem, for no trees grew along this stretch of the river. In the spring of 1860, an army quartermaster engaged the stern-wheeler to carry supplies to a depot at the mouth of the Palouse River, sixty miles up the Snake. The next summer, June 1861, Seth Slater, a Portland merchant, offered a full cargo of supplies to be taken upriver to the closest landing point feasible near the Idaho mines. Working as a cabin boy for his father aboard the *Carrie Ladd* on the lower river, Lars Warren was amused by a news item in the *Oregonian* relating an adventure that was old hat to him:

> After entering the Snake River the captain touched at an island where an enormous tree had lodged from a former high water, and the crew and volunteer passengers were landed with axes to add to the supply of fuel. Upon disturbing the trunk of the tree a nest of rattlesnakes was also disturbed and a vicious war ensued in which a dozen snakes were killed, two of tremendous size.

"I'll bet the one that tried to bite me was bigger," Lars boasted to his father.

"Likely it was," Tommy laughed. "But you didn't have a reporter along as a witness."

"If I could get a job as cabin boy aboard the *Colonel Wright*, would you let me take it?"

"What's wrong with the job you've got?"

"Nothing, Dad. It's just that being aboard a boat on a new section of river would be more exciting."

"I know what you mean, son. But you'd better ask your mother before you apply."

Truth was, the first trip of the *Colonel Wright* up Snake River did turn out to be an exciting one. Below the mouth of the Palouse, a water-powered ferry had been recently installed, with a cable stretched between two tall wooden towers carrying pulleys attached to a big wooden wheel on the flat-bottomed ferryboat by which it was angled into the current and propelled across the river. Sagging low over the water, the heavy rope cable was beneath the level of the boat's pilot house, mast, and stack, so Captain White reduced power and brought his boat to a halt a few yards downstream.

"Ahoy the ferry!" he shouted into a megaphone after coming out on deck. "You're impeding navigation on my river. Will you be so kind as to lower your goddam cable?"

"Beggin' your pardon, Cap'n, but you're wrong on several counts. First place, this ain't your river. Second place, it ain't navigable. Third place, I got a franchise from the Territorial Legislature to operate this ferry. Have you got a license to operate your boat?"

"The Snake is a federal river, you damn fool, and I've got a right to sail my boat wherever it flows. If you'll lower your blasted cable, I'll show you how navigable the river is."

After several minutes of heated argument, the owner of the ferry grudgingly slacked off the cable so that it sagged a few feet under the surface of the water in the center of the channel up which the *Colonel Wright* would pass. Unfortunately, the threshing stern-wheel picked up the slacked-off cable as the boat crossed over it, snapping it in two. Left behind and temporarily out of business, the angry, disgusted ferryman could only watch, curse, and hope for the worst as the boat churned on upstream into the white-water rapid just below the mouth of the Palouse.

And the worst nearly happened. Running in full early summer flood, Palouse Rapid was the strongest the boat had encountered during its maiden journey up the Snake. For two hours the stern-wheel threshed and the engines labored under a full head of steam, while Captain White used all his considerable skills, trying first one channel, then another, until he finally managed to coax the boat through the rapid.

After a few miles of relatively quiet water, the boat found itself battling yet another rapid, this one so bad that the square sail was raised to utilize a favoring wind, and a line was put out and carried ahead. With the threshing stern-wheel, the power capstan, and the wind all working together, the boat climbed foot by foot through the thundering, pounding, tossing current. Just as it appeared that the *Colonel Wright* would be successful in its attempt to ascend the rapid, a sudden gust of wind from astern filled the big square sail, driving the boat ahead with such a surge that it overtook the cable before its slack could be reeled in, causing the heavy wet rope to wrap itself around the paddle wheel in a hopeless snarl. Cutting off power, Captain White nosed the boat into the bank, where its crew spent an hour cutting the line free. The *Oregonian* reporter wrote:

> A little farther up the river, the boat overtook a party of mounted Indians who were engaged in trying to ascertain its speed by first walking their horses, then trotting, then galloping them. Their experiments amused the passengers for some miles until a rocky bluff shut them off from view.

After tying up for the night, which was made much shorter by music, song, and improvised entertainment by the passengers and crew, the steamer proceeded on upriver at dawn the next day, reaching the mouth of the Clearwater in the middle of the afternoon. Despite the difficulties encountered ascending a dozen rapids, the *Colonel Wright* had needed only two days to cover the same distance that William H. Gray and his clumsy barge had required forty to traverse.

Just as the Snake River carried one-third the volume of water that the Columbia did, the Clearwater, in whose watershed the goldfields lay, was less than half the size of the Snake. Even though his new boat required only twenty-eight inches of water under her keel, Captain White doubted that it could go very far up the Clearwater. Still, he decided to keep going until he ran out of water.

Reaching Agency headquarters at Lapwai, twelve miles upriver, he stopped to pick up Chief Lawyer of the Nez Perces, who cried when he saw the boat: "Look! Here comes a water wagon!" Taken aboard with the head chief was Agent Cain, which added considerable weight to the boat, for he weighed over three hundred pounds. As the boat chugged on up the narrowing, increasingly shallow river, whose white granite reefs and gravel bottom could be clearly seen beneath its translucent waters, the reason for its Indian name, *Kooskooskee*, which translated into "Clearwater," became evident.

Twenty-five miles upstream from Lapwai at the mouth of the North Fork of the Clearwater, Captain White decided he could safely go no farther. Pulling in to the bank there, he unloaded Seth Slater's merchandise, then declared this spot, 507 miles inland from the mouth of the Columbia, to be the head of navigation for this branch of the great river.

During the next three weeks, the *Colonel Wright* and another steamer recently built and launched above Celilo Falls, the *Okanogan*, made two trips to what was first called Slaterville, then renamed Orofino, which was Spanish for "fine gold." As the water level fell in midsummer, it became evident that the practical head of year-round navigation must be the tongue of land where the Clearwater joined the Snake, thirty-seven miles downriver. Adjacent to this spot, which still legally lay within the boundaries of the Nez Perce Reservation—upon which no white man could trespass without permission from the Indians—a boom town named Lewiston came into being.

Though the first trip of the *Colonel Wright* had required three and a half days from Deschutes to Slaterville, the return trip downriver riding the crest of the early summer flood took only eighteen hours. Beyond all doubt, Captain Leonard White had proved the Snake to be a navigable river.

Even so, it turned out to be a cantankerous, treacherous river during much of the year, mute testimony to which were the names exasperated steamboat captains gave its many rapids: Perrine's Defeat, Three Island, Copeley's Cutoff, Haunted House, Gore's Dread, Almota Dead March, Steptoe Canyon, and Texas—the last being a euphemism for what one angry captain had called the bare rear end of the proprietor of a much hotter place.

Following the original strike in the Orofino district north of the Clearwater, other strikes were made at Orogrande south of the

Clearwater, and at Florence, still further south in the Salmon River country. In each case, prospectors by the thousands stampeded to the new fields, ignoring all efforts of the agent, the military, or the Nez Perces to stop them, even though the entire area had been designated as reservation land.

Considering the large number of white trespassers violating their territory, surprisingly little friction arose between the Indians and the whites. There were several good reasons for this, Sitkum told Tommy Warren. One was that the streambeds where gold was found lay in high country, which the Nez Perces used only for hunting, summer pasturing for their horses, and seasonal harvesting of roots.

A second reason for their choosing peace rather than conflict was that many of them had become "settled" Indians. Not only had they built up their farms and herds so that they could feed themselves, they now had a surplus to sell for cash. In one of his trips as Chief Engineer aboard the *Colonel Wright*, Sitkum said he had overheard Chief Reuben, a Nez Perce, lecturing a group of his people gathered around him at the Lewiston boat landing.

"He was there telling them to let the whites prospect wherever they wanted to in the high country. Digging for gold was hard work, he said, so let the white men do it. After they had dug the gold, they would bring it to the Indians, who then would sell them horses, cattle, corn, and fresh vegetables without exerting themselves or getting their hands dirty."

Still a third, and probably the most important reason for the Nez Perces keeping the peace, was that long years of association with the whites had taught them tolerance and caution. Since the time of Lewis and Clark, they had seen plenty of pushy, greedy white men, and had learned to put up with them. They had also observed how dangerous, ruthless, and deadly white men could be when given the least excuse, so they had learned to be careful.

"They saw what happened to Chief Kamiakin and the warriors he led at the end of the Yakima War," Sitkum said. "They do not want the same thing to happen to them."

"Have you heard any word of Kamiakin?"

"Only that he still wanders like the wolf, with no home to call his own."

In order to give a semblance of legality to the white invasion of Nez Perce Reservation land, a board of commissioners appointed by the federal government met with the tribe's head chief, Lawyer, and negotiated an agreement putting the land on which the towns of Lewiston and Clarkston had been built outside the reservation boundaries. Designated as white islands within the Indian reservation were the mining settlements of Pierce City, Orofino, Orogrande, Elk City, and Florence.

"Our esteemed government is behaving the same way it did down in California," Emil observed cynically to Tommy. "Where the native population is concerned, the lands granted them by treaty have rubber boundaries. The government is like the farmer who dedicated an acre to God."

"Where did this happen?"

"Down in Georgia, they say. The way I heard the story, a poor, religious farmer tried to impress his neighbors by dedicating an acre of his hardscrabble farm to his church, pledging to donate all its income to the Lord. He called it 'God's Little Acre.' But he kept moving it around. When he had a good crop on most of his farm, 'God's Acre' turned out to be the one hit by a flood, boll weevils, or drought. God could stand a disaster, he said, while he couldn't."

"Sounds like a hypocrite to me."

"Exactly. And so is the government. It operates on the principle: 'We made a treaty with the Indians and we're going to keep it—until it interferes with the diggers. Then we'll just change the boundaries.'"

"How do you think the government ought to treat the Indians?"

"Like they treat everybody else. Put us all on equal terms, I say. Let us all scramble to make a living, with the devil taking the hindmost. That's the only system that will work in this country."

Certainly Emil was applying his dog-eat-dog philosophy with a great deal of success as a substantial stockholder and attorney for the Oregon Steam Navigation Company. After giving the question of running for the State Legislature serious consideration, he had finally decided against it, telling Tommy with mock seriousness: "It's easier to buy a legislator than to be one. Dolores and I have decided to move to Portland, build ourselves a nice house, and concentrate on having kids and getting rich."

With Portland's expanding maritime industry, rapidly growing mercantile trade as principal supplier to the inland country, and the downriver flow of gold from the fantastically rich Idaho mines fueling the local economy, Emil had put together a combine of financiers against which no individual or small operator could stand. On both sides of the Columbia at the Cascades, the portage tramways now were owned and operated by the O.S.N. Company. So were all the steamboats running from Portland to The Dalles. The fourteen-mile portage railroad around Celilo Falls also was owned by the O.S.N., as were the two stern-wheelers now running on regular schedules between Deschutes Landing and Lewiston.

Stimulated by the gold pouring out of Idaho, the town of Walla Walla was growing rapidly as a supply center and a wintering spot for miners who had made their strike and were eager to spend their substance on fun and easy living. To supply the entertainment needs of the miners and the soldiers stationed at Fort Walla Walla, a number of saloons and theaters opened, importing companies of professional actors, musicians, and "hurdy-gurdy" girls who would dance with a heavy-footed miner if he purchased drinks each dance, the girl's drink being well-watered tea, the man's raw whiskey aged at least three days and so strong it would peel off paint.

Because most of the newcomers to the area were single men from the Border States who were fleeing being drafted as soldiers to fight for the North or South in the Civil War, prejudice and passion had come West with them. Fights in saloons, theaters and the street were commonplace. Because law enforcement was lax while easy money was plentiful, a class of men called "roughs" became increasingly troublesome. Thefts, beatings, and murders became so frequent that the local newspaper routinely reported "a man for breakfast" every day. In response, the "better" citizens of the town—meaning members of the Ancient and Honorable Order of Masons—began to hold secret meetings, have secret trials, and mete out their special kind of justice— banishment or hanging.

Presently, the daily newspaper stories were not of a "man for breakfast" but of who had been given a "suspended sentence" in a secret trial the night before, then been found "hanging around" from the limb of a big elm tree on South Second Street convenient to the newly established cemetery. When a second chapter of the Ancient and Honorable Order of Masons was established in Walla Walla a year or so later, rumor had it that the schism in the organization had been caused by a difference of opinion among the better citizens as to whether an accused criminal should be given a private or public trial before being hanged.

But by then the question was moot, for most of the criminal element had fled to the gold boom settlements of the newly organized Territories of Idaho and Montana, where law and order had yet to be established.

In addition to the fortunes in gold that were being extracted from the mines of the interior country, a new and more lasting kind of treasure had been discovered in the nutritious native grasses and the deep, fertile soil that covered the valleys and hills of southeastern Washington Territory. Comparing the region to California, which had become the garden spot of the West fifteen years ago, Emil Warren told Tommy that the upriver country was bound to boom.

"Cattle, wheat, fruit, vegetables—they all do well here. This part of the country has the soil, water, and climate to make its ranches and farms the best in the Pacific Northwest. The Walla Walla Valley looks particularly good to me. That's why I'm making a substantial investment in land there."

"Don't tell me you're going to become a farmer!"

"Why not? There's money in it."

"The only time I've ever known you to get dirt under your fingernails was when you had to pick up a deck of cards from an unswept floor."

Emil laughed good-naturedly. "All I intend to do is own the land, Tommy, not farm it. As a matter of fact, our first venture will be into cattle, not farm products. We plan to bring a herd of cheap Spanish cattle up from California as Ewing Young did twenty years ago. Then we'll drive them across the mountains, sell most of them to the Idaho mining settlements for a quick profit, then use the rest to build up our local herd."

"Who is 'we'?"

"What I've done," Emil said, deliberately ignoring Tommy's question, "is buy up half a dozen abandoned land claims in the foothills southeast of Walla Walla. These are claims settlers have filed and proved up on, then had to sell cheap for one reason or another because they couldn't make a living on them."

"Why did they fail?"

"Lack of capital, poor management—lots of reasons. When I offered them cash, they were glad to sell out. So I got clear title to several thousand acres of good range and farm land without having to live on it. All I needed was a partner with the energy and know-how to develop a ranch."

"That's my question, Emil. Who is 'we'?"

"Carlos Ibanez."

Tommy stared at him in amazement. "Your wife's kid brother? You're taking him in as a business partner?"

"That's right."

"You must be out of your mind, Emil! He's barely out of his teens, with no more business sense than a rabbit—"

"He's twenty-one years old, Tommy, and a lot smarter than you think."

"But he'll be way over his head trying to run a ranch in raw, newly settled country. Why, he's so shy he blushes like a schoolgirl every time an older man speaks to him."

"I know he does, Tommy. That's why Dolores asked me to take him under my wing, so to speak. Here's what happened ..."

15.

EFORE THE SENSELESS WAR between Mexico and the United States destroyed his beautiful, sun-drenched, lotus land called California, Don Alonzo de Varga y Ibanez had lived an idyllic life. A transplanted Catalonian, he was descended from a long line of *conquistadores* who had found the balmy clime of the New World so pleasant that they had remained as permanent residents. In the years following 1820, Don Alonzo had seen first Spain, then Mexico, lose their grip on California because of the greed, corruption, and sheer stupidity of myopic rulers in distant capitals whose endless edicts and laws ignored the realities of life in this marvelous land.

Good Catholic though he was, he had to admit that even the devout, well-meaning priests who had labored so hard to bring God's word to the local Indians and teach them the enlightened ways of the True Faith, had proved themselves to be abysmal failures, except for their skills in raising grapes and making wine. To his way of thinking, a peaceful revolt of the *californios* against first Spain, then Mexico, after which a government administered by landholders such as himself under civil and ecclesiastical laws made by the dons and the priests would be the best of all possible worlds.

Because of the tragic war between Mexico and the United States, it did not happen, of course. Even so, few battles of any consequence took place on California soil, despite the strutting and posturing of military leaders on both sides. For many years, Americans and Californians had traded, mingled, and associated with one another as friends. Knowing how far away the City of Mexico and Washington, D. C., were from this far western empire, which now by treaty had become part of the United States, the local citizens—*americano, californio,* and *indio*—assumed that they would be left alone to work out the sort of government all parties concerned could live with.

But when gold was discovered at Sutter's Mill on the Sacramento River, their peaceful world ended.

The vast estate deeded to Don Alonzo de Varga y Ibanez, first by the Spanish crown then confirmed by Mexican law, covered a large portion of the Napa Valley to the north of Sacramento. Though Don Alonzo's *abogado* immediately began the legal work required to transfer title to his holdings from Spanish-Mexican into American jurisdiction, there seemed to be no way rude, lawless, gold-hungry prospectors could be kept from despoiling the creeks and arroyos of his land without his resorting to violence, which he did not wish to do, nor from stealing his cattle and horses, which until now had roamed freely over the grassy hills and plains of this verdant land.

Bit by bit, piece by piece, Don Alonzo saw his empire crumble and dwindle, just as the gold-streaked ridges of the Mother Lode country were being washed down into the creeks and rivers by the nozzles of the Big Tom hydraulic mining equipment that soon replaced the individual prospector's pick, shovel, and pan.

After bearing him two beautiful children, Dolores and Carlos, six years apart, the *duena* of the family, Senora Maria Elena Ibanez, had given Don Alonzo no more offspring; so it was with them that the future of his family lay. Both he and his wife had at first strongly opposed their daughter's falling in love with and marrying the brash young *americano*, Emil Warren. But the newcomer to their country proved to be so congenial, so helpful in legal matters, and, most important of all, such a fine prospect for a husband because of his political power and growing wealth, that both father and mother finally had given their unqualified blessing to the union.

"She loves him, *mamacita*," Don Alonzo told his wife. "He is going to be rich. True, he is not a Catholic yet. But he has promised Dolores that he will counsel with the priest about converting to our faith."

"That he will be rich is good," the *senora* agreed. "But what matters most is that he will vow to raise the children as good Catholics. Knowing this, we can die happy."

At that time, Don Alonzo had not contemplated dying in the near future, but only two years passed following the ceremony uniting Dolores and Emil before he suffered a fatal stroke. Brought on by an argument with a drunken, ill-mannered *americano* who had taken illegal possession of a piece of Don Alonzo's land, the massive blockage of a vital artery to his brain had occurred so suddenly that he tumbled out of the saddle from his horse, dead before his body struck the ground.

Had it not been for Emil Warren's political power and legal know-how, Senora Maria Elena and her nineteen-year-old son, Carlos, would have been stripped of the entire Ibanez estate, for the greed and rapacity of the American newcomers and the venality of the court system they had established made stealing from the Spanish-Mexican owners of the land a legitimate blood sport. Like all Spanish matrons, the *senora* had never handled money or managed property in her life. As for young Carlos, he was being raised as a *caballero*—a gentleman—which meant that he was a marvelous dancer, possessed impeccable manners, was a magnificent horseman, and had been trained in the fine art of bullfighting by a famous *toreador* from Madrid, who had been a frequent guest at the *hacienda* for the express purpose of teaching Carlos bullfighting, as well as being a suitor for his sister's hand until the *americano* came along and convinced the father and mother that it would be more useful to have a rich *americano* lawyer in the family than a *toreador*.

Because of the prejudice of American frontiersmen against rich Spanish landholders, it had taken all the legal skill and political cunning Emil Warren possessed to save enough of the Ibanez estate to give the bewildered, helpless, aging *senora* a home in which she could live out the rest of her days in peace. This he accomplished by producing and updating a will Don Alonzo had made some years ago in which he had referred vaguely to deeding the family hacienda and the 160 acres of vineyards surrounding it to the Church. Suggesting that it become a haven for aging nuns and priests, with income from the winery on the property to be used for its support, he had not intended for the bequest to go into effect until after his own and his wife's demise. Making the will effective immediately, Emil assured the widow of the donor of the property, Senora Maria Elena, that she would be permitted to live out her days in what had always been her home.

By the time all the details of this arrangement had been settled, Carlos Ibanez had celebrated his twentieth birthday and was six months along toward his twenty-first.

What he was going to do for a living presented a problem. Truth was, he had been trained for nothing but the task of becoming a caballero—a gentleman. In today's rough, ill-mannered, dog-eat-dog world run by pushy, rude Americans, the demand for that sort of person in California ranged from nil to nothing.

To describe Carlos merely as handsome would be a serious misuse of words, Emil admitted. The simple truth was, he was beautiful. Slim, supple, with curly black hair, soft, expressive black eyes, and the classical facial lines of a young Greek god, he possessed an attractiveness dangerously close to being feminine. A proud, extremely sensitive young man, he was further handicapped when dealing with the kind of loud, raucous Americans that dominated local society by his habit of speaking very softly and gently, then blushing furiously at their coarse replies.

"He is old enough to be a man," his sister Dolores told Emil on their final visit to the family hacienda. "But he has not yet learned how to act like one. If he tries to compete in this crude society, he will be destroyed."

"I know," Emil said sympathetically. "But what can we do to help him?"

"We must take him back to Portland with us, where we can protect him."

"He won't stand for being coddled, Dolores. He's far too proud for that."

"He admires you very much, Emil. Could you not set him up in a business of his own? I'm sure he would do anything you tell him to do."

"That's just the problem. What can he do?"

"He is an excellent horseman. And he knows a great deal about fighting bulls—"

Stifling his impulse to point out that there were no bullrings in Portland, Emil told his wife he would give the matter some thought. Going out to the corral behind the hacienda, where a dozen dark-skinned vaqueros were hooting and cheering as they watched an impromptu bullfight, Emil admired the grace and skill with which Carlos evaded the charges of the angry young bull which a pair of riders playing the roles of banderilleros had taunted into attacking by pricking the skin of his neck with lances. Keeping him pinned between their nimble-footed horses, they forced him to charge time after time at the banner-waving young man who was flaunting his square of red silk cloth in the bull's face.

"*Toro, toro!*" the watching vaqueros shouted. "Stick a horn in his ribs, black bull! Make him bite the dust!"

"En la leche de su madre!" Carlos jeered back, using language so
profane and a tone of voice so rough that Emil stared at him in amazement. This bold, self-confident, aggressive young man twirling the
red silk cloth under the bull's nose was not the shy, soft-spoken, gentle heir to the Ibanez fortune that he knew. This was a very tough,
very virile kind of man, who could hold his own in the roughest kind
of masculine company.

During the next ten minutes of frenzied action, the angry bull
charged time and again without touching his tormentor. Tiring at
long last, the frustrated animal dropped its head and stood spread-
legged and trembling, completely beaten. Gracefully moving in, Carlos raised on tiptoe between the bull's horns, made a simulated killing
thrust with the tip of his blunted sword, then turned and bowed to the
watching crowd.

"How do you like that, senores? Am I awarded two ears and a
tail?"

"Ole! Ole!" shouted the vaqueros.

"Le mato! Le mato el toro! He killed the bull!"

"Que hombre! Don Carlos esta el matador grande!"

Obviously these men regarded young Carlos with great respect,
Emil mused. Without doubt, they would follow wherever he chose to
lead them. Even to eastern Washington Territory. Thus, the idea for
the joint cattle-raising enterprise was born ...

Obtaining a thousand head of California cattle turned out to be no
problem, for the lean, agile, wild-as-deer animals had been roaming
the grass-covered valleys and hills untended and breeding prolifically
for many years. Since neither Carlos nor the vaqueros he would be
employing as drovers knew the trail north, it was imperative that Emil
find an American who could act both as their guide and as a buffer between them and the settlers along the way. While Carlos was rounding up the cattle and making ready to begin the drive next spring,
Emil went back to Portland and asked former United States Marshal,
Joseph Meek, who knew a number of ex–mountain men living in the
Willamette Valley, if he could recommend such person.

"You bet I can!" Meek exclaimed. "Fact is, he's one of the men who
made that very same drive with Ewing Young twenty years ago."

"Who is he?"

"Joe Gale."

"Seems to me I've heard of him. Didn't he and some of his ex–mountain men friends try to build a boat on the Oregon coast a few years ago?"

"Try, hell! They done it! Purty good boat, too. Joe Gale kin do anything he sets his mind to. He's prime beaver, Joe is, a good man on any trail."

"Where could I find him?"

"Last I heard he was down in Californy near a town called San José. He's gettin' sick and tired of that part of the country, I hear tell, and thinkin' about comin' back to Oregon. He's got relatives in Salem. Likely they can tell you how to get ahold of him."

Eventually locating Joe Gale in California, Emil found him to be a tall, rawboned, quiet-spoken man in his midfifties. Coming west from the hill country of Virginia in the 1830s, he had trapped for a number of years, had married and still lived with a Umatilla Indian woman, and had traveled all over the wilderness West. After Emil had explained his plan to drive a herd of California cattle north, Gale nodded his approval.

"No reason why it can't be done," he said laconically. "Fact is, I been thinkin' about claimin' a piece of land up in that eastern Oregon country and startin' a ranch myself. You got any breedin' stock in your herd?"

"I haven't seen it yet. My brother-in-law, Carlos Ibanez, is putting it together."

"He's Mex, I take it?"

"Spanish, Joe. And mighty touchy about racial slurs."

Giving Emil a long, unblinking, steely-eyed look, Joe Gale said gently, "In my time, Mister Warren, I've ridden a lot of horses and known a lot of men. Long ago, I learned that color or breed don't make a damn in either one, when your life depends on what they can do. It's what they got under the skin that counts."

"He's a good man, Joe, and he's got a damn good crew of vaqueros. But I thought you should know what kind of company you'll be keeping. Likely you'll run into some Border State rednecks along the way."

"Don't worry about that, my friend. I've never yet seen a redneck I couldn't handle."

Because of the heavy winter snowfall in the Sierras, the Siskiyous, and the Cascades, it was late May before the herd was put on the trail. Taking Joe Gale's advice, Carlos made sure that two hundred cows were included in the gather, while the rest were a mixed lot of steers and two- to-four-year-old bulls which had been too wild to catch and cut. It would be a good investment, Carlos and Joe agreed, if Emil would buy half a dozen Durham bulls from ranchers in southern Oregon when the herd reached that area.

"Probably cost you five hundred dollars apiece," Gale said. "Compared to the five dollars a head you're payin' for wild stuff, that's a lot of money. But they'll be worth it when it comes to breedin' up the quality of your herd."

When Ewing Young and his crew of ex–mountain men had driven their bunch of wild California cattle north to Willamette Valley twenty years ago, trail losses had been heavy, for the ex–mountain men had not been expert drovers. But on this drive, which was guided by Joe Gale, ramrodded by Carlos Ibanez, with an experienced crew of indio, mestizo, and *mexicano* drovers, the losses were minimal, for the men in charge were experts, so familiar with the spooky Mexican cattle that they anticipated what the animals were going to do even before the cattle themselves decided to do it.

Keeping in touch with the progress of the trail herd as it moved north out of the Napa Valley and threaded its way through the rolling foothills and tree-covered heights of northern California's Sierras and southern Oregon's Siskiyous, Emil was pleased to see that it was having no problems, though its pace seemed very slow. With Joe Gale selecting a route offering the best water and grass and the least infringement on settled areas, while Carlos and the vaqueros handled the herd itself, there had been no conflict with people along the way.

Instead of crossing the Siskiyous into the upper portion of the Willamette Valley and then following it north to Portland and the Columbia River, Joe Gale chose a northeasterly route up the Klamath River through the lake country east of the Cascades, which missed the Willamette Valley completely. To Emil's inexperienced eye, this high desert country was dry, barren, and worthless, its sagebrush and seared brown clumps of scattered grass incapable of supporting any kind of livestock. But when he expressed that opinion to Joe Gale, the ex–mountain man laughed.

"Grass don't have to be green to be nourishing, friend. To these Mex cattle, dried-up bunchgrass tastes as good as sun-cured hay."

"You've been through this part of the country before, I take it?"

"Several times. Once when Kit Carson and me worked as guides for Cap'n Fremont back in '43. Again when me and Old Bill Williams were in a trappin' party and had a fracas with some Modoc bucks in '44. And another time when I guided the Applegate party by way of the desert cutoff route into southern Oregon in '46. The trick is to stay close enough to the mountains to be clear of the desert and close enough to the desert to be clear of the mountains. That way, you get the best and avoid the worst of both kinds of country."

Telling Carlos that he'd arranged to buy half a dozen Durham bulls from a rancher near Eugene in the upper Willamette Valley, Emil asked his brother-in-law if he wanted to send a couple of vaqueros to pick them up, drive them across the Cascades, then put them in with the main trail herd.

"*Madre de Dios, no!*" Carlos exclaimed, giving him a horrified look. "We cannot put Durham bulls in with Mexican cattle on the trail!"

"Why not? It'll give them a chance to get acquainted with the cows they're going to breed."

"*No, no, hermano!* It does not work that way. It would cause terrible fighting in the herd."

"The cows would fight the bulls that are trying to breed them, you mean?"

"*Mira, amigo*—look, my friend. I will tell you some things about cattle you apparently do not know—"

"You've got a lot of ground to cover there."

"Bulls and cows do not fight. Bulls and steers—*pues*, sometimes they will fight, if the steer has not been altered until he is three or four years old. You see, he still remembers how it was when he was a bull."

"That I can understand."

"But when tame bulls like the Durhams are put into a trail herd containing wild bulls like the Mexicans, you may be very sure that there will be many fights. This we cannot permit."

"Being so much bigger and stronger than the Mex bulls, the Durhams would do a lot of damage, I suppose."

"No, no, brother! It would be the Durhams that would suffer the most. After all, the Mexican bulls have fighting blood in their veins."

"Well, I suppose you know. So how do I do get my prize Durham bulls to the Walla Walla Valley?"

"There are boats on the Willamette and Columbia Rivers, *verdad?*"

"Sure. Lots of them."

"They carry freight as well as passengers, true?"

"Of course they do! But if you're suggesting I ship those six Durham bulls down the Willamette and then up the Columbia to Wallula Landing—"

"That is exactly what I am suggesting."

"At the rates the O.S.N. Company charges, it would cost a fortune!"

"You own the company, do you not?"

"Only a small piece of it, Carlos. And the O.S.N. is carrying so much freight at premium rates these days, the stockholders will scream to high Heaven if I displace it with six Durham bulls, which will take up a lot of space and require special handling."

"Even so, you must do it. We cannot put them into the trail herd."

Since Emil had agreed that all decisions regarding the welfare of the cattle would be made by Carlos, the six Durham bulls went down the Willamette from Eugene and then up the Columbia to Wallula Landing on boats owned by the O.S.N. Because it was a strict Company rule that the purser aboard each boat appraise and set the rate for each and every piece of freight, the only thing Emil could do was squirm and pay when he was charged the highest possible fee for his shipment of bulls. When he complained about it to Tommy, who was now captain of the *Oneonta* on the run between the Upper Cascades and The Dalles, his brother laughed and gave him no sympathy whatsoever.

"Now you know why our farmer shippers call us highway robbers for the way we set rates on their teams and wagons."

"I wasn't aware that we charged them unfairly. It's simply a matter of weight and space, isn't it?"

"That's what our pursers tell them. But the shippers don't like the way we measure freight."

"Why not?"

"We call forty cubic feet a ton, no matter how much air is in it. Before a team and wagon come aboard, the purser measures the rig from the nose of the lead horse in the team to the tailgate of the wagon."

"What's wrong with that?"

"After the horses pull the wagon aboard, they're unhitched. The tongue of the wagon is turned to one side horizontally to give a second dimension, then vertically to give a third. Multiplying the three measurements together, the purser gets a cubic foot total, divides it by forty, and comes up with the rate to be paid."

"Sounds fair enough to me."

"Then he stalls the horses side by side below decks, takes the wheels and tongues off the wagons, puts them inside the wagon bed, then stacks the stripped-down wagons on deck three-deep. But by then the freight rate has already been determined by the maximum dimensions."

Shaking his head, Emil said philosophically, "Well, Tommy, it's a sound business principle to charge all the traffic will bear. As long as we've got a monopoly on the rivers, the landings, and the portages, our shippers will just have to grin, bear it, and pay."

16.

*S*NOW FELL THICKLY from the gray November sky, and the wind was bitter cold. Though it was high noon, the sun provided little light and no warmth, making Emil Warren shiver despite the sheepskin coat and thick gloves he had donned before driving a rig rented at a Walla Walla livery stable out to the sagebrush-covered flat southwest of town, where the thousand head of Mexican cattle driven up from California were being held.

Having kept in touch with Carlos Ibanez and Joe Gale by frequent visits to the herd as it moved north and east, blazing a new cattle trail across bleak desert and rugged mountain country as it went, Emil was aware of the hazards and hardships the cattle and men had endured for the past five months. He did not fault the drovers because the drive had taken so much longer than they had anticipated it would. Certainly, Carlos, Joe, and the crew of *vaqueros* were to be complimented on the fact that only a few animals had been lost along the way. From what Emil had been told by the local settlers about regional weather patterns, it was unusual for the first snowfall to come in mid-November. With a foot of the white stuff already on the ground, and snow still coming down, getting the crew settled into winter quarters and the cattle onto the best-protected foothill rangeland available were urgent matters. Still, Emil was hoping that Carlos would agree to driving a few hundred steers to the Idaho mining settlements so that they could take advantage of current high prices for beef on the hoof, helping Emil recoup some of the substantial investment he had made in the California cattle and the Durham bulls.

"Well, Carlos, what do you think?"

"It is a long drive to Idaho, Senor Gale tells me," Carlos answered, shaking his head. "In this weather, I hate to risk it."

"My idea was we could split the herd. Take a couple of hundred head and leave the rest here. The mining camps are crying for meat.

We should be able to sell our five-dollar-a-head Mex cattle for three or four hundred dollars apiece on the hoof. That's a hefty profit."

"We would be pushing our luck, *hermano*. If we got caught in a blizzard, we would lose the whole bunch."

"This storm may be over tomorrow."

"And it may last for weeks. Dead cattle and frozen *vaqueros* would be too high a price to pay for the chance of a quick profit."

Whether Joe Gale, who knew this inland country better than any other man, would have sided with Carlos or Emil himself was a moot question, for the ex–mountain man was not present to take part in the discussion. Urged by his Indian wife to visit the Umatilla Indian Reservation twenty-five miles to the south, where a number of her relatives and friends lived, Joe Gale had left the herd soon after its arrival in the Walla Walla Valley. Next spring, he had told Emil, he intended to wander down into what was called the "Big Canyon" of the Snake River 150 miles to the east, where he'd heard gold had been found along one of the creeks.

"Likely the strike don't amount to much," he said. "Still, I'd like to have a look. One thing I do know—the Big Canyon country is a great place to raise horses and cattle. Lots of grass there, a mild climate, and nobody using it but Old Joseph's band of Nez Perces. They're related to my wife's people, so we'll have no trouble if we homestead down along the Snake and start a ranch."

Having learned to trust his brother-in-law's judgment and not wanting to overrule Carlos in what really was his decision to make, Emil nodded reluctantly.

"What do you think we should do?"

"Drive the herd to the land you've bought and get ready for what may be a hard winter. From what you've showed me of the ranch, there are some log buildings and barns we can fix up as a place to live and give shelter to the Durham bulls, which we cannot afford to lose. The Mexican cattle are used to taking care of themselves out on the range in California, but they may need shelter here."

"There's plenty of forage for them in the foothills. The trees and bushes along the creeks will give them some protection from the weather. I took your advice and bought all the harvested wild hay I could persuade our rancher neighbors to sell. They were glad to let me have it for cash. Some of them even laughed behind my back, I gather, calling me a fool greenhorn because I didn't seem to know that the winters in this part of the country are usually so mild cattle don't need to be fed hay."

"There is an old Spanish saying that it is better to have unused food in the pantry while eating well," Carlos said with a smile, "than to starve while the cupboard is bare. If the weather moderates during the next couple of weeks, perhaps we can risk driving a hundred steers to the Idaho mines. If it does not, they should winter well on the ranch. When spring comes, they will be strong and healthy, ready to drive to an early market."

"Well, Carlos, do as you like with them," Emil said, slapping the team with the reins. "Me, I'm heading back to town before I freeze to death. I'll be going downriver to Portland tomorrow. I hope you and the cattle winter well."

"I'm sure we will. *Vaya con Dios, hermano.*"

Contrary to what Carlos had been told about the mildness of the climate in this part of the country, the winter of 1861–62 turned out to be the worst the Walla Walla Valley had ever known. Morning after morning from early December on he and the crew of *vaqueros* opened the door of the big log cabin, which they had repaired and made livable as a bunkhouse, on a white, frozen world, to find the paths to the barn, the corral, the woodshed, and the creek—which they had shoveled clear the day before—drifted level with a new fall of snow.

Blizzard followed blizzard, the storms sometimes continuing for days at a time with such violence that he and his men dared not go more than a few yards from the door of the bunkhouse for fear of getting lost in the white swirling world outside. Though unused to this cold, snowy weather, the *vaqueros* did not complain, for they all were of stoic *indio, mestizo,* and *mexicano* blood, tough as well-tanned leather, willing to endure whatever hardship their *patron* asked them to, so long as he endured it with them.

As the weeks wore on and the snow drifted ever deeper on the range, Carlos became concerned for the cattle. Stalled in a weather-tight barn and being given daily rations of hay, the six Durham bulls were doing well. But out on the range, the majority of the cattle had to fend for themselves. Now and then when the weather cleared sufficiently, Carlos, his *segundo,* Ramon Gutierrez, and the leader of the *vaqueros,* Pancho Onate, rode out to see how the cattle were faring, their horses plunging with difficulty through the shoulder-high drifts. Frequently they found small groups of cattle huddled together for warmth in some sheltered coulee or draw, gaunt and lean from hunger. Taking along a wagon bed fitted with runners and filled with hay, they doled out a few mouthfuls of feed to the animals they found still alive, giving them nourishment for a few more days, which was all they could do in the deep drifts of snow.

Many of the cattle had wandered far from their original range, seeking the cover of bushes and trees along the creeks, where, in their hunger, they had stripped the bushes bare, then pulled off all the low-hanging branches they could reach. In more exposed sections of range, the riders discovered cattle frozen to death on their feet, held erect by the deep drifts, their gnawed tails showing mute evidence of cannibalism. As the bitter winter weather drove the timber wolves and the coyotes down from the mountain heights, the riders found grisly evidence of their work.

Infrequently, Carlos and several of his men bucked the crusted drifts to ride into Walla Walla for food staples, tobacco, kerosene for the lamps, and reading material with which to while away the long, dreary days. On each such occasion, Carlos heard grim tales of the severity of the winter. All over the valley cattle were freezing or starving to death. Running short of food, many of the settlers were dipping into their store of wheat, barley, and rye which they had been saving for spring seed, laboriously grinding it into flour with small hand coffee mills or simply boiling and eating it whole.

No boats had come upriver for the past six weeks, unable to breast the crushing ice floes. One Walla Walla man who had just completed a harrowing overland journey from Portland said that in many places the Columbia was frozen over so solidly from bank to bank that a team and wagon could be driven across it.

Now and then men from the Idaho mines made the dangerous trip on snowshoes from Lewiston to Walla Walla, bringing word of the near-starving conditions of the upriver settlements. Beef literally was worth its weight in gold there, Carlos knew, but until winter loosened its grip on the land a cattle drive was out of the question.

On his occasional visits to town, Carlos had become aware of the fact that the principle business of the merchants and saloon owners was separating wintering Idaho miners from their accumulated riches and the soldiers stationed at the nearby military post from their pay by providing them with alcohol and entertainment. Staffed by a handful of regular Army officers and noncoms, the fort was garrisoned with two companys of dragoons and one of artillery. Consisting of Oregon and Washington Territory Volunteers, these were men who had evaded service in the Union Army by enlisting to "protect the home front" rather than being drafted for the greater conflict now raging so fiercely a continent's breadth away.

Like many of the Americans Carlos had known down in California, the soldiers were an equal mix of Northern and Southern sympathizers, Republicans and Democrats, anti- and-pro-slavery advocates. Some of them argued their beliefs loudly and passionately when sober; when drunk, they erupted into sudden, mindless violence, starting barroom brawls whose participants sometimes were injured or killed.

Also present among the saloon hangers-on was a more dangerous criminal element of roughs and thieves, mean, surly men, ready to prey on any drunken traveler, miner, or soldier who might foolishly give them a chance to steal his horse, gold, or gun.

Like all newly settled Western communities, one of the first business enterprises to be established in Walla Walla was a newspaper. Leaving no doubt as to where his loyalties lay, the publisher named it the *Walla Walla Statesman*, then emphasized his politics by declaring in a line of large, italicized type that ran as a banner at the top of the front page of every issue:

THE CONSTITUTION & THE UNION

Published three times a week, the paper's every word was read and reread all over the valley. Taking a strong stand in favor of law and order, its publisher minced no words in stating:

> During these long, dull winter days, we know that barroom quarrels over politics or war may lead to a few scuffles and bloody noses. But we give warning that this community will not tolerate the sort of violent crime that has become so common in less civilized Idaho mining towns. We expect the commandant of Fort Walla Walla, Major Howard Richardson, to set a strict standard of behavior for his soldiers when they come into town, disciplining them severely if they violate it. We also expect our city's law officers to make our civilian population behave in a reasonable manner. To those few arrogant newcomers who think themselves above the law, we issue this warning:

The sturdy old elm tree on South Second Street, which has served the cause of justice so well in years past, still stands. The organization which used it still exists. Much as its kind of vigilante justice may be deplored, it could be employed again, if the roughs get out of line.

Though Emil Warren had told Carlos that some of his neighboring ranchers resented the fact that an attorney for the Oregon Steam Navigation Company had bought the claims of failed settlers and stocked the range with Mexican cattle, he had seen no outward signs of antagonism on the part of his neighbors. The fact that none of them had come to call was caused, he supposed, by the bad weather and snowbound trails. In any case, three days before Christmas he decided to visit the nearest neighbor, Matthew Kent and his family, who lived just two miles away.

Knowing that the rancher and his wife, Mary, had an eighteen year old daughter named Margaret, a ten year old son, Luke, and a six year old daughter, Susan, Carlos selected and wrapped presents for the mother and the children. Suspecting that Matthew Kent himself might resent a personal gift and knowing that the rancher could not afford the luxury of butchering one of his own steers for beef, Carlos had his men dress out a quarter from one of their own beeves, which still had a reasonable quantity of fat on it, that had recently been butchered for their own use. Surely Kent would not refuse food being offered to his whole family, Carlos reasoned.

Loading the presents and the quarter of beef into the runner-equipped wagon bed pulled by a team of strong horses, with Ramon Gutierrez driving it while Pancho Onate and Carlos rode ahead to break trail through the hard-crusted snow, the pre-Christmas visiting party left the home ranch at ten o'clock in the morning. Under a wan winter sun whose pale light gave off no heat at all, the two-mile trip took almost two hours, for few travelers had passed this way recently to break trail.

Reaching the Kent cabin, Carlos noticed the fresh tracks of a saddle horse leading into the yard from the direction of town. Since no animal was in sight, he assumed that the horse had been led into the shelter of the nearby barn, getting it in out of the near-zero cold. Before swinging out of the saddle, he announced his presence by halloing the house, a custom in frontier country where strangers were regarded with suspicion. After a few moments, the door opened and Matthew Kent appeared.

"Yes?"

"I am your neighbor, Carlos Ibanez," Carlos said with a smile, touching the brim of his hat. "I live just over the ridge to the south."

"I know who you are and where you live. What do you want?"

"To wish you and your family a warm, merry Christmas, senor."

A solid, muscular man of fifty, Matthew Kent was rumored to be one of the leaders of the vigilante committee that had brought law and order to the valley a year or so ago by warning a gang of roughs led by a man named Henry Plummer that they were not immune to vigilante justice. After several known murderers and thieves had been hanged by the nightriders, Plummer and the rest of his crowd had left town rather than suffer the same fate, transferring their base of operations first to Orofino, Idaho, and then to Bannack City, a few hundred miles to the east.

"Give me a bit of warm weather and I'll be merry enough," Kent said gruffly. He hesitated, then added," You want to get down and come in?"

"Not if I am imposing upon you, Senor Kent. I merely wish to give you and your family a few small presents."

"For Heaven's sake, Matthew!" a woman's voice exclaimed behind him. "Where are your manners? Invite him in!"

"Get down! Get down!" Kent grunted. "Your men, too. We can share a little heat with you, at least."

Swinging down out of the saddle, Carlos jerked his head at Ramon and Pancho, murmuring, "*Vamanos, compadres.*"

The three men went inside, all of them removing their hats immediately as they crossed the threshold, as was the custom in California. Stiffly, Kent introduced his wife, Mary, their two daughters, Margaret and Susan, and their son, Luke, then the uniformed visitor, Major Howard Richardson, whom Carlos knew to be commandant of Fort Walla Walla. From the looks exchanged between Margaret Kent and Major Richardson, Carlos suspected that they were romantically involved.

"Please sit down," Mrs. Kent said, motioning them into homemade, rawhide-bottomed chairs. "We're out of coffee, I'm sorry to say, but I've made a substitute out of chicory and dried elderberries that isn't too bad if you drink it when it's hot."

"Anything hot will be most welcome, *senora.*"

"I'll help you," Margaret Kent said, rising and following her mother into the kitchen, which was adjacent to the main room of the cabin.

For some moments, an uneasy silence prevailed, then Major Richardson, a tall, handsome, blonde-haired young man in his late twenties with a neatly trimmed blonde mustache, gave Carlos a challenging look.

"I understand, sir, you run the big cattle ranch owned by the Oregon Steam Navigation Company, which they recently stocked with a thousand head of scrub Mexican cattle."

"Begging your pardon, Major Richardson," Carlos answered politely, "but the statements you have made are not quite accurate."

"Oh? How so?"

"The land and the cattle are owned by my brother-in-law, Emil Warren, and myself in an equal partnership. As for their being scrubs, it is the nature of Mexican cattle to be lean and muscular. But when bred to our Durham bulls, they will become ideal stock for this part of the country, I can assure you."

"But O.S.N. Company money is backing the ranch?"

"No, *senor*. My brother-in-law, who lives in Portland, is an attorney for the Company. But the money being risked by him, as well as the work by me, are strictly our own."

Returning from the kitchen with three steaming mugs of the chicory-elderberry coffee substitute, Mrs. Kent and her daughter served Carlos, Ramon, and Pancho. She had been right in saying that if drunk hot enough it did taste something like coffee, Carlos agreed. After drinking half a cup, he set his mug down on the floor, picked up the used flour sack in which he had placed the presents he had brought along, them took them out one by one.

"I must apologize for the poor quality of the wrapping," he said as he rose and gave the first present to Mrs. Kent, "but all I had were pages of a used newspaper."

Accepting her package with a smile, Mrs. Kent said, "Thank you so much." She looked down at the wrapped present, whose surface showed a faded pattern of red roses and was tied with a pale pink ribbon. She frowned. "Newspaper, you say? This looks like wallpaper."

"It is, *senora*. According to the publisher of the *Walla Walla Statesman*, he ran out of newsprint stock a few weeks ago because no boats have come up the Columbia since the river has frozen over. He had to use the only paper he could get—wallpaper—printing it on only one side."

"How clever of him! And how thoughtful of you, Mr. Ibanez. After we open our presents Christmas day, we can catch up on the local news."

Giving a wallpaper-wrapped package of equal size to Margaret Kent, a somewhat smaller one to Susan, and a much smaller one to Luke, Carlos accepted their thanks with a smile and a murmured, *"De nada,"* which he quickly translated into English as, "It is nothing."

Truth was, the lovely black lace mantilla he had given Mrs. Kent, the bright yellow silk reboza he had given Margaret, the cupid-like muchacha doll he had given Susan, and the many-bladed pocket knife he had given Luke, were priceless imports from Spain which had been in his family for years. But Spain, Mexico, and California were distant lands now, so if these presents to a neighbor's family would create a bit of good will, giving them was well worth the time and effort. Turning to Matthew Kent, he said, "It is a custom in California, Senor Kent, to invite one's neighbors to a fiesta during the Christmas season. Because of the weather, you do not wish to travel, I know. So I brought you the quarter of the beef I would be serving you at the dinner in my home. May I leave it with you?"

"We're not starving, Mr. Ibanez—"

"Matthew!" Mrs. Kent exclaimed. "He's only being neighborly."

"Yeah, I suppose he is," Kent said grudgingly. "Thank you, Mr. Ibanez. We'll accept it."

Ever since the military post of Fort Walla Walla had been built and garrisoned in 1856, daily logs of highs and lows in temperature, direction and intensity of the wind, and the amount of rain or snow falling each day had been recorded. With little else to do on these bitterly cold winter days, Major Howard Richardson, who had been transferred here from New England only eighteen months ago, spent a couple of hours one mid-January afternoon thumbing through the notebook in which the weather log was maintained, searching for a hopeful clue as to when winter would end. Coming into the dayroom, Sergeant Liam O'Flaherty, who had been stationed here since day one, asked cheerfully, "Anything I can help ye with, sir?"

"There certainly is, Sergeant. How much longer is this damned winter going to last?"

"Well, sir, 'tis most unusual for it to stay so cold for so long in the Walla Walla Valley, which has been called the 'banana belt' of the Pacific Northwest because of the mildness of its climate."

"You call this mild?"

"No sir, I don't. What it is, sir, is the exception that proves the rule. Five winters out of six, the grass starts turnin' green on the lower flats and wildflowers start bloomin' on the south banks of the creeks in the foothills in early February. By the middle of March, ye can usually see grasshoppers jumpin' all over the valley."

"You don't expect me to believe that, Sergeant O'Flaherty."

" 'Tis God's truth, Major. Faith, an' I've seen it happen meself. All we need is for one good Chinook wind to blow."

"What in the devil is a Chinook wind?"

"Why, sir, it's a freak change of weather, when a hot wind from the southeast comes pourin' down from the heights of the Blue Mountains and sends the temperature soarin' from zero or below up into the fifties or sixties in a matter of minutes. The name comes, I'm told, from an Indian legend relatin' how Chinook Indian gods of the North, East, South, and West fought a war—"

"Now I know you're pulling my leg, Sergeant. There's no part of the country where the weather changes that fast."

"Here it does, sir. I'll take oath to that." Sergeant O'Flaherty gave him a sly, sidelong look. "In fact, sir, if the Major would care to make a small wager—"

"You bet I would! Say a keg of Dutch beer out of my pay against a quart of Irish whiskey out of yours, to be paid and drunk on the day when the temperature rises fifty degrees in the space of twenty-four hours. Fair enough?"

"We should set a deadline, sir, as to when the Chinook will or will not come."

"All right. Let's make it George Washington's birthday. If it hasn't happened by then, you pay off. If it has, I pay."

"Very well, sir, February 22nd it will be. I'll note the day in the weather log. Meanwhile, I'll be havin' a talk with the post chaplin, Father Paddy Ryan, who has a taste for both Dutch beer and Irish whiskey ..."

By the end of January, with the bitter cold hanging on and deep drifts of snow still covering the ground, the winter kill of livestock in the Walla Walla Valley had reached disastrous proportions. The supply of hay bought and stored by Emil and Carlos was so diminished that it now was being used only to keep the six Durham bulls and the horses needed to work the ranch alive in the shelter of the barn. Out on the range, the extent of the animal losses was as yet unknown.

Making the weekly trip into Walla Walla for supplies one morning in early February with Ramon Gutierrez and Pancho Onate, Carlos treated them and himself to a substantial noontime dinner at the town's best hotel, the Dacres, afterwards lingering at the table for half an hour to indulge in the luxury of expensive Brazilian coffee and Cuban cigars. In the well-appointed dining room, some eyebrows were raised when, after removing their tall Mexican hats and heavy sheepskin coats, the three men were revealed to be wearing cowboy garb. Most of the other diners were dressed in formal black broadcloth suits. This did not bother Carlos in the least. As long as a customer paid the exorbitant prices being charged here with the gold Mexican pesos used as hard currency all over the West—which he did—no discrimination because of dress, race, or skin color was apt to occur.

As Carlos and his two *companeros* finished their coffee, put out their cigars, and rose to go, Major Howard Richardson and Matthew Kent came into the dining room. After being seated by its manager at a table on the far side of the room, both men nodded stiffly to Carlos, though neither of them crossed the room to speak. This did not particularly offend Carlos, for the dining room was crowded and no place for small talk. For that matter, Kent owed him no special courtesy, for, despite the subzero cold and deep drifts of snow, he had stopped by the ranch house a week after Christmas, staying just long enough to accept a cup of real coffee and to thank Carlos for the quarter of beef. He also had given Carlos brief thank-you notes from his wife, two daughters, and son for the Christmas gifts he had brought them ten days ago. That Matthew Kent now was at least being polite, if not overly friendly, was all that Carlos could expect under the circumstances.

Before walking the two blocks to the livery stable at the west end of Main Street, where they had left the runner-equipped wagon bed, the team of horses, and their saddle mounts, Carlos said, *"Una copita, compadres?"*

"*Como no?*" Ramon grunted. "It will be a long, cold drive home."

"*Dos o tres copitas,*" Pancho chuckled. "With two or three drinks in my belly, *los vaqueros* who did not come to town will know from my breath how much I enjoyed the trip."

"For such an insult, they should strip you naked and throw you out in the snow," Ramon growled. "I will suggest it, then help them."

"I have not forgotten the *vaqueros,*" Carlos said. "I am taking home a box of cigars for them. In the Blue Mountain Saloon, after we have our drinks, I will buy them a gallon of whiskey."

"*Ah Chihuahua!*" Ramon exclaimed. "There will be singing in the bunkhouse tonight!"

Even this early in the afternoon, the barroom of the Blue Mountain Saloon was crowded, smoky, and noisy. Sitting on a raised platform in one corner of the room, the piano player seemed to feel it his duty to drown out even the loudest of conversations, while the people who were talking regarded it as their task to overwhelm whatever noise the piano player was providing as music. Unlike the dining room of the Dacres Hotel, there was no pretense of a formal dress code here. Standing with their booted feet on the brass rail of the long bar were half a dozen blue-uniformed soldiers from the nearby fort, an equal number of shaggy, unwashed civilians, and, at tables set as closely together as possible around the room, groups of men talking, drinking, and playing cards.

In a small cleared space on the sawdust-covered floor, two husky blonde hurdy-gurdy girls were doing their best to give their booted, bearded partners their money's worth for the three-minute dance, the glass of strong whiskey for the customers themselves, and a much milder libation purchased for the girls, at three dollars a round. Finding a vacant table between the dance floor and the bar, Carlos and the two *vaqueros* took off their heavy sheepskin coats, which they draped over the backs of chairs, and then sat down. One of the three burly, red-faced bartenders working the room came to their table and asked,

"What'll it be, gents?"

"Three whiskeys to drink here, please," Carlos said. "Then a gallon jug to take with us when we leave."

"You want ordinary bar whiskey or prime stuff?"

"Bring us your best. My men have earned it."

Returning to the table carrying a tray with three small glasses of whiskey on it in one hand, and, in the other, a gallon jug of Valley

Tan, an excellent Mormon-brewed whiskey distilled in Salt Lake City, the bartender set down the glasses and the jug.

"That'll be twenty bucks, mister. In gold."

Because of the shortage of American gold or silver coins in the West, the big Spanish peso, which contained half an ounce of gold, was universally accepted at five to eight dollars a coin. Stacking four of them on the table without taking his hand off them, Carlos smiled questioningly up at the bartender as he clinked them together.

"If we have one more round of drinks before we go, will this be enough?"

Pursing his lips and scowling as he did a bit of mental arithmetic, the bartender reached a favorable conclusion, nodded, and said, "Yeah. That'll be just right."

Carlos removed his hand and let the bartender pick up the heavy coins. As he returned to his post behind the bar, the fat bartender clinked the pesos together, as Carlos had done, showed them to the other bartenders, and chuckled good-humoredly.

"Got to give them Spaniards credit, boys. They sure mint good coins. Likely these are worth eight or ten dollars apiece—which means I got thirty to forty bucks for a twenty-dollar tab."

A shaggy, bearded, unkempt civilian standing at the bar between two blue-uniformed enlisted men blinked bleary eyed at the pleased bartender, then grunted, "You mean t' say that dirty greaser gave you all that money fer his whiskey? Where d'ya reckon he stole it?"

Casting a quick sidelong glance at Carlos, in hopes that he had not heard the remark, the bartender said uneasily, "He's a local rancher. He came by it honestly enough."

"The hell you say!" the man muttered. Turning his head to stare directly at Carlos and the two *vaqueros*, he sneered, "What've ya got to say fer yerself, greaser? Where did ya steal it?"

Carlos gave no sign that he heard. Though neither he, Ramon, or Pancho wore a gun, each man did have a slim, sharp, well-balanced knife sheathed in a leather scabbard close-fitted to the hip. The shaggy civilian was wearing a holstered .36-caliber cap-and-ball Navy Colt, while the two soldiers were armed with regular Army issue, .44-caliber, paper cartridge, Dragoon revolvers. Facing the table at which Carlos and the *vaqueros* were sitting, the civilian and the two soldiers seemed to relish the fact that the piano playing and the talking had stopped; the attention of every

person in the room now was focused on them. One of the soldiers laughed harshly.

"Reckon the bastard is stone-deaf, Jake."

"Or scared spitless," jeered the other soldier. "Wonder where he picked up them two Injuns he's got sittin' with him?"

"In this part of the country you may call 'em Injuns, Pete," the civilian addressed as Jake replied contemptuously. "But back in Missouri where I was raised, we called anybody that dark 'niggers.' Likely that's what they are. So what we got here is a no-good Mexican greaser and a pair of uppity niggers sittin' at a table in a white man's saloon, pretendin' they're just as good as we are."

"Hey, gents, don't start no trouble," the fat bartender pleaded. "They got a right to be here—"

"Shut your goddamn mouth before I blow your head off!" the civilian called Jake roared, snatching his revolver out of its holster and slamming its butt down on the bar. "We're gonna have us a little fun!"

Exchanging glances with Ramon and Pancho, Carlos murmured softly, *"Toman cuidado, compadres.* Take care."

Carefully removing his tall Mexican hat, he placed it on the floor beside his chair. Reading his warning to get their headgear out of harm's way before the action began—which was a barroom brawl custom in California—Ramon and Pancho did the same. Carlos raised his empty glass and motioned to the fat bartender. "We will have our second drink now, senor. Then we will go."

"Hey, ain't you the purty one!" Jake declared. "Why, you're almost as purty as a girl. If I pucker real nice, will you give me a juicy kiss, greaser?"

Looking directly at him for the first time, Carlos smiled and said coldly, "No. You are far too ugly. Also, you smell bad."

"Well, you can talk, can't you? Can you dance?"

Realizing that trouble was not to be avoided, Carlos got to his feet. On the other side of the table, Ramon and Pancho did the same. Pointing the barrel of his Navy Colt at a spot on the sawdust-covered floor, Jake thumbed back the hammer, then pulled the trigger.

"Dance, greaser! Dance!"

Somewhat befuddled by drink and slow in pulling the long-barreled Dragoon revolvers out of their holsters because they first had to unsnap the protective flaps, the two soldiers who tried to emulate their civilian friend barely had drawn their weapons before Ramon and Pancho were on them with flashing knives. A split second later, Carlos leaped forward and seized Jake's right wrist, turning the barrel of his revolver upward so that its second shot blasted toward the ceiling. Then the point of the sharp knife in Carlos' hand drove deep into the shoulder muscles of the man's left side.

Before anyone in the room was aware of what had happened, the two soldiers and the civilian lay prone on the sawdust-covered floor, bleeding profusely. Picking up the revolvers which they had dropped, Ramon, Pancho, and Carlos put their backs to the bar, then stood facing the men in the crowded room, each with a knife in his right hand, a revolver in his left. Over his shoulder, Carlos spoke to the fat bartender.

"We did not seek trouble, senor. Will you bear witness to that?"

"Yeah. All you done was defend yourself."

"We will put the revolvers we took from these men on the bar. If you wish to send for a doctor to treat their wounds, we will not interfere. If you want to call a law officer who will question us about what we did, we will talk to him and explain our actions. But we will not let him arrest us and take us to jail."

"Sounds fair enough to me."

"Hey, are you people going to let this fancy-talkin' greaser get away with slicin' up three white men right in front of your eyes?" demanded a trooper who had been standing at the bar but had taken no part in the fracas. "Ain't you going to insist he answer to the law for what him and his nigger cowboys done?"

"Back off, soldier!" cried a man on the far side of the room. "We saw what happened clear enough. Jake and his drunken friends got exactly what they deserved."

"That's what you say! What I say is we oughta get a rope and hang 'em to the nearest tree! If you townspeople are too gutless to do it, I'll go out to the fort, by God, and round up a bunch of my buddies. They'll see justice done—"

In the midst of the trooper's tirade, the saloon doors opened and closed, letting in a blast of frigid air, as well as the figures of Major Howard Richardson and Matthew Kent. Dead silence blanketed the room. Stepping forward, Major Richardson snapped, "As you were, soldier! Now—will somebody please tell me what the hell happened here?

17.

$\mathcal{W}$HILE THE FAT BARTENDER and a number of eyewitnesses told Major Richardson and Matthew Kent how the attack on Carlos and the *vaqueros* had begun and ended, Dr. Walter Lyman, who happened to be playing cards in the saloon and was an expert at patching up men wounded in barroom brawls, took a look at the civilian, Jake Pitzer, and the two soldiers, Privates Wendall Manning and Allen Clayton.

"They're gonna need some stitches," he said upon completing his examination. "Otherwise, they ain't damaged much. Fetch me a basin of hot water and some soap. As much booze as they've got in 'em, they ain't gonna need nothin' to deaden the pain."

Intending to cripple rather than kill, Ramon and Pancho had thrust their knives into the upper right arms of the two soldiers, while Carlos had inserted his with the expertise of a skilled *matador* into the left shoulder muscles of the Border ruffian who had tried to make him dance. Putting on a fur cap, gloves, and overcoat, the fat bartender responded to Matthew Kent's request that a law officer be summoned, returning presently with both City Marshal Brett Donegal and County Sheriff Tim Kimbrough. To anyone interested, he explained: " 'Cause it happened inside the city limits, the crime is in Marshal Donegal's jurisdiction, he says. But with Fort Walla Walla being located outside of town, he figured the County would be interested, too. So we stopped by and picked up Sheriff Kimbrough."

"Give 'em both a drink on me!" grunted an amiable, bewhiskered prospector. "It's good to know the law is on the job!"

"The soldiers are under my jurisdiction," Major Richardson said curtly. "I'm putting them under arrest. They'll stay in the post brig until their punishment is determined. If the city or county want to bring charges, the Army will cooperate."

"Our local Law and Order Committee has had its eye on Jake Pitzer and several of his friends for some time," Matthew Kent said

grimly. "If the city or county will hold him in jail until he's well
enough to travel, the Committee will have a talk with him. We may be
able to save the expense of a trial."

"We don't want no more hangings, Mr. Kent," Sheriff Kimbrough
said uneasily.

"I said 'travel,' not 'hanging,' Sheriff," Kent interrupted. "The
Committee will suggest to Jake Pitzer and his friends that a change of
air and climate might be good for their health."

After warding off the chills caused by their walk in the frigid air by
downing drinks bought by the friendly prospector, Marshal Donegal
and Sheriff Kimbrough took out notebooks and wrote down accounts
of what had happened, the names of a dozen eyewitnesses, and the
identities of the men involved. Because this was tedious work, both
law officers welcomed the fat bartender's suggestion that they have another drink "on the house."

"Appears to me what we got here, Marshal," Sheriff Kimbrough
said as he studied his notebook, "is a clear case of self-defense. Do you
agree?"

"Absolutely, Sheriff. That's just what it is."

"We'll hold the man who started the fracas in jail till there's a hearing. D'ya suppose we could let Mr. Ibanez and his men go free if they
promise to show up for the hearing?"

"Might be better if a substantial local citizen gave *his* word as bond
for them."

"I'll be glad to do that," Matthew Kent said quickly. "Under the
circumstances, I'm sure Mr. Ibanez is going to be staying around for
quite a while."

"Thank you, Senor Kent," Carlos said quietly. "You are a good
neighbor."

Matthew Kent smiled, then replied in such a low tone of voice that
only Carlos heard him.

"*De nada*," Kent said.

On the night before President George Washington's birthday, Major
Howard Richardson was so bored and disgusted with the subzero cold
and the deep drifts of snow that still held the Walla Walla Valley in its
paralyzing grip that he downed several more drinks of Irish whiskey

before, during, and after dinner than he usually did. By 9:00 P.M., he broke up a poker game with four fellow officers when he cursed the local climate and the cruel turn of fate that had given him a tour of duty here in this frigid post instead of fighting a civilized war in a balmy southern clime. Staggering to his quarters, he stripped off his clothes down to his long underwear and fell into bed. An hour later, he was wakened by a thunderous pounding on the door.

"Major Richardson, sir! Wake up! By all the Holy Saints, it's happened!"

Since Sergeant Liam O'Flaherty was too seasoned a soldier to commit the cardinal sin of waking up his commanding officer with any emergency short of a riot by the troops or a raging fire, Major Richardson's first groggy reaction upon awakening was: "Good! Riot or fire, now I can close down the goddamn post and go back to civilization!"

Swinging his bare feet to the floor and staggering to the bedroom door, he opened it and demanded, "What's happened, Sergeant?"

"The Chinook, sir! It's come!"

"*The what?*"

"The Chinook wind, Major! The warm wind! It's here!"

"You woke me up to give me a weather report? Sergeant, I'll have your balls—!"

"But we've got a bet, sir! You've lost! Come outside and listen!"

If he had not still been half asleep, Major Richardson would have donned a greatcoat and put on his slippers before going outside, for he knew from experience how quickly a person could get frostbitten by stepping out into below-zero cold. Groggily, he followed Sergeant O'Flaherty out the front door, barefoot and clad only in his long underwear. Once there, a strong wind from the southeast struck him directly in the face, taking his breath away.

"A Chinook wind, you say? It's a hot wind, Sergeant!"

"So it is, sir. The post thermometer reads fifty-eight degrees."

"Good Lord! It read ten below zero at suppertime."

"I know. That's a sixty-eight-degree rise in four hours, sir. It's now ten o'clock the night of February 21st, leavin' still two hours to go before George Washington's birthday. Our bet was—"

"Oh, shut up, Sergeant! I know what our bet was. I concede. Tomorrow, we'll celebrate George's birthday by throwing the damndest party you ever saw. Beer for the men, Irish whiskey for me. Tell the post sutler to put it on my tab."

An hour earlier, Carlos Ibanez had been wakened by Ramon Gutierrez, who had the innate weather sense of a wolf when it came to pre-
dicting impending changes in the humidity, wind direction, or
temperature.

"*Patron!* Wake up! You will not believe what is happening!"

Opening his eyes and sitting up in his bunk, Carlos asked, "*Que
pasa?*"

"The warm wind has come, *patron!* Listen!"

Before coming in from the barn just before dusk after making sure
that the horses and the Durham bulls had been fed a few mouthfuls of
hay, Carlos had stood for a moment outside the bunkhouse, studying
the sky. It had stopped snowing during the afternoon; save for a low,
gold-tinted cloudbank in the west, the sky was clear now. The wind,
gradually dying during the latter part of the day, was completely still,
and the hush brought him an odd feeling of expectancy.

The 21st of February. Spring in California, he mused, but you had
only to look at the deep drifts beside the barn to realize that in this
land spring was far away. Pancho Onate came along the path from the
woodshed carrying an armload of logs. Carlos held the door open for
him.

"Not quite so cold this evening," Pancho said.

"Cold enough," Carlos answered, and followed him inside.

After supper he sat up for a while reading a week-old paper he had
perused so many times before that he had memorized all its news. A
restlessness made him throw the paper aside. The bunkhouse seemed
suddenly a prison and the long months of cold and snow a remorse-
less jailer. The knowledge that day by day his cattle were dying and
there was nothing he could do to save them brought him the torment
an active man feels when there is no tangible thing he can fight.

Damn the snow!

He lay long awake after the lamps were extinguished, his thoughts
chasing one another in fruitless circles. Then, a little before nine
o'clock, he fell into a fitful sleep, from which Ramon had just wakened
him. Throwing back the blankets, he sat up, answering crossly, "What's
the matter?"

"Listen!"

He heard it then. A low moaning in the air. A wind rising and falling, like the sighing of a sad, lost ghost. Something hissed in the fireplace as water splattered the coals and from the eaves outside he heard a steady dripping. He got to his feet and went to the door, threw it open, and stared out into the night. Wind struck his face, a vigorous, warm, southeasterly wind, and the air held the damp feel of melting snow. Faintly from down the slope he heard the rising murmur of the creek, a sound long stilled by winter. The long-awaited Chinook had come.

After a while he closed the door and went back to bed. From across the bunkhouse, Ramon said happily, "Winter is done for now, *patron*. Soon we will be out on the range again."

"I hope so," Carlos murmured, and fell into a deep, peaceful sleep.

All the next day and the following night the Chinook wind blew, accompanied by a warm, melting rain. When it was done, winter's grip on the land had been broken. Drifts had dwindled into gray, sodden masses of snow from which water ran in rivulets. Every coulee, every draw became a stream, and below the bunkhouse the creek turned into a roaring torrent that spread a hundred yards over the bottom land.

Riding with Ramon, Pancho, and the *vaqueros*, Carlos spent long hours in the saddle rounding up the scattered cattle. It took ten days to tally them all. By then, the ice floes had broken up on the Columbia River between Celilo Falls and Wallula Landing. Taking the first boat to navigate the upper river, Emil Warren came to Walla Walla, rented a saddle horse, and rode out to the ranch to receive the bad news.

"We have four hundred head left of the thousand we took into the winter, brother," Carlos said somberly. "Most of them are walking skeletons."

"What about the Durham bulls?"

"They are all in good shape, for we kept them in the barn and fed them hay."

Emil shook his head. "We've taken a beating, Carlos. Well, we're not the only ones. A lot of ranchers in the valley were completely wiped out."

"I know."

"It'll be two or three weeks until the ice goes out on the Snake so that boats can get upriver to Lewiston. People in the mining country are starving for meat. Even the poorest kind of beef cattle are selling for a dollar a pound on the hoof. If we could drive our four hundred head to the Idaho market, we could make a killing."

"They are very thin, brother. They will have to wait for the grass."

"How long?"

"A month, at least. Six weeks would be better."

"Hell, by then the river will be open and beef will be coming up from Portland. We won't be able to get half what we'll get now. Make it a week."

"That is too soon. Perhaps in two weeks, if we drive them very slow and let them graze as they travel, we could take a small herd of steers to Lewiston."

"No, let's take the whole lot. Let's make a killing while we can."

"That would be foolish, brother. Some of the cattle that survived are bred cows, which will be calving soon. Also, several of my neighbors like Matthew Kent have offered to buy a few steers for beef, as well as bred cows with which to rebuild the herds they lost."

"Will they pay a dollar a pound on the hoof—in gold?"

"They are my neighbors, brother. We have not discussed price or terms."

"Let's not get softhearted about this neighbor thing, Carlos," Emil said curtly. "We need money to recoup our losses. Let's get all the cattle we can to Lewiston as soon as we can and sell them for the best price we can get. After all, that's the American way."

Reluctantly Carlos agreed to start at least a small trail herd to Lewiston in two weeks. "I will put Ramon in charge and send along half a dozen *vaqueros*," he said, "while Pancho and I and the rest of the men stay here and take care of the ranch."

"Good enough," Emil said, nodding. "I've got to go down to Portland tomorrow and tend to some business there. But I'll be back in time to go on the drive with Ramon and the trail herd. Much as I dislike playing cowboy, I want to be in Lewiston to make sure we get top dollar for the cattle."

"That I can understand, brother."

"By then, I hope you'll decide to drive every animal that can walk to the market place. The way I see it, we'd better accumulate all the cash we can now while beef prices are high. Later, we can restock the ranch with cattle driven across the mountains from the Willamette Valley or California."

After Emil had gone, Carlos went thoughtfully about his work, thinking not about the promised drive to Lewiston but about his neighbors. Few of them had any money. Most were short on food and could not pay the prices the merchants in town were demanding—and getting—from the wealthy miners who had wintered in Walla Walla. Most of them had been in the valley only a short while and were just beginning to build up their herds to the point where they would pay off. Now they were right back where they had started, all their work, all their bitter struggle to carve out a home for their families in this new land gone for naught. It was a heartbreaking blow.

That evening, he rode over to see his nearest neighbor, Matthew Kent ...

The evening before the herd was to start for Lewiston two weeks later, Emil Warren sent word out from town that he would be staying at the Dacres Hotel that night, then would ride out to the ranch in time to take part in the drive. Next morning when he joined Carlos, Ramon, and the crew of drovers on the flat where the cattle were being held, he cast a quick glance at the animals being held, then turned and scowled at Carlos.

"Where are the rest?"

"I sold them."

"To who?"

"Matthew Kent and a few of my neighbors."

"What did you get for them?"

"Enough."

"I'll bet they gave you nothing but promises—"

"I'm satisfied."

"Well, I'm not! You had no right to sneak around behind my back and sell me out—"

"Half the cattle were mine," Carlos cut in, a coldness coming into his voice. "That is what I sold them. The rest are yours. There they are, *hermano*, two hundred of them. Do what you want with them, then keep all the money. But do not accuse me of selling you out."

"For God's sake, Carlos, all I'm trying to do is teach you a little business sense!"

"I appreciate that, Emil. But these people are my neighbors and friends. I had a chance to help them and I did." Smiling gently, he added softly, "After all, brother, this too is the American way."

18.

$\mathcal{M}$ UCH TO THE DELIGHT of Lars Warren, his father and mother let him apply for the position of cabin boy aboard the *Colonel Wright*, which was slated to be the premiere stern-wheeler on the run from Celilo Landing to Lewiston. Since he was the only twelve-year-old boy who could say that he had swum every rapid in that portion of the Snake, he got the job with no contest and was put on the payroll of the Oregon Steam Navigation Company at the respectable salary of twenty dollars a month.

Because the boats of the O.S.N. Company these days all had full passenger and freight lists on every upriver trip, while downriver they carried hundreds of thousands of dollars worth of newly mined Idaho gold, the Company certainly was able to pay good wages to its help. Between Celilo Falls and the mouth of the Snake River, three sets of rapids—Deschutes, John Day, and Umatilla—required a skilled pilot at the helm. Even more dangerous was the 140-mile sector of river between the mouth of the Snake and Lewiston, for melting snows in the mountains to the east, the breakup of ice floes in the river, and the dislodgement of log jams and landslides along flood-swollen tributaries could change the character of the river overnight.

In recognition of this fact, the O.S.N. Company had reluctantly acceded to the demand of Captain Leonard White that he be paid the outrageous salary of five hundred dollars a month. To the limp management complaint that on no other American river—not even the mighty Mississippi—was a steamboat captain being paid that kind of wage, Captain White laughed and replied, "On no other river, gentlemen, does a steamboat carry half a million dollars in gold bullion each trip. Let a greenhorn pilot wreck one of your boats carrying that kind of cargo and the O.S.N. Company would be out of business overnight."

Since the rule: *Charge what the traffic will bear* was part and parcel of unstated O.S.N. policy, management yielded to Captain White's demand for the time being, then initiated long-range plans to make sure that the elevated wage scale did not infect the entire system. Aboard the *Colonel Wright* on her first trip upriver following the spring breakup in late March 1862, was short, stocky, black-haired-and-mustached First Mate Thomas J. Stump, an experienced riverman on the Sacramento in California who had recently gone to work for the O.S.N. Company. No secret was made of the fact that after three or four trips between Celilo and Lewiston aboard the *Colonel Wright*, Tom Stump would be perfectly capable of taking command of this—or any other O.S.N. Company boat—as captain for the more reasonable salary of $350 a month.

Also aboard as Second Mate was William Polk Gray, a well-qualified Snake River rapid swimmer. Though only seventeen years old now, he was bound to be captain material in the not too distant future.

So proud of his new uniform and job that he could barely contain his elation, Lars Warren was pleased that his boyhood friend, Willie Polk, was aboard, for it gave him a chance to ask questions that he would not have dared bother Captain White or First Mate Stump with because they might judge him naive. For example, when the *Colonel Wright* reached Wallula Landing in midafternoon, where its scheduled two-hour stop for unloading was extended to an overnight stay, a number of impatient Lewiston-bound passengers, who found Lars to be the most readily accessible crew member available, demanded to know the reason for the delay. Feeling he could not run up to the pilot house and question the Captain or the First Mate, Lars asked Willie Polk what the problem was. After his friend explained it to him, Lars then was in a position to pass on the answer to the passengers as if he had received it directly from the Captain himself.

"Lot of ice floes coming downriver," he said. "We've got to pull into a sheltered bay till they pass."

"Ice floes, you say? What're a few chunks of ice in a river as wide as the Columbia?" one passenger remarked.

"It's not the Columbia we're worried about, sir. It's the Snake."

"How far away is that?" another man asked.

"Eleven miles upstream."

"Why is Snake River ice worse than any other?" the first passenger asked Lars.

"Yeah, boy," added another. "If the ice floes are in the Snake, why are we waiting here?"

Because Willie Polk had explained the problem in detail to Lars—after having it explained to him by Captain White—Lars was only too glad to pass on the explanation as if it were drawn from his own personal fount of knowledge.

"Well, you see, gentlemen, what happens is …"

During the rest of that afternoon and evening, passengers all over the boat were sharing the new river knowledge they had recently acquired from the cabin boy, who, despite his youth, they had found to be "bright as a button" when it came to knowing the vagaries of navigation on the inland rivers.

"A mighty mean river, the Snake is, from what the cabin boy says."

"Lot of rattlers along its banks. Fact, that's how it got its name."

"The Nez Perces call it *Ki-moo-e-nim*, the cabin boy says. That's Injun for 'Snake.'"

"Worst winter this part of the country has ever seen, accordin' to the cabin boy. Them upriver canyons along the Clearwater and the Snake are so steep, he says, that when the snowdrifts melt and slide down into the river, they build up a wall of ice that can rip the bottom clean off a riverboat. That's why Captain White holes up in some sheltered bay till the ice floes pass."

Having heard that the *Colonel Wright* was due, a squad of soldiers from Fort Walla Walla eager to pick up the post's mail began to appear, as did half a dozen merchants looking for fast freight ordered from Portland and a number of bachelors who had heard a rumor that a bevy of unattached young ladies was aboard. When they learned that the boat would be tied up overnight at Wallula Landing, they besieged Captain Leonard White for permission to throw a party. Among the leaders of the bachelor group and acting as spokesman for them was a man whom Lars Warren admitted to Second Mate William Polk Gray was a shirttail relative of his, Carlos Ibanez.

"That slick-talking Spaniard is a 'sort of uncle' of yours, you say?" Willie Gray demanded. "You'd better explain that one to me, Lars."

"You know my dad's brother, Emil Warren, don't you?"

"Sure. He's head lawyer for the O.S.N."

"He's my *real* uncle. He married a Spanish woman from California named Dolores Ibanez. Carlos Ibanez is her younger brother, so that makes him a 'sort of uncle' to me."

"Well, whatever relation he is to you," Willie Gray said as he and Lars watched Carlos and Captain White chatting together in the pilot house like old friends, "he seems to have talked Captain White into opening up the main saloon for a party. There'll be hi-jinx aboard tonight."

Because Willie Gray was five years older than Lars and much more knowledgeable about the ways of the world, Lars listened with rapt attention as Willie told him the nature of the female passengers aboard the *Colonel Wright* this trip.

"One bunch is hurdy-gurdy girls," he said. "The other is hoors."

A hurdy-gurdy girl, Lars knew, was a young lady who worked in a saloon and would dance with any man who would buy a drink for himself and for her, then pay her a fee of a dollar or so a dance, most of which went to the proprietor of the establishment. Though he had a vague suspicion of what Willie meant by "hoor," he risked his friend's disdain for his ignorance by asking,

"Is 'hoor' the same thing as 'whore'?"

"However you pronounce it, Lars," Willie answered primly, "it means a bad woman who takes money for doing what a good woman refuses to do until after she gets married. Least, that's what Pa tells me. I've never had anything to do with hoors or hurdy-gurdy girls myself. All I know about them is what I've heard rivermen say when they brag about what *they've* done."

Despite Wille's disavowal of firsthand personal experience, he seemed to have acquired a broad knowledge of the subject by listening closely to the accounts of men who had dallied with both classes of women. In charge of the six blue-eyed, flaxen-haired, well-scrubbed young German girls aboard the *Colonel Wright*, he told Lars, was a middle-aged couple named Hans and Marta Stohlhofen. They were headed for the gold boom town of Orofino, forty miles up the Clearwater River from Lewiston, where they planned to establish an eating house serving good German food, a saloon, and a dance hall. Traveling with them were their nineteen-year-old son, Fritz, who played the tuba, their seventeen-year-old son, Johann, who played the clarinet, and their fourteen-year-old son, Wolfgang, who played the accordion. In addition to providing a wide selection of danceable polkas, waltzes, marches, and drinking songs, the three young men would also serve as waiters, keeping the income from the entire enterprise within the family.

"What's really interesting," Willie said, "is the deal they've made with the six girls. Before their ship sailed from Germany, Hans

Stohlhofen told me, he and his wife made each girl sign a contract binding her to work for one year without letting a man touch her except on the dance floor. Each girl will be given her room, board, clothes, and everything else she needs, so long as she stays pure. When her year is up, she'll be given one thousand dollars in gold and released from her contract. If she wants to stay in the United States and get married, Hans and Marta Stohlhofen will help her find a good husband. If she wants to go back to Germany, they'll buy her a boat ticket home."

"Who gets the money she takes in?"

"They do. Hans Stohlhofen bragged to me that he expects every girl to earn at least five thousand dollars a year, so they'll make a nice piece of money on each one."

"I've heard that gold boom towns like Orofino have some pretty rough men living in them. What will happen if a drunk miner abuses one of the girls?"

Willie Gray laughed. "I asked Hans how he intended to keep order in his place. He's a big, husky man, as you can see. He reached into his hip pocket, pulled out a tool he uses to knock the bungs out of beer barrels, then he told me: '*Das ist mein* bung starter, Willie. Vhen a customer tries to get fresh vith vun of my girls, it vill become my bum stopper. One clunk on de noggin vith dis, und he suddenly vill remember to mind his manners.'"

Though the other group of young ladies, which numbered a dozen or so, was much prettier and better dressed than the six hurdy-gurdy girls, Willie said they were all "hoors," who would do whatever a man wanted them to do if he paid them enough money. In charge of the group was a slim, shapely, dark-haired woman who appeared to be in her early thirties. She was French, Willie said, having come to San Francisco soon after the Gold Rush began to work as a "hoor" in a high-class bordello. Because of her great beauty, she had become the favorite consort of the man who owned the establishment, a Frenchman named Francois deBeauchamp. Falling in love with her and wanting her all to himself, he had married her and made her a partner in the business. Unfortunately, a year after she gave birth to a lovely girl christened Daphne, Francois deBeauchamp had been killed in a gunfight over a card game, leaving her a well-to-do widow in charge of a thriving business.

"She's on the passenger list as Ma'm'selle Lili deBeauchamp,"

Willie said. "That's too much of a mouthful for most men. So they just call her French Lil."

"She looks too beautiful to be a whore. So do the ladies traveling with her."

"That's why they're such high-priced hoors, Lars. Unless a man has a lot of money, he can't even afford to go into her place and buy a drink and a cigar, let alone pay for going to bed with a hoor."

Feeling that the San Francisco area was beginning to decline, French Lil had sold her business there and was moving north and east into what she felt would be a more lucrative area as long as the gold boom lasted. Probably, she would relocate in Lewiston, where many prosperous miners wintered. In addition to the dozen or so working girls in her entourage, she had brought along several male and female employees who had worked in the San Francisco house as hairdressers, musicians, and bartenders. Acting as a bodyguard for her and the girls was monster of a man with the ominous name Goliath Samson.

"Anybody looks cross-eyed at French Lil or one of her girls," Willie said, "Goliath will break him in two with his bare hands, tear him up into little pieces, and toss him over the side to feed the fish."

Standing six feet, six inches tall, weighing close to three hundred pounds, and wearing a perpetual menacing frown on his dark, swarthy face, Goliath Samson grunted rather than spoke with what sounded like a thick Greek accent, had black, piercing eyes, and moved with a catlike grace despite his bulk. Whenever a male passenger crossed the deck to within half a dozen paces of French Lil or one of her girls, Goliath was there to let the man know that he was being watched closely and would pay dearly for any indiscretion of word or deed. The giant bodyguard was particularly protective, Lars noticed, of the lovely, ethereal, black-eyed girl Daphne deBeauchamp, French Lil's daughter.

She would be about ten years old, Lars guessed, with a bright, sparkling smile, a lilting laugh, and a mischievous tone to her musical voice. An hour after the *Colonel Wright* tied up at Wallula Landing, Lars encountered her unexpectedly when he went into the ladies' section of the small forward lounge, where two small tables, several comfortable chairs, and a rack of magazines and newspapers had been placed for the exclusive use of the fair sex. Nearly tripping over the broom he had brought in to sweep out the lounge, Lars blushed furiously as he backed away from the chair in which she was sitting.

"Pardon me, ma'am. I didn't mean to intrude."

"Oh, don't mind me!" the girl exclaimed, tossing her head and giving him a brilliant smile. "I was just looking for something to read."

"We don't have much of a selection, I'm afraid."

"Phoo! Who cares? Just being on a riverboat is more fun than reading anyhow." Tossing the magazine aside, she got to her feet, crossed to the cabin window, and gazed at the shoreline to the southwest. Over her shoulder, she said, "I suppose you know all the landmarks along the river?"

"Well, I have traveled on the river quite a bit."

She pointed at two pillars of basaltic rock looming upward against the skyline just beyond the gap where the Columbia River made its big bend to the west. "Do those tall rocks have a name?"

"Why, yes, they do," Lars said, crossing the cabin to stand at her side. "The Cayuse Indians call them 'The Sisters.'"

"Why?"

"It's one of their legends, I've been told. You see, their guiding spirit is *Speelyi*, which means "coyote" in their language. As I heard the story, two beautiful Indian maidens used to live where the rocks are now. Coyote liked them both but he couldn't decide which one he wanted to marry. So he changed them into rocks so that he could look at them and admire them until he made up his mind. Then he went off and forgot them—so there they still are."

"That was awfully mean of him, wasn't it?"

"I suppose it was. But he's always been a fickle lover, the Indians say."

She eyed him speculatively. "That's a very nice uniform you're wearing."

"Thank you."

"What's your job on the boat?"

"I'm a cabin boy."

"My name's Daphne. What's yours?"

"Lars."

"I'm ten. How old are you?"

"Twelve."

"Do you like working on a boat?"

"I think it's the greatest job in the world," Lars said earnestly. "But I don't intend to be a cabin boy very long. I want to work my way up to purser, second mate, first mate, then captain in command of a boat of my own."

"My, that does sound grand!" Daphne exclaimed, blinking her long dark lashes and looking properly awed. "Do you really think you can do it?"

"I don't know why not. All the men in my family have spent their lives on the river. My grandfather, Benjamin Warren, came out with the Astor party and became the first licensed bar pilot at the mouth of the Columbia River. My father, Thomas Warren, is a Senior Captain for the Oregon Steam Navigation Company on the Middle River. I started working on a keelboat when I was nine years old. Someday, I know I'll be a captain."

Why he told her this in such a sudden rush of words, Lars did not know, but as he talked she stood gazing up at him with such an enthralled look in her soft black eyes that he felt like he was relating the history of the world. Suddenly he became aware of the fact that a huge, ominous figure had filled the doorway. Turning, he saw Goliath Samson scowling down at him, his face bleakly accusing.

"He botherin' you, Miss Daphne?" the bodyguard grunted.

"Of course not! We're just talking."

"I had t' make sure, Miss Daphne. Got t' know you all right."

Hastily excusing himself, Lars turned away and began sweeping furiously, his face red as fire. *How dumb can you be?* he raged at himself. *Telling all that foolish stuff to a girl!*

But apparently Daphne did not think him dumb at all, for, as she moved past him to precede Goliath Samson out the cabin door, she touched his arm reassuringly and murmured, "Don't mind him, Lars. Later, we'll talk some more."

Impatient for Emil Warren's word regarding restocking the ranch, Carlos Ibanez had made the half-day ride to Wallula Landing in hopes of receiving a letter in the mail carried upriver aboard the *Colonel Wright*. He was not disappointed, for the letter was there, hand carried by Captain Leonard White and given to Carlos personally when he went up to the pilot house to pay his respects. Offered a drink and the privacy of the pilot house in which to read the letter, he did so. He was pleased to learn that the news from his partner was good.

"Made a killing in the Idaho market," Emil wrote, "so whatever kind of deal you made with your neighbors we've got plenty of capital to use restocking the ranch. Looks to me like our best bet would be to buy some breeder cows and feeder calves in the Willamette Valley rather than in California, so we won't have to make such a long drive. Suggest you bring a crew of drovers downriver in the next month or so, then we'll go on a buying trip up valley, figuring to put together a herd you can trail across the mountains later this spring.

"If you happen to go down to Wallula Landing to meet the *Colonel Wright*, say hello to the new cabin boy, Lars Warren, who will be aboard on his first river job. Like my father and brother, he's got the notion that the only life worth living is steaming up and down the Columbia River. But he's a good kid and proud as punch of his job, so tell him howdy for me."

Finishing the letter and the drink, Carlos smiled at Captain White. "How is my nephew Lars doing, Captain White?"

"Great! He's a fine boy."

"You have quite an interesting passenger list, I notice. More lovely young ladies bound upriver than this country has seen in many a year."

"Well, I will admit they're lovely," Captain White said wryly. "As to whether or not they're ladies, that's an open question."

"I know one who is, Captain. Ma'm'selle Lili deBeauchamp."

"Oh? How do you happen to know her?"

"She and my late father were good friends down in California. On occasions when he took me with him to San Francisco, we visited her establishment on the Barbary Coast. In my father's opinion, the drinks, cigars, music, and entertainment offered in her parlor were the finest in San Francisco."

"So I've heard."

"You plan to stay at Wallula Landing until the ice floes clear the Snake, I'm told."

"That's right."

"Winter in the Walla Walla Valley has been very long and very dull, Captain White. Since your boat will be laying over for a day or two and you have such an intriguing list of passengers aboard, it has been suggested to me by a number of lonely young bachelors that you might be persuaded to open the main saloon this evening for a party."

"I'm not in the entertainment business, Carlos."

"That I know. Still, you do have a bar and a dining room on the boat."

182   "Purely as a convenience for the paying passengers, my friend. As a matter of fact, when the O.S.N. Company first started running boats on the river, serving and selling alcohol was strictly forbidden. But we soon found out there was no way to stop passengers from bringing their own bottles aboard, so we decided we might as well put in a bar and make some money on their drinking."

"Exactly. So while your boat is tied up here, why not open up the dining room and the bar to gentlemen visitors from the Walla Walla Valley who have a great deal of money to spend?"

"If they really are gentlemen, Carlos, I would have no objection to that."

"I will guarantee their good behavior, Captain."

"But there's one thing I won't stand for."

"What is that?"

"I won't permit the hurdy-gurdy girls or French Lil's ladies to charge for their services. Can you make sure of that?"

"I certainly can. This will be a friendly party, Captain White, with only your bar and dining room to be paid for what they serve."

"In that case," Captain White said with a smile, "you have my permission to go ahead. Let the good times roll."

As Carlos had anticipated, neither Hans and Marta Stohlhofen nor Lili deBeauchamp objected to the proposed party or the rules under which it was to be conducted. Both realized that with two hundred male passengers aboard and fifty or so lonely young bachelors from the Walla Walla Valley visiting the *Colonel Wright*, this would be an excellent opportunity to demonstrate to the paying public the sort of entertainment their establishments in Orofino and Lewiston would provide.

Because Second Mate William Polk Gray and Cabin Boy Lars Warren had no other pressing duties to perform while the boat was tied up to the landing, Captain White ordered them to pitch in and help the purser, the bartender, the two dining saloon waiters, and the visiting musicians and entertainers to set up whatever was required to put on an evening of first-class entertainment. Despite his avowed knowledge of what went on in hurdy-gurdy halls and houses of entertainment, Willie admitted to Lars that never in his born days had he seen the likes of the skills this band of professionals possessed as they put together the ingredients for the evening's party.

While Lars and Willie moved and stacked tables and chairs in the main saloon out of the way in order to clear an area for dancing,

Goliath Samson took a couple of helpers below decks and supervised carrying a spinet piano, kerosene-fueled footlights, and sections of a portable stage up to the dining saloon. While these were being set up, groups of musicians, vocalists, vaudeville performers, monologists, and magicians began to rehearse in a cacophony of dissonant sounds, though after an hour or so it became clear that all the performers knew exactly what they were doing.

Still, Lars found it strange to see individuals such as the silver-haired piano player in French Lil's group slap on a bushy-haired wig, a bristling mustache, then stick an unlighted cigar in his mouth, squint pugnaciously at an imagined audience of Club Ladies, and announce in a gravelly voice: "Just to please you ladies, I'll be happy to demonstrate how the Fiji Island cannibals eat their meals, if one of you would kindly pass me a baby ..."

Though Lars could not help giggling at the outrageous remark, he had no idea of which famous West Coast comedian the piano player was mimicking until Willie told him.

"He's pretending to be Samuel Clemens, a Virginia City, Nevada, newspaper writer who's become quite a comedian," Willie said. "When he goes on tour, he calls himself Mark Twain."

By combining the tuba, clarinet, and accordion played by Fritz, Johann, and Wolfgang Stohlhofen with the spinet piano, violin, viola, cello, and drums of French Lil's people, an excellent orchestra took shape, though it took a while before its individual members reached common ground on a leader, a style, and a beat. Much to Lars' surprise, the huge bodyguard, Goliath Samson, demonstrated a marvelously gentle-fingered touch on the cello—which he could have lifted to his chin and played like a violin if he had chosen to do so—then further showed off his musical talents by doubling on the snare, kettle, and bass drums.

By the time the warm spring darkness fell and the music began, lanterns festooned with colored paper streamers had been hung around the rails of the tethered boat, with drinks and buffet-style food being served from tables set along the promenade deck walkways. Landing stages were extended to the shore from both the passenger and the cargo decks, allowing gentlemen and ladies who were unable to get onto the crowded dining saloon dance floor to go for moonlight strolls in the balmy night. Since the adjacent sandy beach was the site of the former Hudson's Bay Company trading post first called

Fort Nez Perces, then Fort Walla Walla, which had been abandoned and partially burned by the Indians during the 1856 war, romantically inclined young bachelors from the Walla Walla Valley had a good excuse to take their lady friends for strolls to "see the sights" in the shadows away from the boat. Whatever "sights" the gentlemen pointed out to their ladies, of course, were nobody's business but their own.

Meanwhile in the dining saloon of the *Colonel Wright*, music such as had never been heard before at this location on the river was making the night merry for the enthralled dancers. Polkas, waltzes, schottisches, hoedowns, square dances—whatever the crowd demanded, the orchestra played. In order to give the musicians and the young ladies a rest now and then, a magic act, a comedy monologue, a few numbers by a male quartet, or a popular song of the day sung by one of French Lil's girls, who had a really fine contralto voice, gave a change of pace to the evening.

Standing on the outskirts of the crowd where they could serve customers milling along the promenade deck, Lars and Willie made themselves useful and watched the dancing couples with unabashed awe. Willie shook his head in amazement as his gaze followed the slim, lithe, handsome figure of Carlos Ibanez as the smiling young rancher twirled a golden-haired hurdy-gurdy girl through the bouncing, exuberant steps of a polka.

"Your Uncle Carlos is quite a dancer."

"He sure is."

"'Course that gal he's got ahold of now is mighty lively herself."

Indeed, she was. Like all the hurdy-gurdy girls, she was blonde, blue-eyed, and glowing with good health, for Hans and Marta Stohlhofen had made sure that the dancing girls they hired possessed stamina. Unlike the other girls, this one was not in the least heavy-footed, floating lightly through the most intricate of steps, responsive to her partner's every move. Already, Lars noticed, Carlos had danced with this particular girl three times, which, considering the number of eager men awaiting their turn, was two more than his share.

Even now as the polka ended and the members of the orchestra put down the instruments prior to taking a break, Carlos kept a firm grip on the girl's arm, refusing to let her leave his side. Raising his free hand, he motioned to the silver-haired piano player and the warm-voiced contralto singer, who filled in the breaks with numbers requested by the audience.

"*Por favor!* Please could you play and sing a special birthday song for this lovely young lady?"

"Sure," the silver-haired piano player said with a smile, "if we know it."

"What's the name of the song?" the contralto asked.

"Annie Laurie."

Nodding his head, the piano player struck a chord, then looked questioningly at the contralto to make sure he was in her range. In gold camps all over the West these days, this was an extremely popular song among men who were far from loved ones and home, for it expressed a sentiment felt by all of them.

Bowing to the young lady, whose eyes were misting with tears as she dropped her gaze in embarrassment, Carlos announced to the crowd: "Her name is Anna Lowehr, which is German for 'Annie Laurie.' Today is her nineteenth birthday, she tells me, and she is a long way from home. Let us all wish her many happy returns."

In her mellow contralto voice, the vocalist sang:

Maxwelton braes are bonny,
Where early falls the dew;
And 'twas there that Annie Laurie
Gave me her promise true.
Which ne'er forgot will be;
And for bonny Annie Laurie,
I would lay me doon and dee.

When the singer motioned for the audience to join her in repeating the song, it did so enthusiastically. Tearing herself loose from Carlos' grasp, the young lady named Anna Lowehr burst into tears, ran and hid her face in Marta Stohlhofen's ample breast as the crowd sang on. But from the look she gave Carlos before she turned her eyes away, she did not seem to be in the least displeased.

19.

$\mathcal{A}$s the members of the orchestra resumed their positions and picked up their instruments following the break, Carlos stood in front of the stage and held up his hands for silence.

"*Senoras y senores.* Ladies and gentlemen. If I may have your attention, please! Honoring us with her presence tonight is a beautiful, talented lady whose distinctive style of dancing in years past made her the toast of San Francisco. I refer, of course, to the lovely, charming, gracious Lili deBeauchamp. She has agreed to entertain us with the solo number with which she used to drive men mad on the Barbary Coast—the tarantella."

"Carlos, please, you must first state my condition!" Lili protested. "I cannot do the dance unless the orchestra plays the proper music."

"Maestro?" Carlos queried the silver-haired piano player, who by popular choice had become the leader of the orchestra. "Can you play the wild Italian Gypsy music which the dance requires?"

Running his supple, well-groomed hands rapidly over the keys to produce several bars of the requested rhythm and chords, with the strings, the clarinet, the tuba, and the accordion soon joining in, the piano player smiled fondly down at his employer.

"Have you forgotten, Miss Lili, that the first night you danced in the Golden Circle, I was playing piano in the pit? You could not yet speak a word of English, as I recall, and were just sixteen years old—"

"Which could not have been more than two or three years ago," Carlos cut in diplomatically. "Lili, the floor is yours."

Standing on the promenade deck outside the open windows to the main saloon, Lars Warren marveled at the magic which these people from what was to him an alien world could create with their music and movement. Exactly what a Gypsy or an Italian was, he had no idea, for he never had seen such people. But when the slim, dark-eyed, beautiful woman called Lili deBeauchamp rose from her chair, stood tall and frozen like a statue for a few bars of music, then tossed the multicolored silk scarf she had obtained from somewhere over first one shoulder and then the other as she walked, stalked, prowled, writhed, and moved sinuously in strict time to the music, he felt he was being lured into a wild, distant, passionate world, where loves and hates and conflicts more intense than any he ever had known existed.

Tentative and a bit stiff the first time through, the orchestra began to get the feel of the rhythm as it repeated the theme, with the accordion, which had meekly followed the piano's lead during the opening bars, now asserting itself and taking off on a musical quest of its own, while the piano alternated between following, trying to take over, arguing, then compromising by playing in tandem in a rising crescendo of blending sounds. Deserting the softer melody line of the cello after the second time through, Goliath Samson rattled first the sticks of the snare drum, then the padded hammer of the kettle drum, and then, obtaining a castenet from some secret store, began shaking it to create a complicated three-way beat with it, the kettle drum, and the bass drum thumped with a hammer operated by his foot.

But it was Lili playing the role of the wild, hot-blooded, Gypsy dancer that became the focus of all eyes. How many years had passed since she had been the toast of San Francisco, no one cared, for now— at this moment, on this night, in this place—for the 250 lonely, entertainment-starved men on the boat docked at the edge of this desert wilderness, she was the Toast of the Western World.

"*God-a-mighty!*" Willie Polk exclaimed as he clutched Lars' arm. "In all my born days, I ain't never seen nothin' like this!"

Strictly religious grammarian that the senior William H. Gray was known to be, he would have peeled his seventeen-year-old son's hide off, Lars suspected, if had been present to hear that remark. But, God-a-mighty, it sure as hell was true!

When at last the dance crashed to its climax and Lili motioned with her scarf for the orchestra to cease and desist, she collapsed in a mock faint into Carlos' arms, exclaiming, "Oh, my goodness! What a spectacle I've made of myself!"

"It was a spectacle none of us will ever forget, Lili. You were marvelous!"

Fanning herself as she tried to catch her breath, she gave him a challenging look. "Now it's your turn, young man. Now you must dance for us."

"*No es posible, senora.* The tarantella is no dance for a man."

"I agree. You must do a special dance with me as your partner."

"With pleasure, Lili. A waltz, perhaps? Or a minuet?"

"Oh, no, you will not get off that easily!" Lili cried with a merry laugh. "Down in California, you were a bullfighter, were you not?"

"This is true."

"Then we will do the bullfighter's dance together—the flamenco."

Carlos frowned. "I doubt if the orchestra knows how to play that kind of music, Lili—"

"Maestro!" Lili called to the silver-haired piano player. "Flamenco music, *por favor!*"

"*Con mucho gusto, senora,*" the piano player murmured, then struck a chord …

Again, Lars found himself carried away into another world, this one full of charging, sharp-horned bulls, screaming, bloodthirsty crowds, and arenas where tense dramas of danger and death were being acted out between brave men and animals. Forgetting where he was and what he was supposed to be doing in order to get a closer view of the dancers, Lars was shocked to discover as the number ended that he had moved from the promenade deck through the door of the main saloon, then somehow had worked his way to the forefront of the crowd, where he now stood directly behind the slim figure of Daphne deBeauchamp. As the dance ended and a thunderous round of applause began, she turned, saw him, and then threw her arms around him impulsively.

"Oh, Lars! Weren't they wonderful?"

Embarrassed, he tried to break away. "They sure were."

"Do you know how to dance?"

"Well, I can polka a little bit—"

"Do you know the gavotte?"

Before Lars could confess that for all he knew, a "gavotte" was something you covered with sugar and cream and ate for dessert, Carlos and Lili moved to their side. Again, his uncle held up his hands for silence.

"Now the young people must have their turn. Do you not agree, Lili, that your daughter, Daphne, and my nephew, Lars, should dance with each other?"

"I certainly do," Lili said, smiling at both Daphne and Lars. "What kind of music would you like, *cheri?*"

His face turning scarlet, Lars tried to back away, but the crowd kept him hemmed in. "I can't dance now," he protested. "I'm on duty."

Carlos scowled at Leonard White, who had been watching the festivities with a bemused smile on his face. "Is this true, Captain White?"

"Why, yes, it is, Carlos. But right now, I would say his duty is to dance with the young lady, showing all these nice people that the employees of the O.S.N. Company know all the latest steps."

The best Lars could make out as the orchestra started playing and he gingerly touched Daphne's hands and waist where she indicated he should take hold, a gavotte was somewhere between a dignified minuet and a lively polka. Once he conquered his fear of stepping on his partner's feet, tripping over his own, and falling flat on his face, he began to accept the exciting fact that for the first time in his life he was grasping the hand and touching the body of the most beautiful girl he ever had met. Not only that, but her warm black eyes and her brilliant smile as she gazed up at him were letting him know that she was enjoying every moment of it.

All too soon, the dance ended. Minding his manners, Lars bowed to his partner and thanked her as an enthusiastic round of applause filled the room. Returning Daphne to her mother, Lars even managed to compliment her, too, before forcing himself back into the real world in which his primary duty as cabin boy was to serve drinks and food to the passengers and guests as the party went on.

By midnight, the hurdy-gurdy girls, the orchestra members, and French Lil's ladies were all so exhausted that the party ended for the night, so far as music, dancing, and entertainment in the dining saloon was concerned. A few first-class passengers ticketed to Lewiston retired to their bunks in comfortable staterooms, while deck passengers bedded down wherever they could find space aboard, leaving the fifty or so bachelor visitors from the Walla Walla Valley, the city, and the fort, to spend what was left of the night ashore in wagon beds, buggies, or blankets removed from saddle horses and placed randomly on the warm sands of the sloping beach or within the crumbling walls of the abandoned fort.

With large blocks of ice still floating down the river the next morning, Captain White's announced decision to lay over for another day

or two at Wallula Landing set off an immediate clamor from the passengers and visitors for another party that night. But to this idea, both
Hans Stohlhofen and French Lil raised strong objections.

"*Mein Gott*, Captain, already dese voman-starved men are trying to
steal my girls! If de boat stays tied up here for anodder day or two, dey
may run away and get married, in spite of their contracts. If dis happens, I vill sue de O.S.N. Company for damages!"

By midmorning, it was common gossip that two of French Lil's
ladies had left her, giving in to the sworn promises of two male visitors from the Walla Walla Valley that before they took the ladies
home with them they would stop at the county courthouse, obtain a
wedding license, go to a minister and marry the ladies in a legally
binding ceremony. It was firm policy with Lili deBeauchamp, Willie
Polk told Lars, that no girl in her house would be started on her career there, nor would she be bound to stay if she wished to leave. Having known a good marriage herself, French Lil always was pleased to
have her girls better themselves, so long as their new station in life was
an honorable one.

"Please, Captain White, can't we move on toward Lewiston?" she
pleaded. "Already I've lost two of my best girls. If we stay tied up here
any longer, I'm sure I'll lose more."

"I know you have a problem, ma'am. But I can't endanger the
safety of my passengers and my boat."

"Couldn't you at least leave the dock and pull out into the river so
that these wild Walla Walla Valley men can't come aboard? Yesterday,
there were only fifty of them. Today, there are at least a hundred—and
more arriving all the time."

"Well, I suppose I could cast off and go upriver as far as the mouth
of the Snake. If I don't tell the visitors what we're doing, they'll think
we're heading for Lewiston."

Casting off her lines at noon, the *Colonel Wright* steamed eleven
miles up the Columbia, turned east up the Snake, then gingerly picked
her way through increasingly dangerous floes of floating ice for ten
miles, until she finally was forced to seek shelter in a half-moon bay
adjacent to the south shore. Here, sheer lava bluffs rose five hundred
feet into the air behind a narrow strip of sandy beach. Since there
were no roads, trails, or settlements in this remote sage-covered desert
country, Captain White was sure he had shaken the Walla Walla Valley men. After nosing the boat into the beach, tying off bow and stern

lines, and putting out landing stages so that the passengers could stretch their legs ashore, he announced confidently, "Those pushy bachelors will never find us here."

Standing in the pilot house beside him, First Mate Thomas Stump took his half-smoked cigar out of his mouth and gestured with it at a distant line of riders wending their way down a goat-like trail cutting across the face of the nearby bluff. "Oh no? Look yonder."

Leading the band of Walla Walla men, Lars learned a few minutes later, was his uncle, Carlos Ibanez …

Because for two days there was no way the boat could be moved without danger, there were two more nights of parties, music, and appeals from lonely bachelors to young ladies to desert their employers and embark on the lower-paying but presumably more honorable seas of matrimony. Because Hans and Marta Stohlhofen did have ironclad contracts with their six young German hurdy-gurdy girls, which they refused to cancel for less than five thousand dollars a girl, they lost none of their portable assets. But three more of French Lil's young ladies left her, which reduced the working staff of her proposed Entertainment Parlor from twelve to seven.

Since he had few other duties to perform other than waiting on the paying customers while the partying went on, Lars talked, danced, and took long strolls ashore with Daphne deBeauchamp, whose mother gave her tacit approval so long as the two young people talked, danced, and strolled under her or Goliath Samson's watchful eye.

By the morning of the third day, the worst of the ice floes had passed, so Captain White ordered the lines cast off; the stern-wheel started churning, and the *Colonel Wright* proceeded cautiously up the Snake River. In the boat's log, it was recorded that for two nights she had sought shelter in a bay to be called then and later "Ice Harbor," in which, during spring breakup, upriver-bound craft could safely wait for the ice floes to pass.

Crying her eyes out as she stood at the rail waving farewell to Carlos Ibanez, the lovely blonde-haired, blue-eyed, young hurdy-gurdy girl, Anna Lowehr, made no effort to conceal the fact that she was hopelessly in love with the dark, handsome, Spanish rancher she was leaving behind for at least a year, just as he made no secret of the fact that he was in love with her as he forlornly waved his hat.

At the end of that day, when the boat docked at Lewiston and Lars and Daphne parted, she cried, too, though he did his best to keep a stiff upper lip and let no emotion show on his face other than a slight misting in his eyes.

"It's been nice knowing you," Daphne said, holding out her hand.

"Me, too," he blurted, the warmth of her palm and fingers making his own hand tingle. "I mean, I'm glad we met."

"Mother says she'll enroll me in a good Catholic school, if she can find one. But I'm sure they'll let you visit me when your boat is in."

"Yeah. I suppose they will."

"We could go for a walk, maybe. I'm sure that would be permitted."

"Yeah. Probably it would."

Remembering all the dumb things he'd said at their parting, Lars was miserable for the next two weeks, as the *Colonel Wright* made several runs up and down the Columbia and Snake between Celilo Falls and Lewiston. Despite Daphne's prediction that she was sure the authorities of the Catholic school in which her mother planned to enroll her would permit visits from boys like himself, he was sure they would not. Furthermore, he was positive he had lost the first and only girl he had ever loved or would love during the rest of his life.

So it came as a very pleasant surprise when three weeks later Lili deBeauchamp, the silver-haired piano player, Goliath Samson, all of her staff, seven of her girls, and beautiful Daphne herself came aboard the *Colonel Wright*, headed downriver for Wallula Landing.

"Mother found out there's no Catholic school in Lewiston," Daphne told Lars happily. "But there is a good one in Walla Walla, she's been told. So that's where we're going to live."

"Hey, that's great! My Uncle Carlos owns a ranch near Walla Walla. I go there whenever I have a few days off."

"Then we'll be seeing each other a lot, won't we?" Daphne exclaimed, squeezing his hand. "Oh, Lars, we'll have such fun!"

20.

$\mathscr{I}$N THE NEWLY BORN TOWN of Lewiston during the summer of 1862, the spirit of expansion advocated by Alonzo Leland, editor of the local newspaper, the *Radiator*, was running amuck with unprecedented speed and vigor. As the northern Idaho mines boomed and stern-wheeler traffic increased on the Snake and Columbia, the merchants began to dream of commercial grandeur. Discounting all previous reports of rapids, whirlpools, and other obstacles to navigation in the Big Canyon upriver, the town promoters dispatched a scouting expedition in early autumn "to determine the possibility of navigating Snake River with light draught steamers to Fort Boise."

The report turned in by the "three reliable men" was highly favorable:

> The entire distance from Lewiston to Fort Boise is only one hundred and thirty-five-miles!" the editor of the *Radiator* declared jubilantly. "They found nothing in the river to impede navigation whatever, and pronounced it feasible at any season of the year unless it be by ice ...
>
> A new route will now be opened for steam, the results of which cannot now be foretold. We shall penetrate Nevada and Utah Territories by steam, as it is well-known that it is only ninety miles from Fort Boise to Salmon Falls on Snake River. Salmon Falls is within 250 miles of Salt Lake ...
>
> But a few more suns will rise and set before the shrill whistle of the steamer will reverberate along the banks of this noble river, and its echo will be heard for ages yet to come through the ravines, gorges, and canyons, and on the mountaintops of our golden land, as a symbol of ambition, perseverance, and goaheadativeness.

Unfortunately for the goaheadativeness of the Lewiston promoters, Captain Thomas J. Stump, who was now in command of the *Colonel Wright*, felt that a couple of serious misstatements had been made. For one thing, the scouts had underestimated the distance by at least a hundred miles. For another, their description of the country they were supposed to have scouted bore little resemblance to what he had been told about it from rivermen who had seen it.

By now, Captain Leonard White and his $500-a-month salary had moved on to another field—building, owning, and operating a boat on the upper Columbia River into Canada. Thomas Stump had accepted the more reasonable salary of $350 a month, while Willie Gray moved up to the position of First Mate at $200, with Lars Warren now working as Cabin Boy, Assistant Purser, and Second Mate combined for the respectable wage of $100 a month.

After reading the newspaper editorial to Willie and Lars while the boat was docked at the Lewiston wharf one morning, Captain Stump chomped down on his cigar, shook his head, and grunted sourly, "That description of the Snake in the Big Canyon sounds phony to me. What do you fellows think?"

"I've never seen it myself," Willie Gray said. "But from what Pa tells me of a trip he took up to the mouth of the Salmon in an Indian canoe a couple of years ago, the river gets worse the further up you go, with rapids every mile or so."

"I haven't seen it either," Lars said. "But I've read quite a bit about it."

"Where?"

"In a book Grandfather Warren has in his library in the Hilltop House in Astoria."

"Who wrote it?"

"Alexander Ross, a clerk who worked for the North West Company when they built a trading post on the Columbia River near what's now Wallula Landing. This was in 1819. Ross and Donald McKenzie, the factor in charge of the post, were good friends of Grandfather Warren."

"I've heard of Donald McKenzie. He was a big, red-bearded man who weighed over three hundred pounds, I've been told. Everybody he dealt with respected him."

"Grandfather Warren certainly did. He says that the expression 'big enough to go bear hunting with a switch' described him perfectly. Anyway, in the book I read, Alexander Ross tells how McKenzie and six voyageurs took a loaded barge through the Big Canyon in the spring of 1819. The river was full of rocks, rapids, and whirlpools, he said, and they had to use towlines a lot. Since the trip took two months and was awfully hard on the men, he never tried it again."

Captain Stump looked thoughtful. Removing the stub of the dead cigar from his mouth, he peered down at it for a moment, decided its two-inch length was not worth scorching his nose in an attempt to re-light it, so tossed it out of the open pilot house window.

"Well, there's only one way to silence these armchair explorers," he grunted. "We'll have to take the *Colonel Wright* upriver and check it out for ourselves. Next time I talk to your Uncle Emil, I'll ask him to let us take the boat out of service for a week or so, then we'll steam upriver till we run out of water or go on the rocks. That's the only way we'll know how far into the Big Canyon a boat can go."

With passenger and freight traffic between Lewiston and Celilo re-maining heavy and profitable, it was not until late spring of 1864 that the Oregon Steam Navigation Company decided that the navigability of the Snake above Lewiston should be tested. By then, gold and sil-ver mines in the Boise area of what had become Idaho Territory had developed to such a degree that prospectors, businessmen, and politi-cians were pouring into the region, creating a demand for cheap, reli-able transportation. There was even talk of moving the capital of the newly created Territory from Lewiston south to Boise City. While taking no sides in the controversy, the O.S.N. Company was deter-mined to get its share of the business in southwestern Idaho—either by steaming its boats through the rapids of the Big Canyon or by transporting the pieces of a boat to be built on freight wagons across the Blue Mountains, putting them together on the river near Farewell Bend, and starting steamboat service on the upper river from there.

Because Captain Stump wanted all the water he could get under his boat's keel so that the rapids would be flattened out, the time chosen for the attempt was late May, when snowmelt in the mountains upriver would supply a maximum flow through the Big Canyon. Because of the risks involved, only two passengers would be carried aboard the *Colonel Wright:* Alonzo Leland, editor of the *Radiator;* and William H. Gray, Willie's father. Though both men agreed that they would not hold Captain Stump or the O.S.N. Company responsible for their safety, the captain told Willie and Lars that he was not worried about them, for, in his opinion: "They're both too ornery to drown."

Indeed, both were outspoken, cantankerous men. Having come to the Pacific Northwest with the Whitman-Spalding party of missionaries in 1836, William H. Gray had been in on every historical event that had happened since, thus felt it his right to record regional history as he had lived it. As for Alonzo Leland, the fiery-tempered editor carried on a number of feuds with regional people who differed with him.

For instance, he called Superior Court Judge Samuel C. Parks, whom he detested, "judge of a most inferior court."

Carrying on a long-distance feud with James Reynolds, editor of the *Idaho Statesman* down in Boise City over the proposed relocation of the Territorial capital from Lewiston to Boise City, Leland claimed Reynolds "was so lazy he never worked but once—and that was when his mistook castor oil for bourbon."

In response, Jim Reynolds refused to capitalize either the name of the town or the editor of the *Radiator*, referring to them as the "lewiston lelander."

Personally disagreeable though the two passengers could be, both men knew that on this exploring trip upriver aboard the *Colonel Wright* they must mind their manners or risk being tossed overboard, for Captain Stump was the undisputed master of his boat. Alonzo Leland told the captain that despite his earlier endorsement of the report turned in by the scouting party a year and a half ago, he was beginning to doubt its truth himself, and would certainly say so in print if it proved to be wrong. Admitting that he could not swim a lick and was deathly afraid of water, he gladly accepted the offer of a lifesaving vest made him by Lars Warren shortly after the boat pulled away from the dock.

"In fact, if you don't mind, I'll take two life jackets," he said, casting an apprehensive glance over the side at the brown, surging current. "That water looks awfully cold, wet, and rough."

After contemptuously declining a flotation device himself, William H. Gray snorted, "A dozen life jackets won't help you if you go overboard in a rapid like Wild Goose."

"Why not?" Leland asked nervously.

"Because the first thing that will happen, you'll hit your head on a rock and be knocked unconscious. Second, there's more foam than water in that kind of rapid, so it won't support you. Third, when you gasp for breath you'll take foam rather than air into your lungs, so you'll drown inside before you do out."

"Well, I do thank you for those reassuring words, Mr. Gray," the editor said sarcastically. "But I'll wear the two life jackets all the same."

Called up to the pilot house soon after the boat got under way, Lars listened intently as Captain Stump told him what his duties would be on this exploratory trip upriver.

"I want the river charted mile by mile, just in case the O.S.N. Company decides to make commercial runs through the Big Canyon. Note the landmarks on each side of the river and give each rapid a name. Don't pester me with questions as to why I'm steering a certain course. But if I say anything about my navigation, write it down—leaving out the cuss words. Can you do that, Lars?"

"Yes sir."

"I've noticed both you and Willie take notes on the way I steer the boat through a rapid. That's good—so long as you don't let your notes turn to concrete in your head. Always remember that a rapid changes day by day and is different going upstream from coming down. Keep reading the river, as well as your notes, and remember what you learn. In time, you both may be become good pilots."

Truth was, both Willie Gray and Lars Warren had been ardent students of the Columbia and Snake Rivers ever since they had been old enough to toddle and distinguish sights and sounds. Like all boys raised along the river, both of them had acquired an encyclopedic knowledge of boat whistles, becoming able to name each boat long before it came into sight. Both were avid readers, learning by heart all the statistics and boat lore they could absorb through newspapers, shipping columns, and journals of early-day river explorers. Because his father, grandfather, and great-grandfather all had been masters of riverboats or sailing ships, Lars Warren could boast of three generations of captains in his family. He was determined to make it four.

As for William Polk Gray, he had become a deckhand and a rapids swimmer at the age of thirteen. Now First Mate of the *Colonel Wright* at the youthful age of nineteen, he fully expected to get his captain's license by the time he was old enough to vote, for he had learned that there was no combination of iron, wood, and water that could frighten him.

Captain Stump's instruction to chart the Snake above Lewiston mile by mile bothered Lars, for he was not at all certain as to how one measured miles aboard a stern-wheeler steaming up a swift-flowing river. Not wanting to bother the captain with what might be regarded as a stupid question, Lars approached the senior William Gray with it, for he knew that the acerbic-natured man was a self-styled expert on every subject under the sun.

"Could you tell me, Mr. Gray," he said politely, "how a person goes about measuring miles aboard a moving riverboat?"

Shooting Lars a piercing look, Mr. Gray scowled as he considered the question, then snapped, "The same way you do at sea, I suppose—by throwing a log tied to a line overboard, then counting the number of spaced knots that run out during a given period of time."

"Wouldn't the current of the river affect the accuracy of that?"

"Yes, I suppose it would. You'd have to allow for the current's speed." He was silent for a time, then added, "Triangulation might be a better way to do it."

"How does that work?"

"You make two legs of a triangle and a space in between with an instrument aboard the boat, pick two landmarks ashore such as a bluff or a tall tree, then relate the known length of the third leg of the triangle aboard the boat to the distance you're trying to establish ashore."

"Wouldn't the vibration of the boat's deck make your instrument jiggle and throw off your calculations?"

"If you used a rigid instrument on a tripod in contact with the deck, yes, it certainly would. But why do that when you've got an arm, a hand, a thumb and four fingers?"

"What does that have to do with it?"

"Stand here, son," Mr. Gray said impatiently, positioning Lars beside him so that both of them were facing the passing shore. "I'll show you a trick that every good carpenter knows—"

The trick, Lars learned, was that by extending his left arm to its full length, folding under three fingers, then spreading the little finger and thumb, an angle of approximately sixty degrees could be formed. By peering along the arm at points ashore known to be a mile apart, it was not at all difficult to establish the distance required to comprise a land mile ashore. In all probability, Mr. Gray said, this was how the term "rule of thumb" came into being. Certainly under the circumstances it would do.

"In any case, I've been up the Snake River as far as the mouth of the Salmon," Gray said, "which is about forty-five miles. If you want to chart the river mile by mile, I'll name the points, landmarks, and rapids for you as we go."

Though the current was strong and the color of the water a murky brown due to springtime erosion and placer mining operations up-stream, no rapids of any consequence impeded the progress of the *Colonel Wright* until shortly before noon of the warm spring day. Goat Island, Swallows Nest, Asotin, and Ten Mile Rapids were traversed and noted on Lars' chart. A quarter-mile wide and contained by low basaltic hills now covered with a lush growth of soft, green bunch-grass—which would turn crisp and brown with the coming of sum-mer—the Snake moved with quiet power through empty, rolling hill country. Except for an occasional white settler's log cabin, a handful of slab-roofed Indian pit houses, or tepees pitched on sandbars, few signs of civilization were visible.

Twenty miles upriver from Lewiston on the Idaho side of the river, several large lava boulders near the water's edge created a swirling pool in which the current turned back on itself, forming what Gray told Lars was called Buffalo Rock Eddy.

"My Indian boatmen took me ashore to show me some picture writings on the face of the rocks. Best I could make out, the pictures were supposed to be mountain sheep, bears, horses, or maybe even people. They were so crude and primitive it was hard to tell."

"Who painted them?"

"Nobody could say. All my Indian guides knew was that they were 'old—very old.' They weren't much as paintings. Just stick figures like kids draw in school."

At Mile 24, the *Colonel Wright* ascended a short stretch of white water near the Idaho side of the river called "Captain John" Rapid by his Indian boatmen, Mr. Gray said, and at Mile 25, one on the Wash-ington side called "Billy Creek" Rapid.

"The Indians told me Captain John was a Nez Perce brave who scouted for Colonel George Wright back in '58 and was proud of it. Who 'Billy' was, nobody knew."

Coming into the Snake from the Washington side at Mile 29, the Grande Ronde River was swollen with late spring snowmelt from the ten-thousand-foot-high Wallowa Mountains to the southwest. Loom-ing above it a mile upstream was a gray, rocky bluff called Lime Point. Here, the foothills on either side of the river grew higher and steeper, compressing the river into a narrowing space which Mr. Gray said was the lower end of the Big Canyon.

"We'll get a sample of what's in store for us when we hit Wild Goose Rapid, a few miles further on. If Captain Stump can drive this

boat up it without using his power capstan, I'll take my hat off to
him."

"Is Wild Goose worse than what we've seen so far?"

"Much worse. When the Indians took me upriver, we portaged around it. Coming down, we shot it at full speed, coming over a six-foot ledge of white water like we were falling out of a barn loft. When we hit the water, it gave us a jolt that shook our teeth loose."

Reaching the foot of Wild Goose Rapid at Mile 33, Captain Stump rang the engine room to slow the speed of the stern-wheel to the point that the boat merely held its own against the current while he peered intently into the glare of the noontime sunlight ahead, study-ing the rapid. Standing beside him in the pilot house and listening at-tentively to what he was saying was First Mate Willie Gray, while Lars Warren, the senior William Gray, and the nervous newspaper editor, Alonzo Leland, stood on the deck outside and below the pilot house, respectfully keeping silent while Captain Stump planned his attack on the rapid.

"Looks like the best bet would be to stay to the right of that long narrow island, which splits the river into two channels. Lots of water pouring through it, but it's coming straight and fast through the right-hand channel. We'll hit it with all we've got and see what happens."

"What do you make of the left-hand channel, sir?" Willie Polk asked.

"Looks tricky to me. The current doesn't appear to be as fast as it is in the right-hand channel, but it's pinched into such a narrow chute that it forms a sneaky back eddy. The water in half of the channel is racing downstream, while that in the other half is turning back on it-self and going upstream. If we hit that spot wrong, we'll lose steerage-way and spin around like a cork."

"Have you considered winching?"

"May have to, Willie. But we'll try straight power first."

For this maiden trip, the *Colonel Wright* had stocked its engine room with high-quality fuel—dry, seasoned pine cordwood well laced with pitch—which would provide maximum steam pressure for the boilers. Designed to operate at 185 pounds per square inch, the en-gines could stand 200 or more for brief periods of time, Chief Engi-neer Chester O'Malley told the captain. What did he mean by "brief"? Ten, twelve minutes, maybe. Beyond that, well, he didn't know.

Dropping back into slack water downriver in order to have room to build up a head of steam and hit the rapid at maximum speed, Captain Stump leaned over toward the engine-room speaking tube and said, "Give me all you've got, Chet! Tie down the safety valve and hope she doesn't blow!"

"Aye, sir! Let 'er rip!"

In addition to a pair of deckhands who were doubling as stokers, the boat carried a supply of spare planking, soft-patch materials, and a master carpenter and two helpers so that quick repairs could be made in case the boat hit the rocks and holed her sides or bottom. Feeling the deck under his feet vibrate as the thundering of the engine increased to a sustained roar, Lars gripped the nearby railing until his knuckles turned white, rising on tiptoe as he urged the boat on.

"Go, baby! Go!"

Three hundred yards in length, Wild Goose was slightly wider at its lower end than its upper. With the momentum she had gained by hitting the rapid running, the *Colonel Wright* climbed the first hundred yards of the thundering white water briskly, the second hundred more slowly, then gradually slowed to the point where she was making no progress at all. For half a minute she hung on a balance point, motionless in the middle of the constricted channel.

Captain Stump leaned toward the speaking tube.

"Got any more, Chet?"

"Sorry, sir. You've got it all."

"Ease off, then. She's shaking herself to pieces."

As the speed of the threshing stern-wheel slowed, the *Colonel Wright* drifted back into quieter water. Letting her rest there for a few minutes to cool down the engine and give the stokers time to build up a new head of steam, Captain Stump then increased power and tested the left-hand channel. Noting that he kept the boat's stem well to the right of where the back eddy turned the current upstream, Lars was not surprised when the captain shook his head, eased off power, and let the boat drift back downstream.

"Too goddamn risky!" Lars heard him mutter. "If we lose steerageway here, we'll be on the rocks before we can correct it."

Pulling in to the right-hand bank, Captain Stump ordered Willie Polk, two deckhands, and two carpenter's helpers ashore with a quarter mile of two-inch-thick line, which they unreeled from the power capstan in the bow as they carried it upstream to a point above the rapids, where they secured it around the base of an immense black lava rock. Leaning out the window of the pilot house, Captain Stump spoke to the senior William Gray, who was standing on the deck just below.

"Did you teach your son how to secure a line, Mr. Gray?"

"By the time he was ten, Captain Stump," Gray answered testily, "If he hadn't learned it by then, I'd have drowned him."

"All right, Lars," the captain called down. "Signal the engine room to tighten the slack, then tell them to give us full power on the winch. We'll see if we can walk her up the rapid."

With the capstan pulling and the stern-wheel pushing, the *Colonel Wright* moved into the white water of the right-hand channel once again. This time, the boat moved through the tumbling torrent without difficulty. After reaching slack water above the rapid, the boat pulled in close to the shore, giving the line looped about the big lava rock enough slack that it could be loosened and brought aboard by Willie Gray and his crew.

"Make a note, Lars," Captain Stump called down, "that Wild Goose must be lined. For future traffic, it would simplify matters if the O.S.N. Company engineers would bury a big iron ring in the face of that rock we tied to."

"Yes, sir," Lars said. The puzzled frown on his face as he wrote the notation on his clipboard made the captain realize Lars was dying to ask for a fuller explanation, so Captain Stump gave it to him. "What the engineers will do, Lars, is cinch one end of a heavy line into the ring, let a quarter mile of line float downstream through the rapid to the quiet water below, with a floating barrel attached to its lower end. When a boat bound upriver comes along—"

"It'll pick up the barrel with a boat hook," Lars blurted impulsively, "fasten the end of the line to its power capstan, then winch its way up the rapid."

"Exactly!"

"That's real clever, sir! I'll write it all down."

Three miles upstream from Wild Goose Rapid, at Mile 36, a moderate stretch of white water toward the Idaho side of the river was encountered and passed without difficulty. Because a cluster of Chinese miners had settled along a gulch running back into the mountains, putting up crude shelters of stacked rocks, assembling sluice boxes, rockers, and hand-panning pools along the creek, the spot was called China Gulch Gardens, Mr. Gray told Lars. Why had the word "Gardens" been added? Because as they always did where good soil, water, sunlight, and fertilizer were available, the Chinese had established a flourishing kitchen garden from which they usually had fresh produce to sell.

Hearing that, the stooped, wrinkled old Negro cook, Mose Titus, perked up his ears. "S'pose they'd sell us some fresh vegetables for supper?"

"Likely they would," Mr. Gray said. "Of course the night soil they use as fertilizer will make them smell to high heaven."

"Do'an make no never-mind to me how bad their fertilizer makes 'em smell, Mr. Gray. Time I wash and bile a few cabbages, beets, and carrots with a big hunk of prime beef in a hot stew, the only smell Cap'n Stump and the crew gonna get is a good-eatin' smell."

With the afternoon almost gone and everyone worn out after a long, tension-filled day, Captain Stump decided that this would be a good place to tie up for the night. When Old Titus asked Lars to go ashore with him to do the bargaining with the Chinese, Lars was glad to do so, for he was curious about this alien race of people which more and more of late had settled in this part of the country. Willing to do any kind of labor for wages below what a white man would accept, the Chinese were not recognized as citizens nor welcomed as prospectors in California or Idaho gold camps. Where they usually appeared as miners was in remote places such as this in the depths of the Big Canyon of the Snake, taking over diggings deserted by white miners after most of the gold had been mined, settling on sandbars where their patient, careful panning produced a couple of dollars' worth of flour gold for a day's work—far too little to satisfy a white man but a decent day's wage for an Oriental.

From the excited manner in which the Chinese were chattering with one another and pointing at the *Colonel Wright*, Lars gathered that seeing a stern-wheeler come this far up the Snake was a surprising event to them. Though they appeared to welcome the opportunity to sell their produce to the boat's crew, the fact that white civilization now had reached this remote canyon gave them a grim foreboding of bad things to come.

Despite the language barrier of singsong Cantonese, Southern Negro drawl, and his own more precise English, Lars found that a

basis for trade could soon be reached. Just as Mose Titus knew a firm
head of cabbage when he felt one, the Chinese were aware of the
value of the gold dust in Lars' buckskin purse, so an accord soon was
reached.

Returning to the boat with a bushel basketful of fresh vegetables,
Mose Titus bustled down to his galley while Lars found a deck chair
forward in the bow of the boat where he could finish recording his
notes for the day. As the late spring sun dropped below the cliffs to the
west and the great river whispered past, he wrote:

> At the end of our first day of exploring the Big Canyon of the
> Snake, we tied up on the Idaho side of the river at Mile 36 just above
> a rapid called China Gardens. Bought some fresh vegetables raised by
> Chinese miners who live here. Mose Titus thinks they're a strange
> sort of people—and so do I. But I suppose they think we're strange,
> too.

21.

$\mathscr{N}$EXT MORNING while the stokers built up the fire under the boilers, the crew ate breakfast. Two hours after sunrise, the boat cast off its lines and the *Colonel Wright* resumed its cautious exploration of the Big Canyon of the Snake. As dark brown bluffs rose ever more steeply on either side of the river, Lars noted rapids and landmarks such as Cougar, Cave Gulch, and Deep Creek at Miles 37, 39, and 44. At Mile 48, the largest, most turbulent river yet seen—the Salmon—poured its raging waters into the Snake from the southeast, breaking through a high, narrow gorge from the Idaho side of the river.

"This was as far up as I went with my Indian guides," the senior William Gray told Lars as he leaned close to his ear and shouted to make himself heard over the roar of the rapids and the threshing of the boat's stern-wheel. "They told me the Salmon heads in high mountain country two hundred miles to the southeast. It's filled with impassable rapids almost all the way, they said."

"That's what Lewis and Clark found out when they came west in 1805," Lars shouted back. "Clark first named the Salmon 'Lewis's River' because Lewis had discovered it. Lewis told him it looked unnavigable but Clark insisted on trying it for himself. Lewis turned out to be right."

"You certainly know your history, boy," Gray said with an approving nod. "Which is only natural, considering the roles the men in your family have played in making it."

"Thank you, sir. It's just that anything that has to do with rivers interests me."

What William Clark had written in his journal was that he had found the steep bank of the river impossible to traverse:

> ... without a road, over rocky hillsides where the horses were in perpetual danger of slipping to their certain destruction ... with the greatest difficulty and risk made five miles and camped ...

After losing three horses to injury or exhaustion, Clark gave up, rejoined Lewis and the main party, and sought an easier way across the mountains further north.

"Just out of curiosity," Mr. Gray told Lars, "I got out of the canoe and hiked a mile or so up the canyon of the Salmon. It was rough going, believe me. Where the Salmon bursts through those sheer lava rocks yonder there's a gap so narrow the Indians call it 'Eye of the Needle.' Just above it is a race of white-water prospectors named the 'Sluice Box' because when you ride downstream through it in a boat it shakes the gold fillings out of your teeth."

Because there was plenty of water in the Snake below the mouth of the Salmon at this time of year, Captain Stump encountered no trouble in the center of the main river channel there. But visualizing future navigational problems, he called down to Lars through the open side window of the pilot house, "Make a note, Lars, that at low stage a boat should stay as close to the rough water on the Idaho side of the river as it can, without actually getting into it."

"Yes, sir."

"What likely will happen at that level of water is that the Salmon will dump whatever gravel its carried down during spring runoff into the Snake, forming a bar that may cause trouble. But there'll always be a deep channel close to the rough water. Write that down."

"Yes, sir. I will."

Above the mouth of the Salmon, the Snake entered a canyon so narrow, sheer, and filled with tumbling white water that the *Colonel Wright* moved against the current only by using maximum power. At both High Mountain Sheep, Mile 49, and Imnaha Rapid, Mile 51, the boat was forced to pull into shore and send a crew ahead with a line so that the *Colonel Wright* could winch its way through the raging white water. Telling Lars to note that at one spot in the middle of this stretch of the Big Canyon the river was only sixty feet wide, Captain Stump added, "If we turned the boat broadside here, both the bow and stern would be high and dry. Of course, the way the Snake pours through this part of the canyon, we'd be driven under in no time at all."

Having found three rapids that must be winched in the first fifty-one miles upriver from Lewiston, Alonzo Leland, formerly a strong supporter of the explorers who had declared rapturously that they "found nothing in the river to impede navigation whatever," had to admit that the report was dead wrong. Anxious to promote commercial travel on the Snake, the editor asked Captain Stump if he thought judicious blasting of a few rocks scattered through the three rapids would make them more easily surmounted.

"Might help," Stump grunted, nodding. "But it would be an awfully expensive job. Who'd pay for it?"

"Perhaps the merchants of Lewiston would pick up part of the cost, if the O.S.N. Company would pay the rest. Or maybe our Territorial Representative could persuade the Corps of Engineers to undertake it as a federal project. After all, the Engineers are in charge of making improvements in the nation's rivers."

"In its navigable rivers, Mr. Leland," Captain Stump corrected him. "We've still got a long way to go before we can say the Snake above Lewiston is navigable."

At Douglas Bar, Mile 56, the terrain on the Oregon side of the river flattened out for half a mile or so back from the water's edge, then began to rise in a series of steep slopes slashed by winding trails which were scarred by the hoofs of many horses. It was at this spot, Mr. Gray said, that the Wallowa band of Nez Perce Indians crossed the Snake on their way to visit their fellow tribesmen living on the Idaho side of the river.

"You mean, they ferry the river here?" Lars asked incredulously.

"Not exactly, boy. What they do is make bull boats out of buffalo hides and willow frames, pile their women, children, old men, and all their belongings in the boats, then pull them across the river behind young bucks mounted on swimming horses."

"Strong as the current is here, I'd think they'd be swept under and drowned."

"They very seldom get into trouble, I'm told by Indians who have crossed here. Usually, they wait till the river is at a much lower stage than it is now. When it goes down, they say, there's a back eddy half way across that will carry a bull boat or a swimming horse straight to the shallows on the Idaho shore. The Indians call this place 'Nez Perce Crossing.'"

Numbering the spot Mile 57 on his chart, Lars wrote that down. Last year, he recalled, over fifty chiefs of the Nez Perce tribe had met with federal commissioners at Lapwai, headquarters of the Nez Perce Reservation, for a week of talks whose purpose had been to reduce the size of the reservation and bring bands now living in the Wallowa Valley to the Idaho reserve. The chiefs of five dissident bands had refused

to sign the new treaty, preferring to dissolve the Nez Perce nation
rather than give up their freedom. The leader of the rebellious bands
had been a Christianized chief named Old Joseph, who was so in-
censed by the revised treaty that he tore up his Bible and rejected the
white man's religion from that time on.

Knowing that Mr. Gray had come West as a missionary in 1836
and had served with the Nez Perces for many years, Lars wanted to
ask him about Old Joseph. But right now he had time for nothing but
exploration of the river.

For three more days, the *Colonel Wright* fought her way up the
never-ending rapids of the Snake River, her captain, crew, and passengers hoping that beyond the next bend the white water would grow
calmer, the confining bluffs would lower and recede, and the way
would open for clear, easy steaming on toward Boise. But it was not to
be. Instead, the water grew rougher, the canyon narrower, and the cliff
walls on either side turned into towering mountains.

At one spot in the depths of the Big Canyon, Lars used his recently
perfected "rule of thumb" to sight vertically instead of horizontally,
estimating that from water level to the mist-shrouded crest of the
peak overlooking the Oregon side of the river the distance was a
straight up-and-down mile.

Ironically, the place where Captain Stump decided to end the attempt to steam any farther up the river at Mile 73 had been named
Pleasant Valley on Lars' chart, for above the sandbar at river level an
attractive vista of flat, fertile-looking land could be seen, a really lovely
spot on which to file a land claim and build a cabin. Certainly neighbors would be no problem, for in the seventy-three-mile stretch of
river between this point and Lewiston only a handful of Indians, Chinese prospectors, and settlers had been seen.

But at water level, the Pleasant Valley Rapid was a bad one; during
a reconnaissance for half a dozen miles upriver along the shoreline,
those ahead appeared to be even worse.

"By my calculations," Captain Stump said, shaking his head,
"there's fifty to a hundred more miles of canyon, rocks, and white
water ahead between here and Farewell Bend, where the Oregon Trail
crosses the Snake. No steamboat man in his right mind would even
consider starting a commercial operation on this stretch of river."

Turning the bow of the *Colonel Wright* downstream at eleven
o'clock in the morning, Captain Stump either got careless or under-

estimated the power of the current pushing the boat downstream. After barreling into a rapid at a high rate of speed, the boat suddenly was caught in a vicious whirlpool circling toward a sheer lava bluff looming above the Idaho shore, yawed sickeningly to the right, then careened into the jagged projecting rocks, ripping her starboard side from stem to stern with a crunching sound of tearing timbers.

As the boat spun around in the quieter water downstream from the point where she had struck, Captain Stump, who was fighting the wheel, shouted frantic orders.

"Stop engines, Chet! Full power astern! Willie, get a crew ashore with a line. Try to snub her off when we float free. In case she heels over and starts to sink, we've got to keep her bow above water!"

"Aye, aye, sir! Lars, Pa, Mr. Leland, everybody lend a hand! Grab hold of the line and take it ashore!"

Never in all his days aboard the *Colonel Wright* had Lars seen a crew pick up a line and carry it ashore with such speed. First Mate Willie Gray, the senior William H. Gray, Editor Alonzo Leland, the Master Carpenter and his two helpers, both deckhands, and Lars himself all grabbed hold of the heavy two-inch line by its ends, its middle, or wherever else they could seize it, leaped over the side and waded up onto the long stretch of sandy beach below the rapid. Turning to brace themselves when the stricken boat hit the end of the line, Lars at one end and Willie Gray at the other each had a fixed loop in his hand, shaped to fit neatly over a bollard aboard the boat or a rock ashore so that the boat could be snubbed off and kept afloat.

Unfortunately, both Willie's and Lars' loops at the line ends were ashore, for each had assumed that the other would drop *his* loop over the boat's bollard.

As matters turned out, it did not matter, for even as Willie and Lars stared at each other with sheepish chagrin, Captain Stump worked the *Colonel Wright* free of the rocks in which she was entangled, moved her out into the main channel of the river, took her downstream a quarter mile, then, finding quiet water there, brought her bow around into the current. Easing her into the shallows off the Idaho shore, he patiently waited for the line-carrying crew to walk down the bank and rejoin the boat.

While Willie, Lars, and the deckhands shame-facedly coiled and stowed the line aboard, Captain Stump and the Master Carpenter

went below to appraise the damage done to the boat's side. The
fifteen-foot-long rupture was well above the water line, it turned out, so an hour's labor by the Master Carpenter and his helpers sufficed to make temporary repairs so that the hull would not leak and the boat could safely embark on its return trip to Lewiston. In his final report on the trip, Lars noted:

> Covered the same distance it had taken us four and a half days to ascend the river in three and a half hours coming down.

While the *Colonel Wright* was out of service undergoing permanent repairs, First Mate William Polk Gray approached Captain Tom Stump and asked for a week's leave to undertake a private venture. When asked its nature, Willie said, "A man named Phil Atwood owns a sawmill just above Clarkston on the Washington side of the river, sir. He says lumber there is worth only fifteen dollars a thousand board feet. But if he can float it down the Snake and Columbia to Umatilla, Oregon, which is booming, he can sell it for fifty-five dollars a thousand."

"Why doesn't he?"

"He's tried several times, he says, making up big rafts of lumber and trying to float them down the river. But his luck so far has been bad. When the rafts hit the rapids, they break up, the lumber is scattered for miles along the banks, and before he can recover it, white settlers and Indians pick it up and carry it away."

"What does he want you to do?"

"I told him, sir, that if his lumber raft was put together right, and if he got the right man to take it downriver for him, it would get to Umatilla in two or three days without a piece missing."

Captain Stump smiled around his newly lighted cigar. "Then you told him you were the right man?"

"Yes, sir. I did. For ten dollars a day, I told him, I'd take on the job and guarantee to float his raft of lumber down to Umatilla within a week without a piece being lost."

"Well, if anybody can do it, Willie, you can. Hop to it."

After supervising, assembling, and lashing together a raft containing fifty thousand board feet of lumber at Phil Atwood's mill just above Clarkston, Willie Gray brought it across the river to Lewiston, where Atwood added ten thousand feet more. A big, red-faced man in his early forties, Atwood hovered at Willie's side, nervously questioning him about each detail of the operation.

"Don't worry about a thing, Mr. Atwood," Willie reassured him. "I know every rock and rapid in the river. I won't lose a single piece of your lumber."

"I'm going to be riding on the raft with you, Mr. Gray. I won't let you go without me."

"If you insist, sir. I'll carry a skiff amidships in case you decide to get off."

"How big a crew will you be hiring, Mr. Gray?"

"There'll be no crew, Mr. Atwood. Only me."

"How will you control the raft?"

"With a single steering oar, sir, which I'll be holding at the stern."

"That sounds crazy to me. On the other rafts, we had three men with sweeps on each side, doing their best to keep the raft out of the fast water. But they weren't enough. Once the rafts got into the rough water, they broke up and my lumber was scattered all over the river."

"Your men didn't know what they were doing, Mr. Atwood. I do."

"You *say* you do. But I'm not so sure."

"Relax, Mr. Atwood. Just sit back and enjoy the ride."

Between Lewiston, Idaho, and Umatilla, Oregon, lay 180 miles of the Snake and Columbia Rivers, with at least half a dozen major and two dozen minor rapids, in any one of which the raft could come to grief. During previous unsuccessful attempts to float lumber rafts downriver, Willie knew, crews had tried to manage them with side sweeps; all he planned to use was a steering oar at the rear. When approaching a rapid, his predecessors had made desperate efforts to keep to the edge of the rapid in order to avoid the faster water; in the same situation, he intended to steer the raft directly toward the center of the rapid, where the current's force would give the clumsy raft such impetus that it would quickly shoot through into slack water. If worse came to worst, Willie knew that for him all the rapids were swimmable—a piece of information likely of small comfort to Mr. Atwood.

As they moved down the Snake at a brisk nine miles an hour,

Willie cheerfully told his employer that they would get along all right until they came to Palouse Rapid.

"There, we might have a serious time of it," he said, "for the water pours through a narrow chute and empties into an eddy, which boils back toward the current from the south shore."

"But you think we can get through it?" Mr. Atwood demanded.

"Yes, sir. One way or another."

"What does that mean?"

Before Willie could answer, the front part of the raft entered the rapid and he was too busy to talk. The current proved to be so swift that it shot the raft into the eddy at breakneck speed. Before he and Atwood knew what was happening, the forward part of the raft went under water, then the current caught the back end of the raft and drove it under, too.

"We're sinking, Mr. Gray!" Atwood screamed.

Indeed, that was exactly what was happening, Willie realized, for the raft was no longer in sight beneath them. Now the water covering it was up to their knees. Seeing the skiff about to float away, Willie grabbed its painter, told Atwood to get aboard, then joined him. Picking up the oars, Willie used them to keep the skiff pointed downstream in the same general direction the lumber raft had been going when it disappeared.

"What happened to the raft?" Atwood shouted in bewilderment.

Too embarrassed to admit he did not know, Willie made no reply. Reaching down with an oar, he could feel only water beneath them, so he continued to concentrate on keeping the skiff headed downstream in the middle of the main channel. Truth was, his confidence was badly shaken, for this had been his first command—and he had lost it. As for Mr. Atwood, his face, his voice, and his words were gloomy.

"I should have known you couldn't do it, Mr. Gray. Running a steamboat through a rapid like the Palouse is one thing. Taking a big, clumsy raft of lumber through it all by yourself is quite another. The raft will bust apart, I'm sure of that. If and when it does come up, my lumber will be scattered all over the river—"

By now, the skiff was half a mile downstream from Palouse Rapid, where the water was deep and quiet. Suddenly Mr. Atwood broke off his gloomy tirade, then exclaimed, "Willie! Do you feel something coming up from underneath us?"

"Yes, sir! I do!"

What they both felt at the same instant was the big, clumsy raft of lumber—still intact—rising out of the depths under them, lifting the skiff—which still was positioned dead center on the raft—clear of the water. Not a single lashing had broken; not a stick of lumber was out of place.

Relating the story later to Captain Stump, Willie concluded: "You never saw a man more pleased than Mr. Atwood."

It was small wonder that Phil Atwood was pleased. For Willie's four days' work, plus a day's bonus given out of the goodness of his heart, Phil Atwood had paid the nineteen-year-old riverman fifty dollars. For this sum, William Polk Gray had brought a raft of lumber worth nine hundred dollars in Lewiston, Idaho, downriver to Umatilla, Oregon, where it sold for thirty-three hundred dollars—a net profit of slightly under twenty-four hundred dollars. Not a bad return on a fifty-dollar investment.

22.

*E*VEN AS THE *Colonel Wright* explored the upper Snake for the O.S.N. Company, the newly established political entity called Idaho Territory was developing its political and legal traditions during the turmoil of the Civil War. Seeking to escape the consequences of that conflict, many residents of Border States such as Missouri, Kentucky, Nebraska, and Kansas had sold their farms or businesses and headed west toward Oregon during the spring of 1863, planning to re-establish themselves in the peaceful haven of the Willamette Valley, where they imagined the war would have no influence on their lives.

A roughly equal mix of Republicans and Democrats, Unionists and Rebels, honest people and crooks, these emigrants were bewildered to discover that even on the Oregon Trail people carried along the excess baggage of their political beliefs and prejudices, just as they overloaded their wagons with unneeded four-poster beds, anvils, ploughs, and pianos they could not bear to leave behind. Because of the threat of Indian attacks along the way, which made it inadvisable for small trains to travel west of Fort Laramie, most wagon trains combined there into larger units of at least fifty wagons, regardless of politics, sectional loyalties, moral uprightness or lack thereof. This assured some lively times on the Oregon Trail, as it also would do wherever the movers eventually settled.

When the wagon trains passed though southwestern Idaho in the late summer of 1863, the emigrants were surprised to hear that big gold strikes had been made in the region and that Idaho Territory had been established March 10, 1863, by the National Congress. Furthermore, they were pleased to learn that the Idaho soil was fertile, sunshine abundant, skilled labor was in great demand, and all kinds of trades and businesses were flourishing. Why travel on to the Willamette Valley, which was filling up with people, they asked themselves. Why not end their long overland journey here?

Why not, indeed. So many of the trail-weary travelers did just that.

Roughly a third of the new settlers assumed that the North would win the war and that Republicans would be the dominant party in Idaho. Another third was positive that the South would triumph and that Idaho politics would be controlled by Democrats. The remaining third, which had no convictions of any kind, decided to hang around just long enough to steal whatever property was not nailed down before law and order could be established. So the lively times enjoyed back in the Border States and along the Oregon Trail seemed destined to continue for a while in Idaho Territory.

In northern Idaho, where the first strikes had been made and the Territorial capital established, a "Get-the-loot-and-get-out" philosophy prevailed. The miner was king and all property rights were secondary to his desires. Each mining district made its own rules, and invariably those rules favored first discoverers. A member of a prospecting party finding pay dirt in a new region could file a creek claim, a bar claim, a hill claim, a gulch claim, and, in some cases, another of each for a nonpresent friend. If a town developed adjacent to a gold-mining district, the prospector could dig test holes big enough to engulf a mule in the center of its main street or undermine its buildings with tunnels to the point of collapse without being liable for damages or responsible for filling up his burrowings when he was done.

Few of the miners took any interest in politics. A week after the organization of Idaho Territory in March 1863, President Lincoln appointed a governor, a secretary, three judges, and a United States marshal, but months passed before they set foot in their domain. Meantime, a virtual state of anarchy existed, for the laws of Washington Territory and the state of Oregon no longer were in effect, and until a territorial legislature was elected, convened, and passed a code of laws, there would be no laws to be violated. This hiatus lasted for nine months.

In late September 1863, Governor William H. Wallace at last arrived in Lewiston. His first official act was to decree that on October 31 an election would be held to select a legislature and a delegate to the national Congress; his second was to declare himself a candidate for the Territorial Delegate position, which inspired a rash of jokes to the effect that even the governor of Idaho, after one quick look at the Territory, figured the best thing to do was mine whatever political gold he could and then get the hell out.

Immediately following his election as Delegate to Congress, William Wallace resigned as governor and left the Territory. Secretary Daniels, as acting governor, issued a call for the First Legislature to convene in Lewiston in early December, the session to last forty days. The first problem it faced was a real puzzler: how to punish theft and multiple murder without a code of laws, proof that a crime had been committed, or corpses.

Because of their employment by the O.S.N. Company, Lars, his father, Tommy, and his Uncle Emil all were involved in the pursuit, capture, and eventual punishment of the criminals in a case that would become legendary in early Idaho history. Known as the "Hill Beachey Dream Murders," the crime became a classic in frontier justice.

An energetic, outgoing man with many interests and friends, Hill Beachey was the builder and proprietor of the finest hotel in Lewiston, the Luna House. Whenever the *Colonel Wright* laid over for the night, Captain Tom Stump, First Mate Willie Gray, Chief Engineer Chet O'Malley, and Second Mate Lars Warren usually had dinner at the hotel, with before-dinner drinks and after-dinner cigars, compliments of the management. In return, Hill Beachey, who was a big shipper, always was given free passage on all O.S.N. Company boats.

Hill Beachey's best friend was a merchant named Lloyd Magruder, who during the past two years had extended his trading area two hundred miles east into Montana, where new gold strikes had recently been made. In August 1863, Magruder left Lewiston with sixty laden pack mules, telling Hill Beachey that he planned to cross the Bitter Root Mountains to the gold camps near Virginia City, where he hoped to sell his goods at a substantial profit. According to business gossip, he had done so, obtaining thirty-thousand dollars in gold, then heading back toward Lewiston in early fall. His party numbered nine men.

As the time came and passed when he should have returned to Lewiston, his hotelkeeper friend, Hill Beachey, grew increasingly worried about his safety. After dinner one evening at the Luna House, he confided his fears to Captain Tom Stump.

"This sounds crazy, I know, Tom. But last night I had a bad dream about Lloyd and his party. It was so horrible I woke up in a cold sweat."

"What kind of a dream?"

"It had a lot of blood and violence in it. I seemed to be seeing Lloyd and his men lying asleep in a camp deep in the wilderness. I saw

217

some other men creep up on them with axes and knives. In my dream, I saw them all murdered." Beachey shuddered. "It was so terribly real, Tom, I tried to scream a warning. But no sound came out of my throat."

Knowing Hill Beachey to be a solid, practical man not given to wild imaginings, Captain Stump eyed him soberly through the smoke of his cigar.

"You say the Magruder party is overdue in Lewiston?"

"By at least a week. Lloyd isn't a man to waste time on the trail when he's traveling light and knows snow may be falling in the high country any day."

"Who's with him?"

"Four of his regular crew, plus four other men who came to him in Virginia City and asked to travel with his party back to Lewiston."

"Do you know who they are?"

"D. C. Lowry, David Howard, James Romain, and Billy Page. The first three have shady reputations, while the fourth is a witless, weak-spined man whose stupidity often gets him in trouble."

"Well, from what I know of Lloyd Magruder he's usually able to take care of himself. Since he has four loyal men with him, he should be all right."

"That's what I keep telling myself, Tom. Still, I had that horrible dream ..."

Next day, Hill Beachey found solid evidence to support his dream. Four suspicious-acting men had stopped at a ranch near Lewiston the night before, left some mules and saddles there, then had taken an early-morning stage to Walla Walla. Going out to the ranch, Hill Beachey identified the mules and pack saddles as having belonged to his missing friend, Lloyd Magruder. When he questioned the owner of the ranch and the manager of the stage station regarding the identity of the four men, they both told the same story.

"Didn't give no names. Just paid cash, kept their hats pulled low and their faces turned away. Had very little to say. Seemed to be in a hell of hurry to get on their way, wherever they were goin.'"

Now Hill Beachey was positive there had been foul play. His premonition was so strong that he went to Acting Governor Daniels, told him what he had discovered, and demanded that he be given requisitions on the governors of Oregon, Washington Territory, and California for their assistance in arresting the four suspects. At first, Governor

Daniels was dubious.

"I'm not sure I have the authority to issue arrest warrants in a case like this, Mr. Beachey—"

"I'm not asking for warrants, Governor. All I'm asking is a request for assistance."

"Well, I suppose that does make a difference—"

Armed with a piece of paper of dubious value requesting assistance by the authorities of two states and a territory, Hill Beachey and a friend named Tom Pike caught the next stagecoach to Walla Walla. Learning there that four men answering the description of the fugitives had passed through yesterday, gone on to Wallula Landing, then taken a downriverboat bound for Portland, Hill Beachey and Tom Pike rented a team and rig and drove to Wallula, where they found the *Colonel Wright* about to depart for Lewiston after having completed her downriver run to Celilo the previous evening. Hill Beachey told Captain Stump what he had discovered, then asked, "Have you seen these men?"

"As a matter of fact, I have," Captain Stump said wryly. "We took them downriver to Celilo Landing yesterday afternoon."

"So they're a day ahead of us. When does the next downriverboat leave Wallula Landing?"

"The next *scheduled* boat isn't due to head downriver till noon tomorrow, Hill. But I'm changing the schedule as of right now. Lars, tell the Lewiston-bound passengers if they don't want to stay aboard while we go back to Celilo, they can get off and walk. Willie, tell the deckhands to prepare to cast off the lines."

At Celilo in late afternoon, Beachey and Pike took the portage cars to The Dalles, where Captain Tommy Warren, who was overnighting there before making the downriver run to the Upper Cascades tomorrow morning, told Beachy, "Yes, we had four passengers named Lowry, Howard, Romain, and Page aboard yesterday, according to the purser's list. I didn't see them myself. But he tells me they were pretty scruffy-looking characters."

"I'm certain they're murderers, Captain Warren. And I intend to catch them."

"More power to you, Hill. We'll help in any way we can."

At the Lower Cascades, Hill Beachey and Tom Pike learned that the fugitives were still a day ahead, then at Portland were dismayed to discover that twenty hours ago their quarry had gotten aboard an ocean steamer and taken passage to San Francisco. Since there were no telegraph lines between Portland and San Francisco and no steamer fast enough to overtake the fugitives scheduled to sail immediately, it appeared that all chances of catching the fleeing men had been lost. But by now all O.S.N. Company personnel had been alerted to Hill Beachey's problem. Even as Beachey despaired, Emil Warren offered a possible solution.

"The closest telegraphic communication with San Francisco, Mr. Beachey, is at Yreka, California. If you go there, you might be in time"

"How far is it to Yreka?"

"Roughly, 350 miles. And I do mean 'roughly,' for the stage road is terrible."

"But there is stage?"

"You bet there is. And by calling in my cards for a few favors the stagecoach people owe the O.S.N. Company, I can put you aboard their best coach with top drivers and team changes every ten miles. If you travel night and day and don't get your brains scrambled by the worst roads on God's green earth, you may be able to make it in time to wire the chief of police in San Francisco to arrest your suspects the moment they step off the boat."

"I'll be eternally grateful, Mr. Warren."

"Use my name in your telegram to the chief. He's a special friend of mine. Tell him you have warrants issued in the names of the governors of Idaho, Washington, Oregon, and California. That should get his attention."

"Actually, all I have is a requisition for assistance."

"He won't quibble over details, I assure you. Meantime, while you're getting rump-sprung on the stagecoach seat, I suggest you send you friend, Tom Pike, to San Francisco by boat so that he can back up your telegram by identifying the suspects and giving the authorities whatever paperwork they need. Happy hunting, Mr. Beachey."

Leaving Tom Pike to catch the next steamer south, Hill Beachey rode the stagecoach for three days and nights over the worst kind of roads to Yreka and wired a full description of the fugitives and their names to the chief of police in San Francisco. When their ship made port, they were immediately arrested.

A writ of *habeas corpus* briefly delayed the return of the four men to Lewiston for trial, but the San Francisco court—apparently caring no more for legal nitpicking than Idaho did—denied the writ. On December 7, the same day the First Legislature convened in Lewiston, Hill Beachey and Tom Pike arrived home with their prisoners.

There were a couple of legal problems to be ironed out. In the first place, there were no bodies with which to prove that murder had been done. This was neatly solved by a confession from Billy Page relating in horrible detail how Magruder and four other men had been slain and their bodies dumped into a canyon deep in the mountains, where they now lay buried under many feet of snow.

Secondly, Idaho Territory had no code of laws. This the Legislature remedied by enacting a Civil and Criminal Code patterned roughly after the Common Law of England. It took effect January 4, 1864. District Court convened in Lewiston January 5, Judge Samuel C. Parks presiding. Howard, Lowry, and Romain were duly tried and convicted. On January 25, Judge Parks sentenced them to be hanged; and on March 4 the sentence was carried out.

Billy Page, who had turned state's evidence, was permitted to depart. The rumor soon floated back that he had been killed—in what matter or by whom no one knew or cared.

Upon the recommendation of Judge Parks, the Legislature passed an appropriation of $6,244 to reimburse Hill Beachey for expenses incurred in the pursuit and capture of the murderers of his friend. When spring at last melted the snows in the high country of the Lolo Trail to the east, Beachey and a party of men journeyed to the canyon into which Billy Page had said the five bodies had been dumped, found the remains exactly where he had said they would be, and gave them a decent burial.

Following a dinner at the Luna House after Hill Beachey returned from the somber task of burying the remains of his good friend, Captain Tom Stump raised his glass and proposed a grim toast, "Let's drink to Idaho justice, Hill—direct, effective, and not subject to appeal."

23.

*F*OR CARLOS IBANEZ, the cost of his love affair with the beautiful, nineteen-year-old, blonde hurdy-gurdy girl, Anna Lowehr, was becoming almost more than he could afford in terms of time, money, and frustrated emotion. Well established as the bright, glittering jewel of the Bavarian House in the gold boom town of Orofino, Idaho, the lovely, vivacious, blue-eyed Anna Lowehr was something of a gold mine herself. Whenever she was available, the line of eager, hard-breathing men waiting to pay for her services at three dollars a dance was as endless as her energy.

Ground rules established and enforced by the stern-faced Marta Stohlhofen and her bung-starter-wielding husband, Hans, assured the good behavior of Anna Lowehr's dancing partners. That she loved Carlos just as much as he loved her and fully intended to marry him as soon as the year she had contracted to work as a hurdy-gurdy for the Stohlhofens was up, was fully accepted by her employers and the patrons of the establishment. But since the ground rules required: (1) that Carlos also must pay the going rate of three dollars a dance, with no discount for volume; and (2) that following a dance with her, he must go to the end of the line and work his way back up again—which could take all evening—he often found that his 140-mile ride from his ranch in the distant Walla Walla Valley over deeply drifted, muddy, or dusty trails gained scant rewards, so far as precious time with his *novia*—his "sweetheart"—was concerned.

Time and again, he had tried to tempt her into breaking her contract and running away with him. Her horrified response always had been, "But, darling, I cannot do that! I gave the Stohlhofens my promise to work as a hurdy-gurdy for a year. In return, they promised to pay me a thousand dollars in gold when my year is up and to help me find a good husband."

"But you *have* found a good husband, *carisima!* You have found me! As for the thousand dollars, I will pay it to you myself!"

"In gold?"

"Perhaps not in gold, my love. But certainly you will share equally in all my worldly goods, such as land and cattle."

"I love you, Carlos," Anna Lowehr exclaimed, giving him a quick kiss. "Truly, I do! But I will not break my contract with the Stohlhofens."

"Then I will talk to them. Surely they will be reasonable."

In reply to his pleas, the Stohlhofens indeed were reasonable. They would release Anna Lowehr from her contract, they said, if Carlos would pay them the amount of money they expected to make from her services. What was that amount? Five thousand dollars. In gold. Since neither his partner, Emil Warren, nor the bankers in Walla Walla would lend Carlos that kind of money on the land and cattle collateral he offered them, there was nothing left for him to do but wait and suffer.

Sitting at a table near the dance floor in the Bavarian House in Orofino one cold March night, Carlos Ibanez nursed his third glass of brandy in less than two hours as he watched the golden hair of his loved one toss and glitter as she was shoved awkwardly around the sawdust-covered dance floor by one clumsy miner after another. It was part of her job to be pleasant, he knew, and act like she was enjoying the dance, no matter how lead-footed her partner might be. But the knowledge that she was only doing her duty made waiting his turn—which tonight was going to be a long time in coming—no easier.

"Mind if I join you, Carlos?" a genial voice inquired.

"But of course. Sit down, Scott. I will buy you a drink."

Scott Burton was a tall, lanky man in his midforties, a veteran prospector who had taken part in many gold rushes from California to Idaho. A regular at the Bavarian House, he was well aware of the fact that Anna Lowehr and Carlos were in love and that nine more months must pass before they could marry. Raising his glass, he gave Carlos a sympathetic smile.

"It's tough waiting, I know. But nine months ain't forever."

"That is true. But it seems like forever to me."

Hearing the German band, which was made up of a tuba, clarinet, and accordion played by Fritz, Johann, and Wolfgang Stohlhofen, play the opening bars of the crowd's sentimental favorite, *Annie Laurie*, Carlos clapped his hands over his ears and moaned.

"If they play that song one more time, I will go insane!"

"But Carlos," Scott Burton said with a scowl, "twice already this evening you've paid them to play it."

"This I admit, *amigo*. It was Anna Lowehr's birthday song, you see, which the band played aboard the boat the night we fell in love. The first time, I had it played to make her cry, which she did. Then I paid them to play it again, so that we could cry together, which we did. But if they play it a third time …"

"It'll set you off on another crying jag, I know, which you don't want it to do. Well, just stick your fingers in your ears, Carlos, and don't listen." Taking a long swallow of his drink, Scott Burton put down his glass, his eyes misting as he shook his head reflectively. "Minds me of the time my buddies and me sung it with a thousand men comin' down the trail out of the high country." He peered quizzically at Carlos. " 'Course I don't suppose you'd want to hear about that,"

"Hear about what?" Carlos muttered.

"About how a thousand of us men comin' down out of the high country sang *Annie Laurie*."

"Why wouldn't I?"

"Why wouldn't you what?"

"Why wouldn't I want to hear it?"

" 'Cause you just said you didn't want to hear it again."

"*Mira, amigo.* Look, friend. What I said was I did not want to hear the song sung again now. I did not say I did not want to hear your story about how you sang it with a thousand other men coming down the trail from the high country. So tell it, please."

"Well, this is what happened …"

A year or two after the strike had been made in the Orofino district, which was in low-altitude country just over a thousand feet, another strike was made some fifty miles to the south in what became known as the Orogrande region, where the altitude ranged up to seventy-five hundred feet. The Orogrande diggings proved to be so rich that by the end of the summer five thousand men were at work in boom

towns such as Elk City, Florence, and Gospel Hump. Since the only
means of taking supplies into the region meant packing by mule train over narrow, twisting mountain trails, where the snows came early and stayed late, providing food staples with which to support such a large population was going to be an enormous problem when winter came.

"We called a miners' meeting to discuss the situation," Scott Burton told Carlos. "It was decided that each group of five men should appoint one man to stay and represent them on their claim, while the other four men would go out to winter in lower country where food would be more available. Not over a thousand men would go out at any one time …"

Scott Burton and Clay Harlow were selected to lead the first thousand-man contingent on the two-day trek from the high country down to the milder weather of the South Fork of the Clearwater. Their friends, Fi Gilbert and Charley Painter, also were going out of the district to winter, leaving behind a fifth man to represent them on their claim.

Traveling light, they reached the Halfway House the first night. From that point on, it was mostly downhill to the Clearwater, Scott Burton said, which the four men reached in late afternoon the second day.

Up in the high country, killing frost had come weeks ago; tamarack and aspen had turned to gold; and winter was at hand. But here in this low valley as they gathered wood for their campfire and dipped water out of the stream for tea, the air was balmy and mild. In a few days, they would be home—gold in their pockets, exciting tales of adventure to tell their loved ones, and long months ahead in which to talk and dream of the fortunes they would surely make next summer. They built a fire, put water on to boil, then …

We saw the main body of the long line following us coming around the high point where the switchback began. There were three other points where the trail and the men on it could be seen. As I mixed batter for flapjacks, Clay Harlow, who was tending the fire, began singing *Annie Laurie*. Fi, Charley, and I joined in.

The long line of men was soon coming into camp, picking out a spot for a fire, dropping their blankets, and preparing their meal. Group by group, they began singing, too. The song spread up the line of moving men like a fire. Soon from the camp to the highest point at the beginning of the switchback the men were singing in one giant chorus about two miles long—all singing *Annie Laurie*.

Away up on the mountainside, a man would come around one of the points on the switchback singing, and then as he went back into the draw his voice would fade until he would again come out on the next point below, still singing *Annie Laurie*. The singing did not stop until every man was in camp and was wrapped in his blankets, asleep by the fire. Each man recalled a different name, but we all sang *Annie Laurie*.

When Scott Burton finished telling his story, Carlos sat staring down at his empty brandy glass, his eyes brimming with tears. At last, he murmured, "*Amigio mio*—friend of my heart—that is the most beautiful story I have ever heard. I thank you for telling it. But it does not solve my problem."

"What problem?"

"*Anna Lowehr! Mi amor! Anna Lowehr!* How can I live without her until her year is up?"

In some manner or other, Carlos Ibanez did manage to live out the year, at the end of which his beautiful, blonde, blue-eyed hurdy-gurdy girl was given a thousand dollars in gold by her employers, Hans and Marta Stohlhofen. Joining him in Walla Walla, she married her handsome, dark-eyed sweetheart. Giving in to his bride's wish that the ceremony take place in the Congregational Dutch Reformed Church in Walla Walla, Carlos pleaded with his brother-in-law, Emil Warren, who was his best man, to intercede for him with his sister, Dolores, explaining why he had married outside the Catholic Church.

"All I can promise, brother, is I'll try," Emil answered uncomfortably. "Maybe the fact that I married *into* the Catholic Church, while you married out of it, will be considered a fair trade wherever such deals are made."

24.

*A*s a senior captain with the Oregon Steam Navigation Company, Tommy Warren had his choice of boats and runs along the lower and middle river. Living as he and Freda did close to Rooster Rock, Multnomah Falls, and Crown Point—roughly 120 miles east of the mouth of the Columbia River—they had the best of all scenic worlds. In view from their house were the towering peaks and bluffs of the Cascade Mountains upriver, the majestic milewide sweep of the river itself, and the broadening vista downriver to the west of Oregon's beautiful, fertile Willamette Valley to the south and the equally wide stretch of plains, low hills, and prairies of Washington Territory north of the river.

Even this far inland, the rise and fall of the ocean tides could be seen and felt. A spring or summer wind from the west bore the sharp salt tang of the sea. A fall or winter wind from the east carried the acrid odor of the inland desert country's dust and sagebrush or the high mountain chill of impending snow. At any season of year, rolling banks of fog, sudden veils of mist, showers, cloudbursts, or a blinding explosion of sunlight through a rift in the clouds bathed the land in a beauty so intense and fleeting that no artist's brush ever could have moved fast enough to capture it on canvas.

Of all Tommy's commands during the 1860 boom days of the lower Columbia River, the most intriguing was his stint on the *New World*. Like all river captains, Tommy knew the history of the boats he piloted all the way back to the date and place where they had been launched, their tonnage, their speed, their best and worst sailing points, their brushes with near disaster, and the identity of every master who had commanded them in local or distant waters. When asked to take over the *New World* on the run between Portland and the Lower Cascades in the spring of 1864, Tommy knew at once that he was climbing into the pilot house of a boat steeped in history.

"When she first came out to the West Coast in 1850, she was called the 'runaway steamboat,'" he told Freda. "Her captain literally stole her out from under the nose of the sheriff in New York Harbor, then brought her around the Horn to San Francisco. Now the O.S.N. Company has bought her and turned her over to me."

Built for the Hudson River trade in the late 1840s, the *New World* was 225 feet long, propelled by side-wheels operated by a powerful walking-beam engine. She could reel off twenty knots at sea, a speed she needed after sailing without papers out of New York Harbor to avoid a lien and becoming fair game for any privateer able to capture her on the high seas. In Panama, marshals tried to seize the vessel, but Captain Ned Wakeman, who was something of a rogue, enlisted the aid of two hundred men eager to go to the California goldfields, offering to take them aboard if they would persuade the law officers to let his ship weigh anchor. Giving the marshals the choice of letting the *New World* sail or being tossed overboard to feed the fishes, the gold-seekers prevailed.

Off the coast of Rio, the runaway ship outdistanced a British frigate that attempted to take her as a prize, slipping into the safe harbor of the neutral port for three days, then slipping out through a heavy fog and again outrunning a three-ship task force on her way south toward the raging storms of Cape Horn.

At Valapariso, a three-week quarantine was imposed on the ship when it was discovered that a member of her crew was infected with yellow fever. Though eighteen men died before the epidemic ran its course, a few handfuls of gold slipped into the right palms persuaded the authorities to lift the quarantine after eight days, then the ship sailed on north to the Golden Gate.

For fourteen years she ran successfully against competition on the Sacramento River, her fine accommodations, excellent dining room, and great speed attracting a large clientele of well-paying passengers. In 1864, the Oregon Steam Navigation Company purchased her, brought her north to the Columbia River, and put her on the Portland-Cascades run. There, under the command of first Captain John Wolf, then Tommy Warren, she set records for speed, freight, and passenger revenue that would never be equaled.

On one trip from Portland to the Lower Cascades, a distance of 120 river miles from dock to dock, she made the run in a little over six hours. Coming downriver from the Lower Cascades at the height of the interior gold boom, she made history and newspaper headlines when Emil Warren, who was aboard, casually mentioned to an *Oregonian* reporter that on that particular day she was carrying a ton of gold.

"A *ton* of *gold?*" the reporter exclaimed. Being young, new to the Pacific Northwest, and very much impressed to be having a drink with the chief attorney for the Oregon Steam Navigation Company, whose brother was captain of this fabled boat, the reporter was awed by the figure. "Good Heavens, Mr. Warren! What would a ton of gold be worth in terms of dollars?"

"Well, there are sixteen ounces in a pound, two thousand pounds in a ton, and gold is worth around fifteen dollars an ounce at the mint in San Francisco. Figure it out for yourself."

Wrinkling his brow, pursing his lips, and wetting the stub end of his pencil with his tongue, the young reporter wrote down a number of figures, then finally announced reverently, "Best I can figure, sir, that comes to $480,000."

"Sounds about right to me," Emil said casually. "Of course, the ton of gold consigned to us by Wells Fargo doesn't include what our passengers have put in the purser's safe or the pouches a lot of them are carrying on their persons. All told, I'd say we've got half a million dollars in gold aboard."

"Good Lord! What if the boat should hit a rock and sink?"

"Gold is mighty heavy, son. It would sink, too."

"What if somebody tried to steal it?"

"They'd better be prepared to do some heavy lifting. It would take a lot of wheelbarrows to cart away a ton of gold."

TON OF GOLD ABOARD THE NEW WORLD
NO PRECAUTIONS AGAINST THEFT TAKEN

Following publication of the young reporter's story in the *Oregonian* a few days later, it became something of a game aboard downriverboats to sit in the bar and concoct schemes by which a ton of gold might be successfully hijacked. What they all came down to in the end was that "a lot of heavy lifting" would be required.

BILL GULICK
With the Civil War ended and the inland city of Walla Walla beginning to mature as a farming, ranching, and trading center, the pros-
perity of "The town people liked so well they named it twice"
expanded remarkably. The newest showplace of the metropolis was
the luxurious Entertainment Parlor designed, built, and owned by
Ma'm'selle Lili deBeauchamp, more familiarly known to her multi-
tude of friends as "French Lil."

Despite the wide range of music, drinks, fun, and amusement offered in the Parlor, no patron ever got into trouble while visiting
French Lil's. Nor would any visitor ever dare to start trouble himself,
should he be so inclined. One reason for this was the monstrous, menacing bulk of Goliath Samson, who between stints of playing the cello,
drums, and tambourine, routinely patrolled the public rooms of the
place, then made sure that the house rule which decreed that no private room could be locked by a male patron was strictly enforced. Despite his size, Goliath Samson had demonstrated more than once how
quickly he could move and how firmly he could act when a call for
help came from a girl who feared she was about to be abused by an
inebriated customer.

A second reason for the good behavior of the patrons was that the
chief of police, the mayor, the fire chief, the newspaper editor, the
town's leading banker, doctor, and even the priest of the local Catholic
church and private school were regular visitors at the establishment.
Their calls, of course, were strictly platonic, being for the purpose of
enjoying a cigar and a glass of wine when they stopped by to collect
French Lil's generous contributions to the charities affiliated with
their organizations.

Following the advice of the local banker, Lewis Holcomb, French
Lil had invested the substantial funds she had brought north from the
sale of her business on the Barbary Coast in fertile farm and ranch
lands, which now were leased on profitable terms. The four-story red-
brick building in which her enterprise was housed stood just one block
south of Second and Main, the busiest intersection in town. Half of
the first floor and all of the basement were leased to a hardware store
and gun shop, while the other half of the first floor was a temporary
headquarters for the local bank, which planned to erect and occupy its
own building on a corner lot a block to the north next year.

Occupying the second floor were a bar, a theater with a raised
stage, and a parlor where gentlemen visitors and the ladies employed
by the house could meet, chat, and get acquainted. It also contained a

private office for Lili herself, where the mistress of the house could confer with her chief hostess, a tall, statuesque redhead in her early thirties named Anne, or with visitors calling to advise her on business and investment matters.

The third floor was broken up into a number of small, clean bedrooms where the girls employed by the house took their gentlemen friends when both parties decided they wished to get to know each other better.

The fourth floor contained private apartments for Lili, Anne, Goliath Samson, and the silver-haired piano player, Harold Wilson, plus a small two-bedroom apartment for girls who were temporarily indisposed.

Local legend had it that French Lil never would start a girl in the business, even though she herself had become a full-time professional on the Barbary Coast at the age of sixteen. This proved to be true one weekend when Anne came into her private office and said, "I've got a couple of visitors who'd like to talk to you, Lili."

"Oh? Who are they?"

"All they'll tell me is their names are Judy and Jan. They've been living in Portland, they say, where they've been working in one of the best houses in town. But they heard you pay more and need a few fresh young faces. So they hopped on a boat and came here."

Giving Anne a quizzical smile, Lili said, "Do I detect a note of skepticism in your voice, Anne?"

"You sure do. If romps in a hay mow with local boys don't count, this is a pair of vagrant virgins who think it would be wonderful to wear beautiful clothes, make a lot of money on their backs, and live like queens."

"How old are they?"

"Judy is nineteen, she says, while Jan swears she's twenty. But if you want my guess, neither one of the little vixens is very far past her sixteenth birthday. If either one of them ever has been more than fifty miles outside the Walla Walla city limits, I'd be surprised. Shall I tell them to get lost?"

"No, send them in," Lili said with a sigh. "This sort of thing has been happening too often lately. It's time we made an example of them."

From the flushed, nervous look on the faces of the two girls as Lili questioned them in Anne's presence, and the tense, high-pitched giggles punctuating their responses, Lili became convinced that her chief hostess had identified the two girls for what they really were. But she gave no indication that she doubted any part of their story.

"Well, Jan and Judy," she said warmly, "I do believe that you two young ladies are exactly what we need here. We have several handsome, rich gentlemen clients who I'm sure will be delighted with you. Do you have any objection to men who are in their forties?"

Exchanging quick, self-conscious glances, Judy and Jan shook their heads. "Oh, no, Miss Lili!" Judy said, while Jan quickly added, "As long as they pay good."

"I'm sure you'll find they pay quite well," Lili said. Rising from her chair, she ushered the two girls to the door, while Anne followed. "I'll appreciate it, Anne, if you'll see to it that Judy and Jan are bathed, given attractive hairdos, and dressed in the finest of clothes. Please instruct them in what they will be expected to do when they entertain their mature gentlemen friends, which will be tomorrow evening."

"Certainly, Miss Lili. I won't skip a thing."

After Anne and the two new recruits were gone, Lili summoned Goliath Samson, told him about the girls, and asked him to run a check with the chief of police, Abe Browder, as to the identity of the two young ladies. Before the day was out, he brought her a complete report. Reading it, she smiled and nodded. Then she called Anne in and told her what she intended to do.

Local gossip has it that the two girls—who it turned out were barely sixteen years old and never had ventured more than twenty miles outside of town—were the daughters of a local farmer and a staff sergeant at Fort Walla Walla. Both men were in their forties, liked young girls, and were regular patrons of French Lil's.

True to her promise, Lili arranged for the two men to meet the two girls in the privacy of their separate rooms, next evening, with Goliath Samson standing by in case a violent reaction occurred. Discreet as always, Goliath never told anyone except Lili and Anne what happened when the local farmer opened the door beyond which his daughter Judy was waiting or what occurred when the staff sergeant met his daughter, Jan.

All that became known to the other employees of French Lil's Entertainment Parlor and the townspeople was that both fathers and both daughters hastily left the premises—and never returned …

By now, the economy of Walla Walla had changed from that of a supply point and a wintering place for transient miners to the more solid base of a stable farming and ranching community. In addition to French Lil's Entertainment Parlor, three smaller houses patronized by men seeking affection and amusement had sprung up in more modest quarters on the west side of town, which, by common consent, had become the saloon and entertainment district of the city. Although no ordinance covered the subject, it was tacitly agreed that four houses catering to carnal appetites were quite enough for a town of this size.

It was further understood that strict rules of behavior would be imposed by the police and accepted by the proprietors of the houses. Enforcement of these rules would be accomplished and paid for not by a municipal license or tax but by "voluntary" contributions made by the owners of the establishments on a regular cash basis, with no receipts asked or given. Twice nightly a uniformed foot patrolman would climb the stairs of the three lower-class houses, sit for ten minutes or so in the reception parlor smoking a cigar provided by the hostess, discussing whatever problems she might be having with her customers, then be given two silver dollars and sent on his way rejoicing.

Aware of these visits, few patrons were so foolish as to cause problems. If they did and the patrolman was forced to return with reinforcements, the persons causing the disturbance were immediately arrested, jailed, and fined, with an equal or greater fine imposed on the house itself, which invariably banned the instigators of the trouble from the establishment for a long time to come.

Because French Lil's Entertainment Parlor catered to higher-class patrons and had its own police force in the form of Goliath Samson, no foot patrolmen ever visited her place of business nor was she required to pay protection money to insure order. Instead, Chief of Police Abe Browder responded directly to any request for information or assistance that might be required, as he recently had done in the case of the two vagrant virgins. Furthermore, Chief Browder was a regular member of the party of local businessmen and community leaders which took part each Friday afternoon in a custom called "Making the Rounds."

As a substantial part of the local economy, the four houses spent a considerable amount of money each week on food, drink, fuel, jewelry, reading materials, dental, and medical services. Though the local businessmen knew that the houses were good credit risks, they felt it prudent to collect their bills once a week in cash. Since they all were family men who did not want their visits to the houses misinterpreted, they did their bill collecting as a group, moving from place to place together each Friday afternoon, beginning at two o'clock at the plainest of the four houses, giving it half an hour for a drink, a cigar, and a bit of conversation with the madam, moving on to the second house, where forty-five minutes would be spent, then to the third, where an hour would be passed, then finally to the most luxurious place of all, French Lil's.

By that time, it would be 4:00 P.M. Three drinks or glasses of wine would have been consumed, and the merchants and circulating pillars of the community would be ready for the smoked oysters, imported cheese, vintage wine, whiskey, brandy, and the fine Cuban cigars always available at French Lil's. A hostess without peer, she could be depended upon to provide the best of vocal and instrumental entertainment, an hour of highly stimulating intellectual conversation, plus payment in gold of the bills her establishment had incurred during the past week, over which she never quibbled. When asked to make a contribution to the Fireman's Fund, the Policeman's Pension, the Catholic Parish Endowment, or whatever other worthy cause was represented by her visitors, she could be counted on to respond generously. On one occasion when the City Cemetery Association needed financial help, she even bought twelve burial plots so that she and her girls could be interred side by side when they passed on.

Local gossip relates that on only one occasion was the late Friday-afternoon visit to French Lil's anything other than a "happy hour." On that particular day, Father Patrick Flannigan, Police Chief Abe Browder, Mayor Foster Prentice, Fire Chief Karl Sontag, Editor Mike Mallory, Banker Lewis Holcomb, Dr. Walter Lyman, and half a dozen local merchants had been served their food, drink, and cigars, when Lili quietly said to Dr. Lyman, "One of my girls hasn't been feeling well, Dr. Lyman. Would you mind taking a look at her?"

"Be glad to."

Going upstairs with French Lil, Dr. Lyman returned alone some fifteen minutes later, crossed to the sideboard, and poured himself half a snifter of brandy. Turning to face the assembled pillars of the community, he said gruffly,

"Gentlemen, I have an announcement to make."

"Hear, hear!" chortled Editor Mike Mallory, who was feeling no pain. "Doc Lyman's got an announcement."

"The young lady I just examined," Dr. Lyman said, "has scarlet fever. Therefore, in accordance with the law, I am placing this house and all its occupants under quarantine for two weeks."

"The hell you say!" Mayor Prentice exclaimed.

"Quarantine?" Lewis Holcomb muttered.

"Two weeks?" Police Chief Browder snorted.

"Hey!" several local merchants cried in unison. "We better get out of here fast!"

Dr. Lyman held up his hand in a restraining gesture. "On the contrary, gentlemen, nobody—and I do mean *nobody*—is leaving these premises for two weeks. That's what the law requires. As Public Health Officer for the City of Walla Walla, I shall insist that the law be enforced."

"But ... but ... but ... !" a dozen men sputtered at once.

Motioning Goliath Samson into a position where he could block the door and prevent anyone from leaving the room, Dr. Lyman smiled coldly. "We're all law-abiding citizens, I'm sure. None of us wants to be responsible for spreading an epidemic of scarlet fever throughout the community, do we?" He scowled at the men in the room. "Well, *do* we?"

Reluctantly, the assembled pillars of the community agreed that none of them wanted to do that. Individually, what they wanted was for an exception to be made in their particular case, but, being reasonable men, they recognized the fact that if an exception were made for one person, it must be made for all. Mayor Prentice asked the question on everyone's mind."

"What about you, Doc? Are you gonna quarantine yourself?"

"Of course not! I'm a physician. But I assure you I will fumigate my clothes and my person to make sure I do not carry the infection with me when I leave."

"I'm Mayor of Walla Walla. Couldn't you fumigate me, too?"

"The quarantine law permits only medical doctors to come and go from a premise under quarantine, Foster. All of you gentlemen will have to accept that."

In the end, all the gentlemen did. Since even Father Flannigan was caught in the enforced two-week stay in French Lil's Entertainment Parlor and the practice of Making the Rounds was known and accepted

BILL GULICK in the community, no accusations of wrongdoing ever were made by the public at large. In fact, since no scarlet fever epidemic ensued, the dozen or so men trapped in the establishment came to be regarded as heroes, having made the great sacrifice of spending two weeks of their lives trapped in a whorehouse—albeit, a very nice one—for the benefit of the community at large.

True, some inconveniences were suffered—such as city, church, newspaper, and commercial business being done by means of messages passed back and forth in fumigated baskets lowered and raised from the second-story window to the ground. But taken all in all, the parties concerned made the best of the situation—particularly French Lil's girls, who got a pleasant two-week vacation.

25.

$\mathcal{B}$ECAUSE OF THE FORESIGHT of its chief attorney, Emil Warren, the Oregon Steam Navigation Company had a profitable monopoly on the freight and passenger traffic ascending the Columbia and Snake to the north Idaho mines. But following the Boise Basin and Owyhee strikes in southern Idaho, passengers began to favor the water route to Sacramento, thence by stage to Red Bluff, California, and northeast across the Idaho desert.

Over this route, the fare from San Francisco to Idaho City was only $66. By sea to Portland, up the Columbia to Umatilla Landing, then across the Blue Mountains by stage, the ticket price came to $123. Furthermore, since the ocean voyage often was rough and disasters frequent, more and more people bound for the south Idaho mines were bypassing Portland.

"We must leave no stone unturned to divert all the Boise and Owyhee trade this way," Emil warned the O.S.N. Company directors. "Hence the building of a steamboat on Snake River to run from Olds Ferry to a point equidistant from Owyhee and Boise City is not a matter of choice but necessity."

Olds Ferry was located on the Idaho side of the Snake opposite Farewell Bend. By building a steamer that would ply the relatively tranquil 125 miles between the base of the Blue Mountains and the Boise City–Owyhee road, the O.S.N. Company hoped to divert traffic back to Portland, cut into the revenues of the Oregon–Idaho stage companies, and give the owners of the San Francisco–Red Bluff route something to worry about. If the Snake proved navigable as far upriver as Salmon Falls, a connection might even be made with Salt Lake and the transcontinental railroad hopefully soon to come.

A shipyard was established near the mouth of the Boise River, and in late autumn of 1865 lumber to be used in the steamer began to arrive. She was to be a good-sized boat, 136 feet long, and must be built at great cost because her boilers, engines, and metal parts had to be transported up the Columbia to Umatilla Landing, then freighted across the Blues over often impassable roads. Since the Indian troubles of 1866–68 were beginning at this time, arrows and bullets fired by hostiles now and then made workmen scramble for cover. But on April 20, 1866, the *Shoshone*, as the steamer built on the western edge of the Idaho desert was named, celebrated her launching with enthusiastic ceremony.

On her maiden voyage, the *Shoshone* proved the Snake navigable between Olds Ferry and a point a few miles upstream from the mouth of the Bruneau River. During the summer of 1866, she made several runs from Olds Ferry to Owyhee Crossing, and though operating at a loss, did have an effect on the rate war. Coal deposits had been discovered along the banks of the Snake in this area, but the coal was of such low grade that it was useless as fuel.

"Takes a cord of wood to keep a ton of the coal burning," the chief engineer exclaimed in disgust. "It just ain't worth the trouble."

Like most of the country along the lower and middle Snake, the banks were treeless and the supply of easy-to-obtain firewood soon exhausted. Cutting resin-filled pine and fir in distant mountain country, chopping it into boiler lengths, then transporting the fuel down to the steamer was a prohibitively expensive process.

"Our Snake riverboat is laid up for lack of wood," John C. Ainsworth of the O.S.N. Company reported in August, 1866. "We do not think of starting her again before next spring, at which time, if we succeed in getting wood and making proper connections, she will do a fair business."

But the wood problem could not be solved. For three years the *Shoshone* lay idle at her moorings. In 1869, the officials of the O.S.N. Company considered taking a risky gamble. Could the steamer be brought downriver through the Big Canyon and put in service on a more profitable run? they wondered. Emil Warren thought the gamble worth taking. When the Lewiston editor of the *Radiator,* Alonzo Leland, heard it was being considered, he issued a dire warning in print:

> A more perilous and uncertain adventure has never been undertaken in these waters. We shall watch its progress with interest. The canyon between Powder River and the mouth of the Salmon is said to be seventy miles long and is supposed to be a continuous succession of rapids the whole way. River men have always considered it an impossibility to navigate the canyon even with a small boat.

When informed that one of the experts being consulted on the feasibility of the project was nineteen-year-old Lars Warren, Alonzo Leland declared that the O.S.N. Company could not have picked a better man. Despite his youth, Leland said, no one knew the Snake in the Big Canyon sector better than he did.

"Lars Warren charted the river mile by mile when Captain Tom Stump took the *Colonel Wright* into the canyon as far up as a boat has ever gone. He knows all the rapids by their first names. He's the one who named them."

Asked by experienced steamboat captains if the *Shoshone* could be expected to survive a trip through the Big Canyon, Lars repeated the statement made to him and Willie Gray by the senior William H. Gray ten years ago: "The boat will come down through the rapids of the Big Canyon—that I guarantee. She may come down in pieces—but she will come down. The trick will be to keep the pieces as big as possible."

In June, the O.S.N. Company sent veteran Captain Cy Smith and a pickup crew to Owyhee Landing with orders to move the *Shoshone* into the upper reaches of the Big Canyon and test the feasibility of bringing her downriver. Though Captain Smith was capable enough, the crew was a poor one. Faced with low water, exposed rocks, and potential danger, the crew deserted Captain Smith at a spot named Steamboat Creek, leaving the task of bringing the boat down through the Big Canyon to a better crew and a more aggressive captain. Exasperated by the penny-pinching efforts made so far to salvage a substantial investment, Emil Warren took charge of the project himself. Selecting Captain Sebastian Miller, Chief Engineer Daniel Buchanan, and First Mate Lars Warren to supervise the operation, he told them to employ the best men they could find from the ranks of the Company and pay them top wages.

"One way or another, I want the *Shoshone* brought downriver to where she'll start earning her keep," Emil said grimly. "Do it or put her where we can't find her."

Arriving at Steamboat Creek in early April 1870, Captain "Bas" Miller and his crew found that after lying idle for several years the pine-lumber seams of the boat had opened so badly that daylight showed through them. With insufficient caulking material available, Captain Miller ordered Lars: "Rig the pumps and fill her with river water until she barely floats. After we've let her set for a week or two, her seams should swell enough to make her watertight."

"Yes, sir. We'll get at it right away."

"She'll need some ballast to give her stability. What do you think we ought to put in her—rock or coal?"

"Cordwood or lumber would be better, sir. If we hole her sides or bottom, wood will keep her afloat."

"That's what Captain Stump used in the *Colonel Wright*, wasn't it?"

"Yes, sir. And it saved us from sinking when we ripped a fifteen-foot-long gash in her side twenty-five miles above the mouth of the Salmon."

"Then that's what we'll do. See to it, will you?"

Ten days of flooding below decks swelled the seams to the extent that after the water was pumped out no daylight showed through. Replacing the water with cordwood and lumber, Lars set lighted candles in the hold atop the wood so that any remaining leaks would show up. When none did, Captain Miller gave Engineer Buchanan the order to make steam. The lines were cast off and the *Shoshone* pulled out into the river.

With the river running high in early spring flood, the current proved to be very strong. Before the captain got the feel of the controls, the *Shoshone* found herself in the powerful grip of the river. As he rang frantically for full speed astern, the boat was sucked into the trough of a rapid swirling toward Copper Ledge Falls two hundred yards downstream. Still not under control, she spun around three times as she tried to fight clear of the current, failed, then, as she finally got her bow turned downstream, shuddered and plunged at breakneck speed over the middle of the rapid.

Striking the deep pool below, the *Shoshone* careened sickeningly into a sheer lava bluff on the left-hand shore, ripped eight feet off her bow, spun around again, struck the near end of her churning paddle wheel against the rocks, splintering a three-foot section of the wheel. Finally getting control of the boat, Captain Miller pulled her into a quiet cove below Copper Ledge Falls, where Lars Warren got a couple of deckhands ashore with lines by which the craft was secured to convenient rocks.

"Godalmighty!" Captain Miller exclaimed, taking off his cap and mopping his sweating brow as Lars came up to the pilot house to report the boat secured. "That was a mean one! How much more of that kind of river have we got ahead of us, Lars?"

"A hundred miles, more or less."

"Well, we're committed now. One way or another, we'll take her through or put her where the sun don't shine."

As Willie Gray had learned while taking a raft of lumber through Palouse Rapid on the lower Snake several years ago, fighting the tremendous current of the river was wasted effort. Even with the full power of the engines threshing the paddle wheels full astern, a boat the size of the *Shoshone* could not avoid being sucked into the main channel surging downriver; all the reverse thrust of the wheel could do for the boat was give her a little steerageway above and below the rapid.

In half a dozen locations through the Big Canyon—Wild Sheep, Rush Creek, Granite Creek, Imnaha, High Mountain Sheep, and Wild Goose—what were called rapids really were waterfalls dropping eight to ten vertical feet, with sharp bends in narrow, steep-walled canyons just below the falls, making it inevitable that a speeding boat would crash into the rocks bordering the channel and damage her bow, side, or stern. After this happened several times, with the *Shoshone* forced to tie up and spend a day or two making repairs, Captain Miller and First Mate Warren found it prudent to pull into shore upstream from an impending dangerous stretch of river, walk ahead along the bank, spend an hour or two examining the fall or rapid, testing it by tossing pieces of wood into the river and closely watching what the swirling current did to them.

"She'll strike that ledge yonder about ten feet behind the stem, I would say," Captain Miller predicted, pointing at a sheer lava cliff just downstream from the foot of the rapid, where the river took an abrupt turn to the left. "What we ought to do, I'm thinking, is have the carpenters build out a falsework frame of braced two-by-fours, which will take the brunt of the crash and save the boat's hull from being caved in. Do you agree?"

"Yes sir, I do. But we'd better build a falsework frame to protect the stern, too. There'll be a whiplash action, I'm guessing, which will slam the stern into the same rock wall. If we crush a paddle wheel and lose steerageway, we'll be in real trouble."

The fact that the *Shoshone* was making its run through the Big Canyon during the height of spring floods meant that plenty of water covered the sharp, jagged rocks lining the bottom of the main channels, where the deepest water ran, so there was little danger of holing the boat's hull below waterline, which could have proved fatal. Of the ten days it took to negotiate the Snake between Steamboat Creek and Lewiston, Lars noted in the log, only four were spent running the river, and the other six were passed tied to shore while the overworked crew of carpenters and deckhands repaired the damage down to the boat's bow, hull, and stern-wheel.

As the battered steamboat pulled into the dock at Lewiston, Captain Miller leaned on the whistle cord and used up a bit of Engineer Daniel Buchanan's precious steam to announce the triumphant arrival of the *Shoshone* at what until now had been the head of navigation on the upper Snake River.

After a few days' rest, during which more permanent repairs were made on the boat, she moved down through the quieter waters of the Snake between Lewiston and Wallula Landing, where First Mate Lars Warren disembarked. Awaiting the boat there was Emil Warren, so pleased with the success of his gamble that, after enthusiastically shaking Captain Miller's hand, he embarrassed Lars by throwing his arms around him and giving him a bear hug of an embrace.

"I knew you could do it, Lars! So far as I'm concerned, you're the best pilot on the Snake River!"

"Thank you, sir." Lars gave his uncle a questioning look. "Good enough for a captain's rating, would you say?"

"I don't know why not! Certainly, I'll recommend that the next boat we launch at Celilo Landing be given to you."

"When will that be?"

"We're planning to build a grain boat for the lower Snake River run next year. Going to call her the *Inland Queen*. If I have my say, she'll be yours."

"May I tell Daphne that?" Lars said eagerly. "May I tell her now?"

"Why, sure, if you want to," Emil said with a scowl. "But what's the hurry?"

"We plan to get married as soon as I've earned my captain's rating and am given a boat of my own."

"Hell, boy, you and Daphne are too young to get married! You're only twenty and Daphne's still a child."

"I'll be twenty-one years old in six months, Uncle Emil. Daphne will be nineteen."

"Lord, how time flies!"

"With a captain's rating and a boat of my own, I'll be making three hundred dollars a month. Isn't that enough to get married on?"

"Sure it is, Lars. But what about *her* mother? And your mother? What will they say?"

"It's not our mothers who're getting married, sir," Lars said stubbornly. "It's Daphne and me." He gave his uncle a conspiratorial smile. "To tell the truth, Uncle Emil, I'm letting you in on our plans in hopes you'll smooth the way for us with both our mothers—and the rest of my family as well. You're awfully good at that."

"Thanks for the compliment—if it is one," Emil growled sardonically. Then he smiled. "I'll give it some thought, Lars. Maybe I can come up with an idea …"

Though Lars Warren never saw the *Shoshone* again, he followed her wanderings for the next few years with considerable interest. When passenger traffic between Celilo Landing and Lewiston did not prove sufficient to warrant keeping her in service on that run, Captain Bas Miller utilized the last of the early summer flood on the Columbia River and his newly learned skills at running waterfalls downriver to accomplish the unheard-of feat of taking the *Shoshone* over Celilo Falls, whose normal height of twenty feet was lessened to ten because of the tremendous amount of water pouring over the falls at this time of the year.

In the narrow, lava-rimmed, fourteen-mile-long channel between the foot of the falls and The Dalles, where Lewis and Clark had estimated the current to race at thirty miles an hour, Captain Miller asked Chief Engineer Buchanan to give him a maximum head of steam so that he could take the boat into the chute at full speed for better steering control. Since the *Shoshone* had been clocked at twenty-five miles an hour, the land speed related to a stationary object ashore was fifty-five miles an hour, which, by any standard, was flying.

The *Shoshone* made it without once kissing a rock.

Put onto the middle river run between The Dalles and the Upper Cascades during the rest of the summer, fall, and winter—where she again failed to earn her keep—the *Shoshone* registered another "first" under Captain Miller's command next spring when he took her down through the six-mile-long white-water stretch called the Upper, Middle, and Lower Cascades—again with no damage.

For a season, she operated on the Cascades-Portland run. Then, seeking still another river to conquer, she was winched ashore below Willamette Falls, taken around them by land, then relaunched into the Willamette River upstream and put into service on the Oregon City–Eugene run. After plying the Willamette for several years, she was wrecked on a sandbar near Salem in the fall of 1874. By this time, the once-gallant steamboat was beginning to show her age, so no effort was made to tow her back into deeper water and bring her downstream where she could be repaired.

Next spring, when high water cast her hulk ashore, she continued to be neglected. Eventually, a farmer detached her pilot house and converted it into a chicken coop—the final ignominy for a well-traveled lady who never was really at home in any river ...

Meanwhile, Emil Warren was doing some thinking about his nephew's problem. If brought together under the right circumstances, he was sure that all parties involved would come to know and like one another. But scattered as they were from the mouth of the Columbia to the Walla Walla Valley 350 miles inland, the likelihood of their meeting under the proper circumstances was remote.

Unless ...

Unless all parties concerned happened to go on a river cruise together and met one another on a boat.

Well, why not?

With a self-satisfied smile, Emil Warren, the family expert at conniving and smoothing things out, began making arrangements for what would be his greatest challenge.

26.

$\mathscr{I}$N ASTORIA, May could be the most beautiful month of the year. Certainly, in 1871 it was a lovely month for Benjamin and Lolanee Warren, who two years earlier had celebrated their fiftieth wedding anniversary. As a belated present, Emil wrote them, they were to be the honored guests of their children, grandchildren, and the Oregon Steam Navigation Company on a ten-day cruise from the mouth of the Columbia River to the distant port of Lewiston, Idaho Territory, on the Snake River 470 miles inland from the Pacific Ocean.

"Lord almighty, that's a long stretch of river for a saltwater sailor like me," Ben exclaimed after reading Emil's letter at Hilltop House. "The furthest upriver we've ever been is Tommy and Freda's place near Rooster Rock."

"Will we stay on the same boat all the way?" Lolanee asked. "Will Tommy be its captain?"

"From what I know of the river, Lanee, we'll be on at least three different boats on the lower, middle, and upper river. The cruise is to be a family affair, Emil says, compliments of the O.S.N. Company. We're to go first class all the way."

"That's our Emil," Lanee said proudly. "He never stints on anything."

"Particularly when it's O.S.N. Company money he's spending," Ben grunted. "Of course, after all the profitable deals he's made for the Company, he's entitled. Anyhow, it sounds like a wonderful trip and a fitting anniversary present for an old married couple in their dotage."

"What do you mean, in our dotage, Ben? You're only seventy-seven."

"And you're only—"

"Careful, dear. You always do lose track of my birthdays."

"Let's see, you were twenty and I was twenty-five when we got married, right? Of course I've gained a lot of years on you since. You don't look a day over forty-nine."

Truth was, they both had aged well, putting on a little weight, acquiring a few wrinkles called "wisdom lines" around their eyes, and keeping most of their hair, which now was well streaked with white. Since both had been outdoor people all their lives, they still got around well and retained good eyesight, except for reading small print in dim light. Each early morning and late evening, Ben climbed to the third-floor observatory atop Hilltop House and spent an hour or so peering through the nineteen-power telescope mounted there, scanning the wide mouth of the river, the heaving bar, and the endless reach of sea beyond for sails or the smokestacks of steamers.

Though no longer active as a pilot, he kept abreast of the comings and goings of all the ships moving into the river or out to sea, as well as the boats steaming up and down the Columbia between Astoria and Portland. In midmorning and midafternoon, he made the half-mile-long walk down the hill to the waterfront, where he had coffee and shared gossip with both salt- and freshwater captains. Subscribing to Portland, Astoria, and San Francisco papers, he was well versed in what was going on in nautical circles, whether the event be a new sailing or steaming record from or to some far-off port or a disaster such as a collision, sinking, or fire.

When Tommy or Emil came for a visit, as they frequently did, he shared late-night brandies and talk about their freshwater doings up-river, though, as he freely admitted to them, his primary interest was in deepwater events.

As a loving grandmother who kept track of all family birthdays and names—which Ben certainly did not—Lolanee's first question to Emil was whether his six and Tommy's four children would be coming along on the anniversary river cruise. If there had been time, Ben suspected, Lanee would have written to their daughters, Sara Allamanda and Hina Flora, who, with their husbands now lived in Hawaii, inviting them and *their* children—which were numerous—to come along on the river cruise, too.

"Sorry, Mom" Emil replied, "but the O.S.N. Company is not *that* generous. This is an all-adult cruise."

Resigning herself to that, Lolanee settled for a daylong shopping trip to the Astoria stores, during which she bought a special gift for

each and every grandchild she would see along the way, first the three
girls and three boys in Emil and Dolores' ornate home in Portland,
then Tommy and Freda's three daughters in their big house on the
sandy banks of the Columbia near Rooster Rock, with yet another gift
for their twenty-one year old son, Lars, who now was working aboard
a boat on the run from Celilo Falls to Lewiston.

Though Ben grumpily pointed out that going "first class" did not
mean they had to dress for dinner every night aboard the riverboats,
Lolanee insisted on buying three stunning new gowns for herself and
two handsome blue serge captains' uniforms for him, complete with
four gold-braid stripes denoting his rank on the sleeves, just in case
other travelers did not know who or what he was.

"For Heaven's sake, Lanee," Ben protested mildly. "I'm not a
working captain anymore. All I am is a beached bar pilot too feeble to
climb a ship's ladder and bring her in across the bar. My only claim to
fame these days is that I married a beautiful Hawaiian princess,
brought her to America, and made her Queen of Oregon."

"You cheated me, dear. As I recall, you promised to make me
Queen of the Pacific Northwest."

"In those days, the Oregon Country *was* the Pacific Northwest,"
Ben said. He kissed her cheek, then patted her fondly on her well-
rounded rump. "Whatever I promised you, Lanee, you're Queen of
the World to me."

Taking them aboard at the Astoria dock next morning was the
Multnomah Princess, the newest, fastest, and finest steamboat in the
O.S.N. Company fleet. Normally, it was skippered by genial, white-
whiskered, veteran Captain John Wolf. But instead of being up in the
pilot house as they came aboard, Captain Wolf greeted them at the
end of the landing stage with the word that their son, Emil, had de-
moted him to a two-day tour as official greeter. Their captain today,
he said, was a skipper normally assigned to the Middle River run,
Captain Tommy Warren.

"Talk about nepotism!" Captain Wolf snorted indignantly. "It's
running amuck today! But for your sake, I'll put up with it. Happy
anniversary cruise to both of you."

Seeing Tommy smiling and waving down at them from the pilot
house, Ben and Lolanee went up to greet him, then, after giving him
a kiss, Lanee retired to the dining saloon for a cup of coffee and a chat
with several of her Astoria lady friends who were going upriver to

Portland for a few days of shopping. Staying in the pilot house, Ben watched his son make preparations to get under way.

"You're looking real sharp this morning, Dad," Tommy said. "How did Mom manage to get you into a new uniform?"

"The way she always does," Ben growled. "She just bought it and told me to put it on." Noticing that the side-wheels were beginning to turn, giving the deckhands some slack so that they could cast off the lines, he said with concern, "The tide won't turn for an hour. Are you going to sail against it and the current, too?"

"In the lower river, Dad, we steam by the clock, not by the tide or the current. Otherwise, we'd foul up connections with all our upriver-boats."

"I suppose you do have to consider that. But most ocean steamers wait for an ebbing tide before they head out across the bar."

"They've got to consider their fuel supply, Dad. Steaming upriver, all we've got to worry about is the current. There are plenty of wood-lots ashore."

Tide, wind, and shifting sandbars always had made crossing the bar a tricky business, both men knew. Lately, Tommy said, he'd heard that the Corps of Engineers had made a proposal to deepen the channel.

"Have you heard anything about that?" he asked his father.

"As I understand it," Ben said, nodding, "the Engineers think building jetties out from both the Oregon and Washington sides of the mouth of the river will keep it from spreading out so much where it joins the sea. Their theory is that by narrowing the mouth of the river, its flow will be speeded up."

"Sounds reasonable."

"They say that this will flush out a deeper, single channel rather than let sandbars build up near several channels that constantly shift around."

"Have they ever tried it?"

"Such a scheme did work at the mouth of the Mississippi, I've read. A Colonel James Eads was in charge of the project. It supposedly worked like a charm. At least, that's what the Engineers say."

"You sound a bit skeptical, Dad."

"I am. What worked fine at the mouth of the Mississippi, might not work so well on the Columbia, which is a different kind of river. Out here, we get hundred-knot gales blowing in from the west, with

248   seas that have been building across six thousand miles of the Pacific

Ocean. It's not at all uncommon to see waves seventy to eighty feet high on the bar. Mix that kind of power with floods on the lower river that can pick up a hundred-ton boulder and toss it around like a cork, you've got forces the likes of which Colonel Eads and the Corps of Engineers never have faced before."

"Well, I guess we'll just have to wait and see what happens."

Moving smoothly out from the dock into the main channel, the *Multnomah Princess* soon was steaming at full speed up the river, impeded very little by the current and the still-ebbing tide. Flanked by green-timbered hills rising a thousand feet above either shore, the Columbia varied from a mile to three miles in width above Tongue Point, which they soon passed, leaving plenty of room for a mixed traffic of steam-powered riverboats, seagoing sailing ships, and immense cigar-shaped rafts of logs chained together and being towed to market at San Francisco and other ports in northern California.

Sixty years had passed, Ben mused nostalgically, since that cold, blustery, late March day in 1811 when the mad tyrant, Captain Jonathan Thorn, had tried to force a passage of the *Tonquin* across the storm-tossed Columbia River bar, drowning nine men in the process, one of whom had been Ben's father, Thomas Warren. Marooned in this distant outpost as an orphan at the age of seventeen, Ben had made the decision to stay on in the Pacific Northwest: first, to honor the memory of his father; second, because he was the only American left at Fort Astoria; and third, because he liked this part of the world better than any other he had seen. Looking back, he had no regrets, for his had been a long, full life. With Lolanee's help, he had raised a fine family, had completed a good career in a profession he loved, and had participated in many historic events that had played an important role in the development of this part of the country.

Most of the friends he had made as a young man were gone now. But at his age, that was to be expected. The one he missed most was Conco, the slant-headed Chinook Indian whose one-eyed father, Chief Concomly, had been a lifelong friend of the white newcomers and had taught both young men a great deal about the lower Columbia River, the bar, and the wide sea beyond.

Gazing to the northwest across the river toward the spot on the Washington side where the cedar shake-roofed longhouses of the big Chinook village used to be located, he could see only thick-growing forest greenery now, with not a single longhouse in sight. On the beach where dozens of beautifully crafted log canoes used to be drawn up, the only vessel visible was a small rowboat whose clumsy lines indicated it had been built by an unskilled white carpenter.

"Tommy, whatever happened to the Chinook Indian tribe?" he asked his son. "Their village has disappeared."

"They seem to have faded away as a people," Tommy said, shaking his head. "As I understand it, most of the other tribes west of the Cascades agreed to accept pieces of land and go on reservations. But the Chinooks refused. All the lower Columbia River was their territory, they said, and they would not accept any restrictions as to where they must live. The end result was what you might expect. Because they asked for everything, they got nothing."

"That doesn't seem right."

"When did right ever matter in the making of Indian treaties?"

"What happened to Conco's boy, Sitkum, the son he insisted not have his head slanted?"

"He's still around, Dad. As a matter of fact, you'll be seeing him tomorrow."

Even with half a dozen stops at towns along either shore to discharge and take on passengers and freight, the *Multnomah Princess* pulled into her Portland dock at 5:00 P.M., completing the one-hundred-mile run from Astoria in just nine hours, as scheduled. Observing the skill with which his son maneuvered the boat into the mouth of the Willamette River, past the six-mile length of Sauvie's Island, and finally into the heart of the city itself, Ben had to admit that for these kinds of waters steamboats were much better than sailing ships.

Once a ship crossed the bar and got out into the open sea, of course, there was nothing more practical, efficient, or beautiful than a full-rigged Yankee Clipper with a bone in her teeth running before a fair wind for a distant port. Admittedly, life as a sailor on the high seas had never appealed to him after his experiences on the *Tonquin*, where the men before the mast had lived like pigs and been treated like dogs. But of recent years living conditions aboard ship had been vastly improved, he knew. On a long voyage where enough coal to stoke a steamer's boilers could not possibly be carried, there could be no substitute for sail. In all probability, there never would be …

Meeting them with a carriage at the dock, their ever-ebullient son,
Emil, embraced his mother, shook hands with his father and older
brother, then took them up to his showplace home atop the highest hill
on the west side of Portland. There, Dolores, who was still stunningly
beautiful after fifteen years of marriage and six children, treated Lolanee like a queen and made sure that her well-behaved children did like-
wise. With people of Spanish descent, it was traditional that parents be
treated with a politeness verging on reverence, Ben had learned. The
reverent mood was soon broken, of course, when Lanee distributed the
presents she had brought along for each and every child, deteriorating
into undignified squeals, kisses, and hugs, along with smiling com-
plaints from Dolores that Lanee was "spoiling" the grandchildren,
which Lanee insisted was her grandmotherly right to do.

Next morning at dawn, Emil used the carriage again to take his
wife, mother, father, and brother back down to dockside, from which
the party would continue its upriver trip to the Lower Cascades, again
traveling in style on the pride of the O.S.N. Company fleet, the *Multnomah Princess*, whose scheduled downriver trip to Astoria had been
canceled for the time being because nepotism was still running amuck.
In his second day as official greeter, Captain John Wolf had supervised
firing the boilers and getting up a head of steam for the trip, then
turned the boat over to today's captain, Tommy Warren.

"To tell the truth, I could get used to this," he mumbled to Ben, as
he joined Emil and the ladies in heading for the dining saloon and a
sumptuous breakfast, while Ben and Tommy had to settle for rolls and
coffee in the pilot house as Tommy prepared to get the boat under
way. "But Emil says when we get to the Cascades, Tommy will take
you on upriver, while I bring the *Princess* back to Portland."

After descending the Willamette to its mouth, entering the Columbia below Sauvie's Island, then steaming upriver to Vancouver on
the Washington side, the boat pulled into the dock for a twenty-
minute stop during which a considerable number of passengers were
taken aboard for what was billed to be a special late-spring excursion
to the Lower Cascades and back.

Gazing at the sagging vertical log pickets which used to mark the
perimeter of the old Hudson's Bay Company trading post of Fort
Vancouver, Ben recalled how he, Lolanee, and Tommy, who at that
time was only five years old, had come here as uncomfortable guests

BILL GULICK of Sir George Simpson, Dr. John McLoughlin, and Peter Skene Ogden. Being a woman in the British world of gentlemen, Lanee had not been permitted to sit at the dining room table, Ben remembered, a slight she did not even notice, for she was having much more fun eating, talking, and laughing with the Indian, French-Canadian, and Kanaka women in the kitchen. It had been at that dinner, Ben remembered, that Sir George Simpson had proclaimed it to be the policy of the Hudson's Bay Company to "strip the country bare of beaver" because fur was the only possible thing of interest to the United States, which, for the present, was being permitted to share the Oregon Country under the Joint Occupancy Treaty.

Time, religious zeal, and a hunger for land by American emigrants had soon negated that policy. For twenty-five years after taking over Fort Vancouver, the American military had operated it as an Army post, fostering the budding careers of such famous soldiers as Phil Sheridan and Ulysses S. Grant, who, during their tours of duty here, had served as lowly lieutenants. Recently, it had become Vancouver Barracks, training and housing the ill-paid, poorly equipped young recruits hired to fight whichever recalcitrant Indians made trouble. As always happened near a military post, the civilian community that had sprung up nearby had long since outgrown it and taken on a life and vitality of its own.

As the boat steamed east into the early morning sun, the beauty of the late spring day became evident in the flowering trees, bushes, and shrubs along either bank, with the fresh growth of fern, salal, dogwood, and many other plants that Ben could not even begin to name glistening and moist under the spray from waterfalls leaping down from the heights. Here, 120 miles inland from the sea, the influence of the changing tides had diminished toward the vanishing point. Directly ahead loomed the dark, rising heights of the lava bluffs that soon would pinch the river in from its milewide breadth to a narrow gorge filled with tumbling white-water cascades.

Though there was no landing dock with adjacent water deep enough to berth a side-wheeler as big as the *Multnomah Princess*, Captain Tommy Warren pulled the boat inshore on the river side at Rooster Rock, holding her there with the slow-turning port sidewheel, close enough to permit a landing stage to be run out over which Lolanee could walk to the sloping sandy beach below Tommy and Freda's house without getting her feet wet. With Ben steadying her elbow while she carried the presents for the grandchildren, they went ashore and greeted Freda and her three lovely blonde daughters. After exchanging hugs, kisses, and squeals of delight as the presents were distributed and opened, Freda, Lolanee, and Ben came back aboard, the landing stage was pulled in, then the boat proceeded on up the river.

Since Dolores, Freda, and Lolanee had long been friends, it was clear to Ben and Emil that the coffee-and-woman-talk in the dining saloon was no place for them, so they let the genial, gentlemanly Captain John Wolf continue his duties as official greeter while they climbed up to the pilot house and watched Tommy maneuver the *Multnomah Princess* away from the beach and out into the quickening current of the river.

Because the three women Ben and his two sons loved were now aboard, comparisons were inevitable. Matching Freda's yellow-haired, blue-eyed, well-scrubbed Swedish charm against the dark, rich, black-eyed beauty of Dolores, Ben had to admit that both his sons had done well in their selection of wives. Not as well as he had done, of course, but a close second best. For instance, he would bet his bottom dollar that neither one of them had ever experienced the thrill he had gotten the morning after he became a houseguest in Captain Reginald Barker's home in Hawaii when Lolanee ran into his bedroom and cried out exuberantly that he must jump out of bed and join the whole family in a before-breakfast swim. Topless, she had been, as was her still-beautiful mother ...

Because of the early morning departure hour from Portland, the *Multnomah Princess* pulled into the dock at the Lower Cascades on the Washington shore at ten o'clock in the morning. Waiting there with steam up was a newly acquired Baldwin two-four-six locomotive hitched to half a dozen sparkling white, luxuriously upholstered passenger cars and a dozen freight-carrying flats, which would haul passengers, baggage, and freight around the six-mile portage in comfort and style.

For Ben and Lolanee, this would be their first-ever ride on a steam train running on the iron rails of a track laid on land. In the eastern part of the United States, Ben had read, there were many such rail lines operating these days. Two years ago, a transcontinental railroad linking San Francisco, Omaha, and the East together had been completed. There was even talk that soon railroads would reach the Pacific Northwest, putting passenger and freight-carrying steamboat lines out of business.

In Ben's opinion, these were nonsensical fairy tales. Like sailing ships, riverboats would never be replaced by railroads.

By eleven-thirty, the anniversary cruise party had gotten off the portage train and gone aboard the sleek, fast, richly furnished side-wheeler *Oneonta*, which was Captain Tommy Warren's usual command on the run between the Upper Cascades and The Dalles. Greeting Ben as he and Tommy followed the ladies and Emil aboard, was a dark, medium-statured, gray-haired Indian dressed in a blue serge uniform bearing the emblem of the Oregon Steam Navigation Company, with the crossed oil-cans symbol of Chief Engineer on his sleeve. From the way he was smiling at Ben and extending his right hand in greeting, it was clear to Ben that he expected to be recognized.

"Dad," Tommy said, "I'm sure you remember Sitkum, who's been my favorite engineer ever since our days on the old Hudson's Bay Company steamer *Beaver* back in '36."

"My God! Of course I remember you, Sitkum!" Ben exclaimed, seizing and pumping the Chinook Indian's hand. "My good friend Conco was your father."

"That is true, Captain Warren," Sitkum said, beaming with delight at having Ben remember both his father and himself. "You were the best white friend he ever had. And you did me a great kindness when you agreed with my father that the old Chinook custom of head-flattening, which would have marked me forever, must end with me."

"You work for the Oregon Steam Navigation Company, I see."

"He's the company's senior Chief Engineer," Tommy said proudly. "How he learned the trade, I'll never know, but his skill with steam engines is like magic. If he can't make an engine run, nobody can."

"This is my *tah-mah-na-wis*," Sitkum said modestly. "A gift given me by the guiding spirit of my life. In olden times, the spirit might have taught me to be a skilled canoe maker. Since those days are gone, it taught me steam engines instead."

"Just what I said, Dad," Tommy chuckled. "A kind of magic."

Taken suddenly far back into the past, Ben recalled the days of his youth when at times his friend Conco would sniff the barely stirring wind and stare at the tranquil sea, then bluntly refuse to take a pilot canoe out over the bar to guide in a sailing ship lying off the mouth of the Columbia River, even though Ben could see no sign of impending stormy weather. When asked to explain his caution, Conco would simply shake his head and say his "tah-mah-na-wis" told him this was not a good time to venture out across the bar. Since he always proved to be right, Ben soon learned it was as fruitless to question his judgment as it was useless to ask him to explain on what it was based.

"Are you living in this part of the country now?" he asked Sitkum.

"Yes, I am, Captain Warren. I live on the north side of the river, near Celilo Falls. I married a Yakima woman named Spotted Fawn, but I would not let her or our children go back to the blanket. Just as you and Mrs. Warren taught me to read and write so that I could work in the white man's world, so we have taught them."

After the lines were cast off and the *Oneonta* pulled out into the river to resume the cruise, Ben joined Lolanee, Emil, Dolores, Freda, and Tommy for a delicious dinner in the well-appointed dining room. Through the wide plate-glass viewing windows of the upper deck, an ever-changing panorama of river and mountain scenery passed by as the boat steamed over the tranquil waters of the deepest part of the Columbia River Gorge. Though visible only in spots, Tommy said, Mount Adams, which rose to a height of twelve thousand feet, and Mount Hood, which topped eleven thousand, could be seen north and south of the river.

"The fifty-mile stretch between the Upper Cascades and The Dalles is called the 'Middle River,'" Tommy said. "Back in Oregon Trail days, wagon trains had to make a choice between going up and over the Barlow Road on a horrible trail or taking the wheels off their wagons, putting them aboard log rafts, and floating them through the Gorge."

"That I remember well," Freda said, shivering involuntarily. "Even with plenty of money to pay for help, the Mueller family I traveled with had lots of trouble. Some of the people in our wagon train drowned, while others got sick and died."

Dolores gave Emil a reproachful look. "Why didn't the Oregon Steam Navigation Company help them, darling?"

"For two very good reasons, dear. First, because it didn't exist at that time. Second, because it hadn't hired me to solve all the emigrants' problems."

"From what I've read in the *Oregonian* the past few years," Ben said dryly, "I've gotten the impression that the portages at the Cascades and The Dalles were placed there specifically to benefit the O.S.N. Company so that they could charge three tolls on every pound of freight that moves up and down the river. Is that true?"

"Only partially, Dad," Emil answered with a smile. "Somebody had to replace the robber Indians who were stealing travelers blind at the portages. We figured it might as well be us. The difference between us and the Indians is we smile when we rob our customers. Also, we don't have fleas."

Despite being down in the depths of the Gorge between two massive mountain peaks, the Columbia for most of this fifty-mile stretch was broad, deep, and quiet. Coming out on deck and climbing up to the pilot house with Tommy, Ben began to notice a distinct change in the passing scenery. Gradually the towering fir and spruce trees that had covered the heights and foothills had dwindled and vanished. In this country there was more open space between the trees now, fewer shrubs, and less undergrowth. Now the trees were much smaller pine, in some places becoming gnarled and twisted as if nourished with less moisture than the trees on the western slope of the mountains. When he commented on this phenomenon to his son, Tommy nodded.

"We've moved from the wet to the dry side of the mountains, Dad. West of the Cascades, the slopes catch most of the rainfall and wring the clouds dry. East of the mountains, there's not enough rainfall left for anything but scrub timber."

In late afternoon, the *Oneonta* reached The Dalles, where the anniversary cruise party disembarked and went ashore to enjoy overnight accommodations at the Umatilla House, known far and wide as the finest hotel east of Portland. After an excellent supper and a good night's sleep in luxurious feather beds, the party again rose at an early hour, ate breakfast in the hotel dining room, then got aboard the portage cars of the train that would take them on the not very comfortable, jolting, dusty, fourteen-mile ride from The Dalles to Celilo Landing, where they would go aboard the boat that would carry them on up the Columbia and Snake River to Lewiston. Noticing that Tommy Warren was with them on the portage train, Lolanee asked, "Will you be captain of our boat again?"

"No," Tommy answered, shaking his head. "I'm not familiar with this part of the river. But I'm sure we'll be in good hands."

From what Ben could see of the surrounding country, this was bleak, treeless desert, where sheer brown lava bluffs pinched the river into a narrow channel no more than a hundred yards wide, literally turning the Columbia on edge, making it race along in a continuous seething boil of rapids and white water. As the train neared the end of the portage, a series of chutes and waterfalls ranging from three to twenty feet high split the river into a number of channels. Perched like large, crouching predator birds on flat lava rocks overlooking the chutes and falls were dozens of half-naked Indians wielding long-handled dip nets, gaffs, and spears. To prevent their falling into the fast-moving current, which undoubtedly would have swept them to their deaths, each Indian had a length of rope tied around his waist, whose other end was securely anchored to a rock.

"This is Celilo Falls, the great salmon fishery on the Columbia River," Tommy told his father. "All the inland tribes come here to catch their yearly supply of fish."

"I can tell that by the smell," Ben said wryly. "Do they ever fight over fishing rights to a particular spot?"

"Very seldom. They seem to recognize the fact that there are fish enough for all. So they wait their turn."

In the lower Columbia near Astoria, Ben had observed the Indians fishing there, spearing, gigging, and netting salmon so big they were called "Chinook Turkeys" or "Chinook Hogs," selling the surplus they did not need for their own family's use to local white housewives for as little as ten cents. Since the days of the California Gold Rush in '49, fish-packing plants had sprung up in Astoria—the salting and canning know-how supplied by whites, the fishing skill by Indians, and the packing labor by Chinese workers.

In a vague sort of way, Ben had known that the various species of salmon whose runs filled the river ten months out of the year shared a common instinct that impelled females filled with eggs to move from salt- to freshwater, there to spawn in the gravel beds of the distant mountain streams in which they had been born. Just before their own lives ended, the males who had followed them would fertilize the eggs, then both male and female salmon would die. It was this age-old continuing process that had sustained the never-ending food supply of the Indians, he knew. But until now he had never seen the vital life-perpetuating force that compelled these magnificent fish to leap time and again into the thundering face of a chute or waterfall until they either ascended it and continued the journey to the mountain stream in which they had been born or let their battered, broken bodies fall back into pools below the chutes and falls where they would be netted, speared, or gaffed by the Indians.

257

Reaching the upper end of the portage at Celilo Landing above the falls, Ben and Emil followed the other members of the party across the dock toward the spot where the boat they would board for the rest of their journey was waiting. Though he did not wish to offend Emil by telling him so, Ben heartily disliked the drab, dry, empty look of this part of Oregon, where the tallest shrub was a clump of six-foot-high sagebrush, and even the grass underfoot was brittle and dry. Why anybody in their right mind would want to live here was more than he could understand. Of course, as long as a river as magnificent as the Columbia ran through it, carrying boats as beautiful as the glistening white stern-wheeler they were about to step aboard, he could understand why a corporation like the Oregon Steam Navigation Company would want to exploit the country.

Noticing that Ben had paused on the wharf and was shading his eyes against the sun with a hand as he made a visual inspection of the boat, Emil smiled and said:

"We call her the *Inland Queen*, Dad. Isn't she a beauty?"

"She certainly is. She's the biggest stern-wheeler I've ever seen. But why launch her on this particular stretch of river?"

"Because she'll be a moneymaker for the Company. We expect her to pay us big dividends."

"I thought the north Idaho gold boom had pretty well petered out."

"It has, though we still do a good passenger business to and from Lewiston. The freight traffic we're beginning to get now is in the form of sacked wheat, barley, and rye raised in the Palouse Hills country. You won't believe the yields the farmers there are getting. That's why we built the *Inland Queen* and hired the best pilot on the upper river as her captain."

"Anybody I might know?"

"As a matter of fact, Dad, he's a relative of yours," Emil said with a chuckle. "Come aboard. We'll go up and say hello."

But Ben did not move. Instead, he stood staring up against the early morning sun at the pilot house, becoming aware of what Lanee, Freda, Tommy, and Dolores had already seen and now were responding to with cries of greeting and a waving of handkerchiefs and hands.

Standing tall, straight, and proud in his brand-new uniform, saluting them all from the upper deck, was his grandson—Captain Lars Warren.

27.

BECAUSE THE PILOT HOUSE was off limits to nonprofessionals and too small to accommodate many visitors, Lars Warren came down and met his family in the dining saloon on the deck just below. First to greet him with a warm, yet reserved embrace was his mother, Freda, whose bright blue eyes were brimming with tears of happiness she could not begin to express in words. His father, Tommy, was next, giving him a firm handshake, a brisk clap on the shoulder, and a hearty, "Congratulations, son! You've earned it."

Wrapping her arms around him and giving him a hug so vigorous that it took his breath away, Lolanee held him close for a moment, then pushed him out to arm's length while still holding onto both of his hands so that she could inspect him more closely.

"What a handsome man you've grown up to be, Lars! Much handsomer than either your father or your grandfather. Freda must be responsible for that."

Giving him a warm kiss on the cheek, Dolores added her congratulations to the others; Emil grinned and shook his hand; then Ben grasped his hand and grunted, "Nice going, boy! They've given you a fine boat."

"They certainly have, sir. I'm grateful for Uncle Emil's confidence in me."

Lolanee gave Ben a smug look. "Aren't you glad I bought you a new uniform for the trip, dear? Your old one would have made you look shabby compared to Lars when you and he and Tommy have your photographs taken together next week."

"Our photographs?" Tommy said with a scowl.

"Nobody told me anything about photographs," Ben growled.

"How could we?" Lanee said sweetly, "when we just thought up the idea? Didn't we, girls?"

Because both daughters-in-law had learned long ago that when Lolanee decided to do something, it was best to go along, both of them nodded and agreed that the idea indeed had been a mutual one.

"Tommy will have to buy a new uniform, too," Freda said, eyeing her husband speculatively. "Also, he will have to get a haircut so he won't look like an unsheared sheep."

"The best portrait photographer in Portland is at the Charles Conway Studio," Dolores said. "As soon as we get home, Emil will make an appointment for the three of you. Also, he will tell the O.S.N. Company to pay for taking the photographs and giving all the family members framed prints. Won't you, darling?"

Emil winced. "Do I have a choice?"

"No."

"Then I'll say yes."

Taking a gold-plated watch out of his vest pocket, Lars opened its cover, observed the time, snapped the cover shut, then got up from the table at which the steward had served them all coffee.

"It's time to get under way. Excuse me, please."

Though Ben, Tommy, and Emil were eager to climb up to the pilot house and observe the river passage from that vantage point, all of them knew that a new captain on a new boat usually was reluctant to have older, more experienced practitioners of his trade standing at his elbow when he issued his commands. Protocol required that until the new captain extended an invitation to visit him in the pilot house, his fellow steamboat men would respect his space. So the three men stayed seated, sipping their coffee.

"Oh, by the way," Lars said casually, pausing just before going out the door, "if you'd like to come up to the pilot house and watch me run the boat, I'll be glad to see you in twenty minutes or so. By then, we'll be clear of Des Chutes Rapid, and I can talk to you without worrying about running the boat on the rocks."

So far as Ben could tell as he, Emil, and Tommy went out on the upper deck and watched the *Inland Queen* get under way, the performance of the new captain and his crew was flawless. Compared to the *Multnomah Princess* and the *Oneonta*, both of which were side-wheelers and built for speed, the *Inland Queen*, though big and powerful, was primarily a freight boat on whose commodious lower deck a great deal of sacked grain and other cargo could be carried. What passenger accommodations were available on her upper deck were first class, but her principal revenue would come from freight. Noticing that the boat now was angling across the river as it entered the lower end of a white water rapid, Ben asked Tommy, "Is the Des Chutes Rapid a bad one?"

"Not if you keep the boat in the main channel."

"How well does Lars know the river?"

"He's been on it since he was nine years old, Dad. Long enough to know you've got to treat it with respect."

"He has the look of a young man who likes his profession and is good at it."

"Must be something in the blood," Emil said with a smile.

After moving at half speed across the lower portion of the fast water, turning ninety degrees to the right and then churning at three-quarter speed into the main thrust of a river coming into the Columbia from between lava bluffs to the south, the *Inland Queen* pushed through the last hundred yards of white water, then moved on into a quieter section of the river. When Tommy said that Lars would be glad to see them now, the three men climbed up to the top fore deck and entered the pilot house, where Lars had just turned the wheel over to the First Mate. He smiled at Ben.

"Have you been in this part of the country before, Grandfather?"

"No," Ben said, shaking his head. "Until this trip, Rooster Rock is as far up the Columbia as I've ever been."

"What do you think of it?"

"Take away the river, it'd make a mighty fine desert, I'd say."

"That's true."

"Does a boat have to run many rapids like Des Chutes between Celilo and Lewiston?"

"Quite a few, yes. Next on the Columbia are John Day and Umatilla Rapids, which can be bad at times. Once we get into the Snake River eleven miles above Wallula Gap, there's a rapid, a bar, or a shoal every two or three miles all the way to Lewiston."

"How far is that?"

"It's roughly 150 miles from Celilo to Wallula, and about the same distance on to Lewiston."

"How long will it take you to make the trip?"

"Upriver, its a two- or three-day run, according to the season of the year. Downriver, we can make the Lewiston-Celilo run in a long day by running a few hours after dark."

"In a river so full of rapids, night-running sounds risky to me."

BILL GULICK

"Really, Dad, it's not as dangerous as you might think," Tommy said. "An experienced pilot on a known stretch of river can read it just as easily after dark as a sailor can chart his course by the stars on the open sea. A hilltop, a tall tree, a rock formation, a bluff, the way the current sets out into the river from the mouth of an incoming stream—these are all markers to steer a boat by if there's any kind of light at all."

"So I've read in books by that old windbag, Mark Twain," Ben snorted. "But he's talking about the Mississippi, where the only thing a boat can run into is mud or a submerged tree, which have a lot more give to them than the rocks we've got in the Columbia. For that matter—" Feeling Emil's hand on his forearm, urging him toward the wheel, Ben broke off and stared at his younger son. "What in the devil are you up to, Emil?"

"I just had a bright idea, Dad. Humor me. Take hold of the wheel."
"What for?"

"You, too, Lars. Tell the First Mate to step aside and let you, your father, and grandfather take over the wheel. Tommy, you stand on one side of Lars. Dad, you stand on the other. That's it! That's just right!"

Though father, son, and grandson had done as Emil asked, all three of them stared at him uncomprehendingly as he raised both hands, spread them apart with thumbs horizontal as if putting them into a frame, then smiled and nodded enthusiastically.

"What a photograph *that* will make! I'll bet my bottom dollar the Oregon Steam Navigation Company will be glad to pay for that."

Catching on to the idea before his father or grandfather did, Lars Warren turned around and stared at his uncle, his face flushed with excitement.

"Are you going to have the photographer take our pictures together, Uncle Emil, with all three of us standing at the wheel?"

"That's exactly what I'm going to do, Lars. He can't bring his camera aboard, of course. But I can take a boat's wheel into his studio and have him set it up so that he can photograph the three of you together. Think of it, Dad! A family portrait showing three generations of Warren captains on the Columbia River! No other family can boast of that! Won't that make a great picture?"

Standing with his son Tommy on the far side of the wheel, and Lars between them, Ben agreed that photographing the three of them

262

together would indeed make a great picture. But since Emil's statement was not quite accurate, he felt he had to correct it.

"Not three generations of Warren captains, Emil. Four."

"Four?" Emil said, looking puzzled. "Wait a minute, Dad. There's just been you, Tommy, and Lars—"

Before either Ben or Tommy could speak, Lars said quietly, "No, Uncle Emil. Grandfather is right. His own father, Thomas Warren, had a captain's rating in sail, making six trips around Cape Horn before his ship, the *Cotton Mather*, was driven under by hundred-foot following seas during its westbound passage in April 1806—"

"But, Lars," Emil interrupted. "It's a matter of record he shipped out as Third Mate on the *Tonquin* on September 8, 1810. So he was never a captain on the Columbia."

"Yes, Uncle Emil, he did sign on as Third Mate of the *Tonquin*. He drowned at the mouth of the Columbia on March 25, 1811, guiding the *Tonquin* in across the bar during a storm that took the lives of eight other men. What he did not know at the time of his death—and what Grandfather Warren did not know until several years later—was that a Court of Inquiry review board in Gloucester had cleared him of the charges of negligence that had cost him his captain's license. The Court restored that license three months before his death."

In the pilot house of the *Inland Queen*, a silence held for some moments, while the boat threshed her way against the current of the mighty Columbia River, which now was running in full spring flood.

"Good Lord, boy!" Ben exclaimed. "Where did you learn that?"

"It's true, isn't it, Grandfather?"

"Yes, it's true. But I've never told a living soul since I read the Court of Inquiry report two years after it was published."

"I read it, too, Grandfather, when I accidentally ran across it in the library at Hilltop House."

"How did you happen to find it?"

"You and Grandmother Warren have always encouraged me to read anything I found in the library that interested me. Ever since I've been old enough to know one word from another, I've read everything I could find on the Columbia River. Since you'd put the report between the pages of one of your books, I found it and read it ten years ago. It made me feel awfully proud."

Laying a hand on his grandson's shoulder, Ben gave it a gentle squeeze, then turned away, his eyes misting.

"Not nearly as proud as I am of you, Lars," he said softly. "What you just told me, makes it all seem worthwhile ..."

In late afternoon, the *Inland Queen* moved through a broad, tranquil sector of river running between five-hundred-foot-high lava bluffs; here, the Columbia made its big bend to the north toward Canada. To the east stretched bleak, sandy, treeless desert, a country, in Ben's opinion, as worthless as any he ever had seen. Just above the mouth of a small, sluggish stream which Lars told him was called the Walla River, the boat slowed her engines and eased her way toward a dock below a drab, grubby-looking settlement named Wallula Landing.

"We'll lay over here for the night," Lars said, "then head on up-river to Lewiston first thing tomorrow morning."

Noticing that a number of passengers were gathering up their belongings and preparing to disembark, Ben asked his grandson where they were going.

"There's a good-sized town and a fertile valley twenty-nine miles east of here," Lars said. "In fact, the Walla Walla Valley is the most prosperous part of Washington Territory east of the Cascades."

"How can any place be fertile and prosperous in this godforsaken desert?"

Pointing toward a faint line of distant mountains visible through the haze to the southeast, Lars said, "Those are the Blue Mountains, Grandfather, which rise five thousand feet above the floor of the Walla Walla Valley. Just as the Cascades do in western Oregon and Washington, the Blues milk the clouds moving in from the Pacific Ocean of their moisture, causing a lot more rain to fall in the Walla Walla Valley than falls here. This end of the county gets only seven inches of rainfall a year. The Walla Walla Valley gets twenty-five inches in town, with as much as fifty inches falling on the higher slopes of the Blues to the east."

"Didn't Emil and his brother-in-law, Carlos Ibanez, start a ranch in the Walla Walla area a few years ago?"

"They sure did. A big one."

"Has it done well?"

"Very well, Grandfather. As a matter of fact, after Carlos got married and his wife, Anna Lowehr, had a couple of babies, they bought out Uncle Emil. Now they own the ranch themselves."

"Will we be seeing them on this trip?"

"So Uncle Emil tells me. He's invited all the members of the family to come along on your anniversary cruise."

"What about the young lady Lanee tells me you're engaged to, Lars? Will we be seeing her, too?"

Hesitating for several moments before he replied, Lars finally nodded, his face flushed and his lips compressed into a straight line. "Yes, Grandfather, you'll be meeting Daphne deBeauchamp, the girl I intend to marry. Her mother, too. I'm hoping you'll like them both."

"I'm sure we will, Lars," Ben said with a smile. "The men in the Warren family have long been known for their good judgment in selecting wives. I'm sure you'll be no exception."

After the boat had been secured to the wharf and the landing stage had been run out, the crowd of disembarking passengers streamed ashore. A much smaller group, which apparently planned to come aboard for the trip upriver to Lewiston, stood aside and waited for the jam to clear. From his vantage point just outside the pilot house, where he had stood while talking to Lars, Ben could recognize the dark, handsome face of Emil's brother-in-law, Carlos Ibanez, as he removed his hat, flashed his brilliant smile, and waved at Lolanee, Dolores and Freda, who were standing at the rail of the main deck to the left of the landing stage. Beside Carlos stood his lovely blonde wife, Anna Lowehr, who, though not violating Emil's edict that this be an all-adult cruise by bringing her two year old daughter and four year old son along, looked like she might inadvertently break it during the cruise by carrying aboard a soon-to-be-born baby inside her, for she was very, very pregnant.

Beside Ben, Lars gave an exclamation of surprise, blurted a hasty, "Excuse me, Grandfather, they're here!", pushed past him, and then stumbled in a most undignified way down the steps from the pilot house, along the deck just below where Emil and Tommy stood gazing down at the disembarking and boarding passengers, to the lower deck, where he shouldered his way through the crowd toward three people who had just appeared.

By far the largest of the trio was a muscular, broad-shouldered, hulk of a man who Ben judged must be at least six and a half feet tall and weighed in the neighborhood of three hundred pounds. Carrying half a dozen pieces of luggage as if they weighed nothing at all, he was shunting people in the disembarking crowd away from the two women he was escorting toward the landing stage, making sure they were neither jostled nor stepped on. Both women had black hair and eyes, were well dressed, and possessed the kind of beauty that would draw attention to them in any crowd. The older woman with the fuller figure appeared to be forty or so, while the younger, slimmer girl beside her looked to be half her age.

It was toward this girl that Lars was hurrying, Ben saw. The fervor of their embrace as they met made it clear that this was the young lady Lars had just told Ben he was going to marry, Daphne deBeauchamp; the woman standing behind her, smiling her approval, must be her mother.

"Good God, Emil!" Ben heard Tommy exclaim on the deck just below him. "Have you gone out of your mind?"

"Not that I'm aware of," Emil answered lightly. "Why do you ask?"

"You know damn well why! You were stark raving mad to include French Lil in the river cruise party!"

"She's Daphne's mother, Tommy. I invited Daphne."

"Sure, I expected you'd invite Lars' young lady to come along on the trip so that she could meet the family. But to ask her mother, too! That's just plain crazy!"

"I disagree, Tommy. When Lars and Daphne get married—which Lars swears they're going to do whether anybody in the Warren family likes it or not—Lili deBeauchamp will become a member of our clan. So it's important that we all meet her under the best possible circumstances."

"But damn it, Emil, she's a madam! She owns the fanciest whorehouse in Walla Walla!"

"The leading citizens of Walla Walla prefer to call it an 'Entertainment Parlor.' "

"By any name, everybody knows what it is. Even Lars."

"I'm sure Lars knows Daphne's background, Tommy. But he's in love with her. They're going to get married—come hell, high water, or what anybody in our family has to say about it. So what's wrong with our meeting one another under pleasant circumstances and seeing how we all get along?"

"Nothing at all, so far as I'm concerned," Ben said, moving down the steps from the pilot house to join his sons on the upper deck. "But I must admit that the idea of having a madam in the family will take some getting used to. Who is she, Emil? Where did she come from? How did Lars happen to get involved with her daughter?"

"According to Carlos, whose father knew her well," Emil said, "Lili came to San Francisco from France when she was only fifteen years old. She had some talent as a singer and a dancer, but on the Barbary Coast in those days the only shelter she could find from a very rough world was working in a first rate bordello. After a year or so, she married the man who owned the place, taking his name."

"What happened to him?"

"He was killed in a gunfight over a card game, Carlos tells me. Daphne was two years old at the time. By then, Lili deBeauchamp, who inherited the place, knew all the ins and outs of the business—if you'll pardon the expression—and saw no point in giving it up, though she no longer took an active role in the cruder aspects of the trade. After a while, she sold her place on the Barbary Coast for a tidy sum, came north, and eventually went into business in Walla Walla."

"Which was where Lars and Daphne met?"

"As a matter of fact, Lars was working as Cabin Boy on the *Colonel Wright* when Lili deBeauchamp and her troupe came aboard at Celilo and headed upriver to Lewiston. Daphne was ten, Lars twelve. It was love at first sight."

"Was Daphne raised in the—ah, whorehouse?"

"Not at all. When her mother found out there was no Catholic school in Lewiston—while there was one in Walla Walla—she came back downriver and went into business there. Except for occasional visits to her mother's quarters, Daphne has lived a cloistered life under church supervision at the school."

Ben looked questioningly at Tommy. "Have you and Freda met Daphne?"

"No," Tommy answered uncomfortably. "But Lars has told us a lot about her."

"Has he told you anything about her mother?"

"No, he hasn't, Dad. When Freda asked him about her, all he said was that Daphne's mother had come to America when she was very young—just as Freda had—that she'd had no parents to look after her—just as Freda did not—and that she'd had to work hard to survive—just as Freda did."

"Ouch! And then—?"

"Then Freda stopped asking Lars questions. But from other sources, she's learned a lot about Lili deBeauchamp's background and character."

"Who is the big fellow carrying the luggage and looking out for Daphne and her mother?"

"Goliath Samson," Emil said. "In spite of his looks, he's quite harmless—unless somebody threatens his ladies. Then he breaks them in two." Emil sighed, then moved away. "Excuse me, gentlemen. I've got some arrangements to make."

Standing beside Tommy, Ben watched Emil go down to the lower deck, approach Lolanee, Dolores, and Freda, and motioned them toward the upper deck on which the dining saloon was located. As the three women moved toward it, Emil walked off the landing stage, shook hands with Carlos, kissed Anna Lowehr on the cheek, made a joking gesture at Anna's protruding front, then put his right hand under her left elbow as if offering to help Carlos carry her aboard. She laughed and refused assistance, taking her husband's arm and walking as nimbly along the landing stage as if she were unencumbered.

Going on to where Lars, Daphne, Lili, and Goliath Samson waited, Emil took Lili's hand, brushed her fingers with his lips, then gave her his arm and moved her toward the landing stage. Watching the party come aboard, Ben shook his head in grudging admiration.

"Give Emil credit, Tommy. He's some kind of genius when it comes to managing people."

"That I know, Dad. But this time he may have taken on more than he can handle."

Good manager that he was, Emil had seen to it that the dining saloon was closed to all passengers except the Warren family and their guests. Tended by a white-uniformed steward, a silver pot filled with fresh-brewed coffee sat at the center of one table, with fine China cups, spoons, a sugar bowl and a cream pitcher nearby. Seated at the place of honor were she could supervise the pouring, was Lolanee, whom Ben joined at Emil's urging when he came in from the deck outside. Removing his cap and kissing her on the cheek as he took a seat beside her, Ben murmured so that only she could hear, "Feel like a queen, dear?"

"I certainly do. And if the men in my kingdom misbehave, their heads will roll."

Escorting Carlos, Anna Lowehr, and Dolores to a table placed to the left, Emil seated them, then moved back to the open doorway, where Lars, Daphne, Lili deBeauchamp, and Goliath Samson stood waiting uneasily. At a table to the right, four chairs had been placed for them, but before escorting them there Emil seemed to feel that introductions should be made. Looking a bit nervous and ill at ease, he cleared his throat, then said, "Ladies and gentlemen, friends and relatives, in-laws, outlaws, and whoever else may be concerned. This is a special occasion for several reasons. First, the river cruise is a belated anniversary present for Mother and Father, who got married in Hawaii fifty-two years ago, thus starting the Warren family dynasty. Second, we're celebrating Lars' promotion to master of the *Inland Queen*, making him the fourth-generation captain in our family. Last, but certainly not least, we come together to celebrate his forthcoming marriage to the beautiful young lady, Daphne deBeauchamp, who, with her lovely mother, Lili, I now present to you all."

Stepping to one side, Emil motioned Lars and Daphne forward. It was typical of him, Ben knew, to give the lightest possible touch to what very well could be a very serious matter, for if the young lady Lars had chosen to marry, along with her mother, were not accepted into the Warren family without reservation, the emotional repercussions could destroy family unity for a long time to come.

Freda was the first to move or speak. Rising slowly from her chair, looking first at her son, then at Daphne, and finally at Daphne's mother, whom she studied for long moments, she revealed the stress she was under by failing to control the Swedish accent Ben knew she had lost long ago.

"*Ak fy!* Oh, my gootness, Lars, vhat a beautiful girl you have chosen to be your wife! Ve vill all love her so very much!"

Hurrying across the dining saloon, Freda threw open her arms, embracing first Lars, then Daphne, her eyes brimming with tears. Turning to Daphne's mother, she smiled and reached out to her with both hands.

"You, too, are velcome to our family, even though your last name is too much for my clumsy Swedish tongue. May I yust call you 'Lili' while you call me 'Freda'?"

"By all means," Lili deBeauchamp said with a smile.

By now, Lolanee, Dolores, Anna Lowehr, Carlos, and Tommy all had risen and moved forward, taking turns congratulating the young couple and greeting Lili. Soon everyone was talking at once, moving toward the table where the steward was preparing to pour coffee.

"Who in the hell wants coffee at a time like this?" Emil exclaimed. "Steward, break out the best champagne you've got! The Oregon Steam Navigation Company is standing treat!"

Getting up steam an hour after dawn the next morning, the *Inland Queen* churned her way north up the Columbia for eleven miles before turning eastward into the Snake. A third the width of the milewide Columbia here, the Snake appeared to be a much more difficult river to navigate, for its bluff-lined channel was compressed into a narrower space and white-water riffles were more frequent. Standing beside his grandson in the pilot house, Ben asked Lars about the relative length and size of the two rivers, which together drained a major portion of the Pacific Northwest.

"From its mouth to its source in the southeast corner of the Yellowstone country," Lars said, "the Snake is a little over 1,000 miles long. From the Pacific to its source in the Canadian Rockies, the Columbia is 1,250 miles long, I'm told. The truth is, I've never been to the headwaters of either river."

"How far is it from here to Canada?"

"Four hundred miles or so."

"Is the Columbia navigable all the way?"

"That's still an open question, Grandfather," Lars answered, shaking his head as he eased the wheel a few spokes to the right and began a gradual turn into the mouth of the Snake. "A few years ago, Captain Leonard White took a shallow-draft stern-wheeler north to just shy of the Canadian border, I understand. But he had to do quite a bit of winching and grasshoppering to get through some of the rapids."

"Grasshoppering? What's that?"

"Like walking on stilts. What you do is lower spars vertically on either side of the boat, jack up the bow until it's almost clear of the water, then use your stern-wheel to push your boat upstream through the rapid."

"Sounds like it would be hard on boats."

"It is, Grandfather. But Len White has a reputation for treating his boats the same way Indians treat their horses."

"Which is—?"

"If the horse falls down and breaks its leg when it can't go where its rider wants it to go, the Indian leaves it where it falls, then hops on another horse. As a steamboat pilot, all the water Len White needs to navigate a river is a light dew." Lars shook his head disapprovingly. "The truth is, Grandfather, I see no point in trying to establish steamboat traffic on the Columbia above the mouth of the Snake. Practically no white people have settled up there."

Eyeing the wide, endless sweep of flat, barren, sagebrush-covered land visible to the north, Ben said, "From what I can see of the country, it looks mighty useless to me. Why would anybody in their right mind want to live in it?"

"Well, it's good cattle and sheep country, they say. And the soil is very fertile, with plenty of sunshine and an unlimited amount of water available for irrigated crops."

"That doesn't sound like much of an inducement for settlement to me."

"Nor to me, Grandfather. But there is one feature I've heard about that intrigues me—the Grand Coulee."

"What in the devil is that?"

"A tremendous gash in the land which geologists say marks the course of an old channel the Columbia River gouged out of the scablands at the end of an Ice Age ten thousand years ago. What happened, the geologists say, was that ice blocked the flow of the Columbia for thousands of years, forming an immense inland lake that covered the entire Pacific Northwest. When the area warmed up and the ice finally melted, the Columbia poured over a waterfall three miles wide and six hundred feet high, gouging out a coulee fifty miles long."

"Is it still there?"

"So they say. After the ice jam broke, the Columbia went back into its old channel, which is 250 feet lower than the floor of the gouge. So Grand Coulee lies there now, high and dry."

"What earthly use would it be to anybody?"

"None that I know of. Still, it's there. I'd like to see it some day."

Looking at his grandson's tall, lithe figure, his sharp blue eyes, and the clean, strong lines of his face, Ben's mind flashed back to his own youth many years ago, when, as a sixteen-year-old Ordinary Seaman aboard the *Tonquin*, he had stood in the mainmast rigging gazing down at the pudgy figure of John Jacob Astor, who had financed the venture in which Ben was involved.

Lord, how the world has changed since then, he mused. *And for Lars during his lifetime, most of which lies ahead of him while mine is almost done, the world probably will change even more ...*

End of Book Two

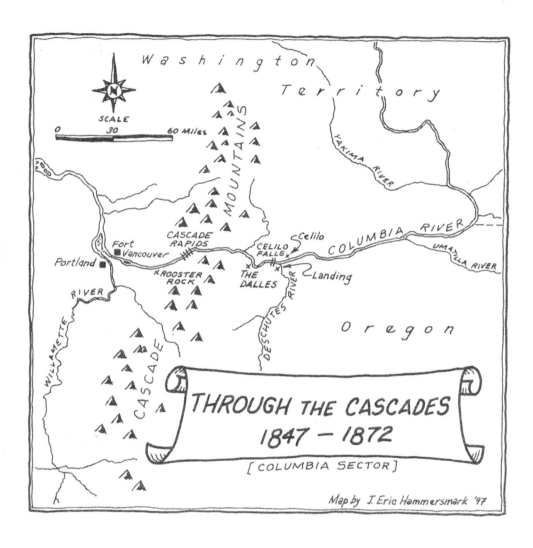